D0938921

CLARENDON LIBRARY OF LOGIC AND PHILOSOPHY

General Editor: L. Jonathan Cohen

IGNORANCE

IGNORANCE

A Case for Scepticism

PETER UNGER

CLARENDON PRESS · OXFORD

1975

Oxford University Press, Ely House, London W.1

GLASGOW NEW YORK TORONTO MELBOURNE WELLINGTON
CAPE TOWN IBADAN NAIROBI DAR ES SALAAM LUSAKA ADDIS ABABA
DELHI BOMBAY CALCUTTA MADRAS KARACHI LAHORE DACCA
KUALA LUMPUR SINGAPORE HONG KONG TOKYO

ISBN 0 19 824408 8

© *Oxford University Press 1975*

*Printed in Great Britain
by Butler & Tanner Ltd, Frome and London*

For
Sidney and Naomi Unger,
my father and mother

Preface

In philosophy, being a sceptic usually means walking a lonely road. It has been my good fortune, however, to have enjoyed serious conversation with a good many friends, critical but encouraging. Their challenges to my sceptical offerings were important events in my coming to produce the present work. While I risk omitting the names of some who should be mentioned, I cannot but take pleasure in now thanking those whose names come to mind. First, as in all my philosophical work, I am indebted, for the model they have set me, to my former tutors, Professor Sir Alfred Jules Ayer and Professor Peter F. Strawson. I have also learned much from association with these following philosophers, to whom I am grateful: William Barrett, George Boolos, Fred Dretske, Bruce Freed, David Lewis, Thomas Nagel, Charles Parsons, Hilary Putnam, James Rachels, Sydney Shoemaker and Dennis Stampe. The linguists, D. Terence Langendoen and Barbara Partee, are also to be thanked for instructive conversations.

There are a few people whom I must single out for special thanks. Saul Kripke has had a great influence on the present work, especially as regards Chapters 1, 3 and 5. I doubt that Chapter 4 would have been of much interest at all but for formative conversations with Robert Gordon. And, without suggestions from Donald Davidson, Chapter 6 would have been very different indeed, and very much poorer. In the actual writing of the manuscript, during 1973-4, scarcely anything came from my hand that was not read and usefully criticized by three good friends: Gilbert Harman, Michael Slote, and John Taurek. In large measure, this finished product is an outcome of my dialogues with these three talented philosophers.

This book is, in rather large measure, based on seven papers of mine that appear elsewhere. By the same token, these papers were written with such a book in mind; in retrospect, they may be regarded as studies for it. For kind permission to reprint this material, I thank the editors and publishers of the following volumes, where these papers appear: 'A Defense of Skepticism',

The Philosophical Review, vol. lxxx, No. 2 (April, 1971) forms the basis of Chapter 2 of the present work. Much of Chapter 3 consists of material originally published as 'An Argument for Skepticism', *Philosophic Exchange*, vol. 1, No. 5 (Summer, 1974). Some of the material in Chapter 4 appeared as 'Propositional Verbs and Knowledge', *The Journal of Philosophy*, vol. lxix, No. 11 (June 1, 1972). Some of the rest, in that same chapter, appeared as 'The Wages of Scepticism', *American Philosophical Quarterly*, vol. 10, No. 3 (July, 1973). The fifth chapter contains material from my paper 'Two Types of Scepticism', *Philosophical Studies*, vol. 25, No. 2 (February, 1974). Certain material in Chapter 6 appears in 'A Skeptical Problem About Representation', being my contribution to *Forms of Representation: The Proceedings of the 1972 Philosophy Colloquium of the University of Western Ontario* (1975), edited by B. Freed, A. Márras and P. Maynard, and published by North-Holland Publishing Company. Finally, Chapter 7 includes material originally published in my paper 'Truth', in *Semantics and Philosophy*, edited by Milton K. Munitz and myself, and published by the New York University Press in 1974.

The sustained essay, while based on these prior studies, took time and effort. For the time in which to make the effort, I am most grateful to the John Simon Guggenheim Memorial Foundation. By granting me a generous Fellowship, they allowed me to spend the academic year of 1973–4 absorbed in the writing of my case for scepticism.

Finally, I thank my philosopher-typist, Mrs. Susan Hank, for her patiently making a legible work of the pages of scrawl she received from me. The moral support provided by her, and her husband Daniel, is something I will always remember with thanks.

New York City
October 1974

Contents

Introduction

I N these pages, I try to argue compellingly for scepticism. In that way, I hope to make a contribution, not only to philosophy, but to our future thinking in general. The type of scepticism for which I first argue is perhaps the most traditional one: scepticism about knowledge. This is the thesis that no one ever *knows* anything about anything. I argue later that as a consequence of this first sceptical thesis, a second type of scepticism must also be accepted: the thesis that no one is ever *justified* or at all *reasonable* in anything. In particular, then, no one will be justified or at all reasonable in believing anything.

Two questions will arise quickly for the experienced reader. First, if I accept this second thesis, how can I hope for anyone to believe what I offer, or even take it seriously? For should someone believe me, then according to my own thesis, he would not be at all reasonable in so doing. As the philosophical literature has, over the ages, accumulated a substantial number of sceptical essays in which these theses are argued, this question is a familiar one. Accordingly, another question arises. With no apparent hope of being believed, why do I bother to fill pages with yet another sceptical essay? I will try to provide brief answers to these two questions. It is my hope that in the process, I will help prepare the reader better to encounter the arguments he will meet in the chapters to follow.

Why have I written this sceptical essay? Over several years, while I have continued to love the subject deeply, I came to have two dissatisfactions with philosophy, at least as I lately found it to be conducted. The first dissatisfaction has less to do with any particularly recent developments; at least it is not confined to these. It is this. After years of thinking intensively on epistemological topics, I could not help but think that the deepest and most compelling arguments I met were those I encountered first, namely, certain classical arguments for scepticism. Perhaps because they were so compelling, there were many arguments I later met which sought to refute the sceptical reasonings. But after a short period when an alleged refutation of scepticism might have a certain heady appeal, it would look shallow beside the original sceptical considerations. Attempts at refutation, it always seemed, missed the main point of the sceptical reasoning. The glare of an appealing fashion sometimes made this failure easy to overlook for a while. The appearance of philosophy's triumph over a negative view allowed for some brief pleasure. But the pleasure was always quite fleeting, lasting only as long as the glare of that fashion might seem to blind.

After recurring episodes of this sort, I had to try to take a larger view. In trying to be more comprehensive, I reckoned that experiences like mine must have occurred over and over again down through the ages. Indeed, what else could so well explain the effort spent to refute scepticism by each new generation of philosophers, and by almost every giant in epistemology who was not himself a sceptic? I reasoned that what might explain both the cycle of the activity, and this underlying cycle of intellectual experiences, was simply the impossibility of refuting scepticism. And, then, I thought, of all the reasons why scepticism might be impossible to refute, one stands out as the simplest: scepticism isn't wrong, it's right. The reason that sceptical arguments are so compelling, always able to rise again to demand our thought, would then be also a simple one: These arguments, unlike the attempts to refute them, served the truth.

If that is why the better sceptical arguments are so compelling, why do they seem, not straightforwardly correct, but so deep? Why do they seem to get us to a level previously covered by the superficial if effective disguise of custom and intellectual lethargy? Being trained in linguistically oriented schools and times, it was natural for me to think that the answer might lie in my language and similarly in the languages of other philosophers who felt the compelling power of sceptical arguments. The steps of the arguments, I conjectured, were based in the real but usually unappreciated meanings of key terms. These steps encourage philosophers to think in the way the meanings dictate, as well they should, if they are interested, not merely in what we take to be cases of knowing, and of being reasonable in believing, but in what is really required for knowing, and for reasonable believing. Sceptical arguments, if they don't immediately make philosophers come to an analysis of the terms, get us to think along the lines that an analysis would explicity provide. In a less explicit way than an analysis would, sceptical arguments may help us to appreciate the meanings of such key English terms as 'know', 'certain', 'reasonable', and so on. Until we encounter sceptical arguments, so far are we from appreciating the meanings of these key terms that we have little or nothing to help us think along the lines they dictate. That is why in everyday life we have no suspicion of any trouble.

If this is so, then the conditions we take to be right for applying these terms differ critically from the conditions of application dictated by the real meaning they have. Now, when something helps us to shunt aside our tendencies to a liberal use of our terms, and thus helps us to get at their real, unsuspected meaning, that is one way, I conjectured, in which we might feel our thought to take on a new depth. Concerning our key epistemic terms, then, the aids which traditionally would make thought seem to take on depth would be sceptical arguments. That is why these arguments have always seemed so deep.

In giving these explanations, of sceptical arguments' depth and compelling power, I was well involved in some ideas which might remedy my second dissatisfaction with philosophy. This dissatisfaction concerns the way in which, in the main, philosophy now seems to be conducted, and what seem to me the likely consequences of this approach to the subject.

In the past fifty years or so, things have come to look bad for the metaphysical insight philosophers so long have sought. It has come to be regarded as an illusion of language. With this I fully agree. But certain dominant trends have developed in the wake of this, and these leave little of substance for philosophy. First, it is assumed that the rather *a priori*, armchair methods of the subject are good for little other than the examination of our ordinary terms. But, second, it is assumed also that our ordinary common sense beliefs, which receive substance in these terms, are by and large correct, indeed, correct almost without exception. Thus philosophers are to be confined to almost nothing but a rather uncritical examination of our common sense beliefs. For, as the beliefs are assumed correct, no substantial result is to be expected from their examination. Philosophy is to leave our view of the world unchanged. Science may add to that view, and substantially so. But philosophy can have no such substantial part to play in the development of our view, of our understanding. Having entered philosophy with nothing like this in mind, I was bound to feel dissatisfied when I felt under the influence of these trends. How could I, with plausibility, think something better of my subject?

If much of our language alters in meaning along with the progress of science, the grip of this pessimistic view would be weak. But I do not think it plausible to suppose that much adaptive change actually takes place. It is true that with the development of physics, old words were appropriated and given new meanings, for example the word 'work'. Of course, the old meaning still stays with the word: in the most ordinary sense, a stevedore who works one afternoon a week does less work than a seamstress who labours fourteen hours six days out of seven. Most importantly, the appropriated words have been comparatively few. The progress of science has left unchanged, it seems, the key epistemic words: 'know', 'certain', 'reason', 'perceive', 'remember', 'true', 'false', and so on. And it has had little impact on connected words pertaining to our 'mental life'; 'happy', 'sad', 'proud', 'sorry', etc. Nor does science look to be holding out a hand for helpful philosophers to do a job of altering the meaning of these words, or of appropriating them for a new use with a new sense. Accordingly, though the progress of science may mean some associated work for philosophers, the amount of substantial work it will afford them looks to be quite limited.

Because there hasn't been much relevant change in our language, the grip of my trend-inspired pessimism seemed unchallenged by the prospect of partnership with science. This is where my ideas about scepticism and our language seemed able to do more. For, if scepticism is right, then all is not well with common sense, however useful those beliefs have been as a basis on which science might grow. If the meaning of our ordinary terms is really so demanding that simple sentences express no truth, and so 'verbal' beliefs have no truth, then common sense cannot be left unchanged. Far from wanting to be left alone, the basis on which our science grows is itself in need of substantial alteration. And if ordinary terms are indeed the cause, then philosophers, linguistically sensitive in relevant ways, may be well equipped to point out where changes might best be made. But, trying to avoid wishful thinking, is it, really, at all plausible to suppose that there might exist for philosophy any such substantial opportunity?

If the meanings of our key terms are impossibly demanding so that the terms don't really apply, the question arises of how things ever developed to this point. How did we come to be in such a conceptual mess, to be, as it were, trapped in it? As it has to other philosophers, there occurred to me the idea of a theory of things embodied in our language, inherited from an ancestor language, or languages. Vague as this idea may be, it seems to provide a framework for explaining why the conceptual mess began and why it has persisted. The theory in our language represents the thinking, conscious or not, of people a very long time ago. These people were instrumental in the development of our language, by way of creative impact on one or another key ancestor of it. Their language was, or their languages were, developed to express an old theory. Language and theory developed mutually: a little language, a little theory, a little language, and so on. The meanings of the key terms were formed, and made to connect with those of other words, in order to accommodate their developing thought. My task, and hopefully that of other philosophers, might be to articulate these meanings, thus articulating the inherited theory in whose terms we now verbally think. This seems a fairly plausible task and one which, if not misguided, might prove philosophy substantial.

This explains, in large measure, why I bothered to write yet another sceptical essay; it is my answer to our question which arose early on. And it provides the makings to answer the other question which arose: How can I, maintaining that no one is ever justified or at all reasonable in believing anything, hope for anyone to believe, or even to take seriously, anything I have to offer?

If our language contains many inapplicable terms, then 'reasonable', along with 'justified' and other similar words, might well be among them. It may be a mistake, then, to think that one must or should be *reasonable* in believing things, for it may be impossible for anyone to do so. What may be desirable, and thus possible, may be to satisfy certain conditions of 'reasonable', without fulfilling entirely the conditions of the term. Of course, this much is allowed for by our sceptical thesis.

But we may say more pointed things to the same general effect. Even if my arguments should terminate in genuine paradoxes, and in plain contradictions, that may be no fault of the arguments; indeed, it may make clear their whole point. For if there is something wrong with the language in which they receive substance and expression, this might be expected. Hence, in such a case, we may best regard the sceptical reasonings as indirect arguments against the suppositions embodied in our language, or against our common sense beliefs, which are given substance in its terms. I will not, then, be overly fearful of contradiction. Rather, I will look at untoward results as possibly indicating good starting points for linguistic reconstruction, and for the attendant alteration of our common sense beliefs.

Should appropriate reconstruction be achieved, then some day some philosopher might write a sceptical essay quite free of essential occurrences of impossibly demanding words, like 'know' and 'reasonable'. Perhaps his essay might then be free of contradictions and of untoward consequences altogether. In what may be very inadequate terms, I write without that opportunity. But even if this means many contradictions run through my own work, I hope that this Introduction helps to provide an atmosphere of exploration in which sceptical arguments may be given a fair hearing; perhaps, even a friendly one.

I

A Classical Form of
Sceptical Argument

T HERE are certain arguments for scepticism which conform to a familiar, if not often explicitly articulated, pattern or form. These arguments rely, at least for their psychological power, on vivid descriptions of exotic *contrast cases*. The following is one such rough argument, this one in support of scepticism regarding any alleged knowledge of an external world. The exotic contrast case here concerns an evil scientist, and is described to be in line with the most up to date developments of science, or science fiction. We begin by arbitrarily choosing something concerning an external world which might conceivably, we suppose, be *known*, in one way or another, e.g. that there are rocks or, as we will understand it, that there is at least one rock. Now, first, *if* someone, anyone, *knows* that there are rocks, then the person *can know* the following quite exotic thing: there is *no* evil scientist deceiving him into *falsely* believing that there are rocks. This scientist uses electrodes to induce experiences and thus carries out his deceptions, concerning the existence of rocks or anything else. He first drills holes painlessly in the variously coloured skulls, or shells, of his subjects and then implants his electrodes into the appropriate parts of their brains, or protoplasm, or systems. He sends patterns of electrical impulses into them through the electrodes, which are themselves connected by wires to a laboratory console on which he plays, punching various keys and buttons in accordance with his ideas of how the whole thing works and with his deceptive designs. The scientist's delight is intense, and it is caused not so much by his exercising his scientific and intellectual gifts as by the thought that he is deceiving various subjects about all sorts of things. Part of that delight is caused, on this supposition, by his thought that he is deceiving a certain person, perhaps yourself, into falsely believing that there are rocks. He is, then, an evil scientist, and he lives in a world which is entirely bereft of rocks. Now, as we have agreed, *if you know* that there are rocks, then you *can know* that there is no such scientist doing this to you. But, no one *can* ever *know* that this exotic situation does *not obtain*; no one *can* ever *know* that there is *no* evil scientist who is, by means of electrodes, deceiving him into falsely believing there to be rocks. That is our second premiss, and it is also very difficult to deny. So, thirdly, as a consequence of these two premisses, we have our sceptical conclusion: you never *know* that there are rocks. But of course we have chosen our person, and the matter of there being rocks, quite arbitrarily, and this argument, it surely seems, may be generalized to cover any external matter at all. From this, we may conclude, finally, that nobody ever *knows* anything about the external world.

This argument is the same in form as the 'evil demon' argument in Descartes's *Meditations*; it is but a more modern, scientific counter-part, with its domain of application confined to matters concerning the external world.[1] Taking the *Meditations* as our source of the most compelling sceptical argument the philosophical literature has to offer, we may call any argument of this form *the classical argument* for scepticism. Arguments of this form may be called merely different presentations of *the* argument, at least when they share the same sceptical conclusion. An argument of the same classical form may also be offered for the conclusion that nobody ever knows anything about the future or even the past, in brief, about other times. And arguments of the same form may also be offered for sceptical conclusions about having reasons for believing certain things, and thus being reasonable in believing them. For example, such an argument may be offered for the conclusion that nobody is ever reasonable in believing anything about the external world, even if Descartes himself might not be much

[1] Rene Descartes, *Meditations on First Philosophy*, 2nd ed., 1642, in *The Philosophical Works of Descartes*, trans. by E. S. Haldane and G. R. T. Ross, vol. I (Cambridge, 1972), Meditation I, pp. 144–9. The crux of what I take to be the main argument occurs near the end of Meditation I. During sections which follow I try to convey the spirit of Descartes's sceptical reasonings, and to extend this reasoning along lines which further convey that spirit. I nowhere claim any expertise on interpreting the works of this great philosopher, nor have I any intention of making a contribution to Cartesian scholarship. Rather, in those sections, I will try to be, or to pretend to be, a latter-day Descartes.

concerned (in any explicit way) with anything so apparently weak as reasonable believing.

These arguments are exceedingly compelling. They tend to make sceptics of us all if only for a brief while. Anyone who would try to further scepticism, as I will try to do, will do well to link his own ideas to these arguments. For, then, the very notable feelings and intuitions which they arouse may serve as support for the theses he would advance.

Unfortunately, I think, these arguments are soon ignored, and the inclinations towards scepticism which they arouse disappear shortly after. On the other hand, they are perennially capable of stirring up again feelings which seem to support the sceptical view. Their being ignored has nothing to do with anyone's finding any serious fault with the arguments, for none has ever been exposed. Nor, then, can anyone's abandoning his sceptical views, however briefly held, be due to that. But though that cannot be the explanation for scepticism's rejection, the explanation is, I think, still quite a simple one: we don't connect the arguments with enough other things of interest to hold our prolonged attention, not even our attention in pursuing our philosophical interests. Lacking any larger connected discussion which favours scepticism, our sceptical inclinations do not remain active and we easily fall back on the comfortable, habitual thinking of 'common sense'. We easily return to think confidently that we *know* all sorts of things, and that we have *reasons* for believing many others, at least quite often then being *reasonable* in believing these latter things.

Being a sceptic, I of course think that we then return to ways of continued error. In every bit of my sceptical work, I will try to do something to remedy this situation. Being much like other people, I too return quickly to supposing that I know quite a fair amount. I do this almost as soon as I cease to think actively about what seems the deeper aspects of these issues. Perhaps even, I must always despair of doing otherwise, not just for fear of losing common ground with others in society, but for fear of disrupting my habitual patterns of thought to the point where my thought itself slows to a halt. Even so, if a sceptical philosophy is the only alternative to massive error, as I suspect it to be, then, at least as a philosopher, I must try to examine our sceptical arguments, and to follow out the implications of their sceptical conclusions. If my suspicions are correct, that will place me, as we are wont to say, in the service of truth. In any case, be they correct or incorrect, this attempt may help us all take scepticism seriously for more than just a moment. Perhaps, then, we will even demand from ourselves a reasonable explanation of those feelings and intuitions which certain sceptical arguments so forcefully and so perennially arouse.

It is hard to believe there to be no good in such an apparently refreshing turn of mind. While grand designs in this direction are needed eventually even for our interest to be held, we may best generate that interest once again by encountering the classical arguments. Accordingly, the first thing for me to do towards either or both of my attempted ends is this: to put forward, in a compellingly clear and explicit way, those arguments which start so many thinking sceptically for the first time.

§1. *Some Problems in Stating a Sceptical Thesis and some Steps towards their Resolution*

The evil demon argument, as well as its more scientific counterparts, works most easily and compellingly for the conclusion we obtained, more or less well, at the outset. No other equally broad, traditionally honoured form of scepticism is so easily or compellingly reached. We may call this concluded thesis, scepticism concerning (alleged) knowledge about any external world there may be, or, following tradition and most conveniently, scepticism about (alleged) knowledge of *the* external world. Anyone versed in philosophy has a pretty good idea of what is intended in this thesis or view, of what alleged knowledge it means to deny. Perhaps a bit too roughly, then, this is the thesis that nobody ever knows anything *about* any concrete entity 'outside his or her own mind'; nobody knows anything *about* any 'external' physical events or mental ones, *about* any such things, processes, properties, and so on. In short, the thesis that nobody ever knows anything *about* 'the external world'. As I have just suggested by all this hesitant verbiage, there is a problem in stating this thesis so that what is stated is the intended, most easily compelled conclusion of the sort of sceptical argument we are to present. Here is the problem, followed, I hope, by some reasonably exhaustive steps towards its resolution.[2]

The words 'nobody knows anything about the external world', in the meaning which would most ordinarily attach to them, will exclude such apparently harmless and unobjectionable cases of alleged knowing as these: First, someone's knowing that any bachelors there may be are unmarried, given of course that we employ 'bachelors' in its most common meaning. For so long as there actually are some bachelors, whether the person *knows* them to exist or not, knowing this will, I fear, count as knowing something *about the external world*. In this case what the person knows is some necessary and, indeed, even analytic or logical truth, though that truth will (happen to) be about some external entities, hence, about the external world. Classical arguments for this sceptical thesis do not, however, mean to exclude knowledge of such analytic material. A second case involves one's knowing something contingent, and so surely not analytic. This is the case of someone's knowing that he himself exists in the world, and also knowing that any external world there may be is part of a world in which he himself exists. Now if there is an external world, perhaps because there are some rocks, then, whether he knows that or not, he would seem to know something *about* the external world, namely, that he himself exists in a world of which any external world is but a part. This is, on the ordinary meaning, a case of someone knowing something *about* the external world. But, our argument is not designed to exclude such knowledge. This should give one some understanding of the problem of stating this thesis.

I propose to meet this problem by an artificial move for the purpose of capturing the point of the relevant sort of classical argument. As will be apparent, this artificiality is no aid for scepticism. I will stipulate what I will here mean by 'someone's knowing something about the external world', trusting that the cases I specify exhaust, or near enough exhaust, those which the classical arguments mean to exclude. So, first, I mean to include any case of someone's knowing something which entails the existence of some concrete entity outside his own

² I was helped in appreciating the difficulties here by discussion with Michael Slote.

mind.[3] Secondly, I will include any case of someone's knowing something which entails that some concrete entity, such that it is not an analytic or logical truth that it does not exist (outside the person's mind), does *not* exist (outside his mind).[4] Thirdly, and I hope finally, I will include any case of someone's knowing something which entails a truth about a concrete entity, which is not an analytic or logical truth, providing only that the entity does exist (outside the person's mind). An example of the first sort of case is someone's knowing that many bachelors are carefree, for that entails that there is at least one bachelor and, so, that a certain concrete entity exists (outside the person's own mind). An example of the second sort of case is someone's knowing that there are no purple bachelors. An example of the last sort of case is someone's knowing that if there are any bachelors, then they are carefree.

I hope that these three cases exhaust those which would be, as the topic is traditionally conceived, considered germane to the topic of scepticism about the external world. If not, one can add further cases to our list, all to be ruled out by a classical argument concerning this easily appealing form of scepticism about knowledge. But even without adding any further sorts of cases to be included in our thesis, we have denied at least very nearly all of the alleged knowledge which a sceptic about such matters might be expected to deny. It is quite clear, then, that any intuitions our classical argument arouses will be in support of a very substantial sceptical position.[5]

[3] By 'concrete entity', I mean to *exclude* such 'abstract' things as Platonic universals, the number four, and so on, in case any such things exist. Roughly, I suppose I mean to *include* anything which exists in time. Thus, I would include Descartes's evil demon, and God, in so far as I can understand what He might be. I take it that if abstract things do exist, and are not 'only in one's mind', then they exist outside one's own mind. In my opinion, our classical argument does not compellingly rule out knowledge of their existence. Later, in Chapter III, I argue that we can know nothing of them anyway.

[4] Please notice that I do *not* say that it is not a *necessary* truth that it does not exist. For several years Saul Kripke has argued in conversation, quite effectively I think, that if unicorns do not exist and never did, it is necessarily true, in the strictest sense, that they do not and never did. And, if Pegasus does not exist and never did, that it is a necessary truth that he did not and does not now exist. But knowing that Pegasus never existed, and knowing that unicorns never did either, apparently *is* knowing something about the external world. As it is no analytic truth that these things never existed, and no truth of logic, our criterion allows this knowledge to be included.

[5] Parallel problems arise with the stating of other sceptical positions, theses

§2. *An Argument Concerning the External World*

Whatever difficulties are encountered, and complexities required, in stating the thesis of this scepticism, they are almost bound to be matched by those in trying to state adequate premisses for a logically valid argument in its favour. Logical validity of the premisses themselves, their holding for all possible cases, is required of any formulation which will seem true to the spirit and the essence of the classical argument, even as Descartes presented it. For that argument arouses, not only the intuition that its conclusion *is* correct, but also the more tutored intuition that *if* its conclusion is true then it is *necessarily* true. We don't come away with the feeling that we *happen* not to know anything about the external world. Rather, we get the feeling that no matter what we do, no matter how our beliefs may change, we will *never* know anything of the sort in question. And, then, we get the feeling that no one, no possible being, *ever can or could* know anything of that sort. To be true to the spirit of the classical argument, we want a formulation which, even on reflection and scrutiny, seems to establish its conclusion as a *necessary* truth.

Fearing complexities, we first present the argument in very brief terms, much as we did at the outset. Thus put, it goes like this: First, if you *know* that there are rocks, then you *can know* that there is *no* evil scientist, a being other than yourself, who, by means of electrodes, is deceiving you into *falsely* believing that there are. (One may notice the qualification that the evil scientist is other than the person on whom the argument is being performed. For you yourself, or I myself, *may* be an evil scientist, one given to self-deception. And so far as this argument goes, one *might know* this about oneself. We are thus specifically excluding such cases, for they do not contribute to the argument in the way we want, or which is wanted by tradition.) But, second, you *can't* ever *know* that all of this is so. So, you *don't know* that there are rocks. The same thing works

with which we will be concerned a bit later, for example in §§ 11 and 12. The measures to be taken are also parallel, and the results equally effective in denying what the sceptic there wants to deny. Accordingly, I will generally write as if these problems don't exist there. In so doing, I will ignore them, I suggest, with almost complete impunity.

for anyone in any situation, and in respect of any external matter. Therefore, no one ever *knows* anything about the external world (nor ever can do so).

I believe that there is very little which escapes this argument, even as so briefly presented. But much modification is needed before a sound argument even *might* be available to us. Indeed, I suspect that there are so many complications here that no sound argument *of this form* will ever actually be before us. At the same time such an argument can give us at least *very nearly* as strong a sceptical conclusion as we might want. But, even for that, we must first overcome some difficulties. The difficulties come in trying to generalize in the quick way just indicated. We cannot validly suppose that because we have covered an arbitrarily chosen case we may similarly cover all relevant cases.

Owing to what I will call Cartesian complications, we need a very complex formulation of the argument. Otherwise the ingenious Cartesian may find trivial but valid ways to escape our conclusion. To see more precisely why this complexity is required, I will motivate the complications by means of an informal discussion. In the fullest formulation we shall give it, our argument will have but two premisses, admittedly very complex ones, from which the sceptical conclusion follows. Even then, the second premiss will not be complex enough itself to validly capture every case. I will present this discussion as a scattered, more informal argument for the same conclusion the formal, more fully stated argument also tries validly to yield.

§3. *The Essential Reasoning*

The first premiss in a scattered presentation is this: In respect of anything which might be known or believed about the external world, say, that *p*, if someone *knows* that *p*, then, *on the assumption that* the person has and can apply at least a moderate amount of reasoning ability to what he knows so as to know other things which follow from it *and that* he will not lack any knowledge (he might otherwise have) because of this ability or its exercise, the person *can or could know* that there is *no* evil scientist, a being other than himself, who is deceiving him into *falsely* believing that *p*. The idea here is that all it takes to get this new knowledge from the older, simpler bit is a rather moderate amount of deductive reasoning. That essential reasoning runs like this: Suppose that I *know* that *p*, e.g. that there are rocks. It follows from this that it is *true* and, so, *not false* that there are rocks. It follows from that that *nobody falsely* believes that there are rocks. And it follows from that, in turn, that *nobody* is being deceived by *anyone or anything*, employing *any* means whatever, into *falsely* believing that there are rocks. Finally, it follows from this last that, in particular, there is *no evil scientist* who is, by means of electrodes, deceiving *me* into *falsely* believing that there are rocks, even if I am myself an evil scientist given to self-deception in various matters. This reasoning is deductively valid and sound. In so far as anything is *a priori* reasoning, it is that. It lies well within the grasp of an ordinary person, indeed, of anyone who can reason even moderately well. If one's own reasoning is at least that good, and on the assumption embedded in this first premiss, then, through repeated checking of the reasoning, one *can know* that there is *no* evil scientist who, by means of electrodes, is deceiving one into falsely believing that there are rocks.

§4. *The Assumption of Reasoning*

Why do we have a complicated assumption about reasoning embedded in this first premiss? The premiss now seems right, and it also seems that it should be more simply put to the same effect. To get our premiss to cover every logically possible case, however, the embedded assumption, or some equivalently complicating idea, must be employed. For we want to avoid any way out for, e.g., a small child, or a mystic. With the assumption, we may allow that a small child might know that there are rocks even while *not* being able to know various logically related things, like this thing about scientific absence. For I do not say that if the child knows the former, he must be able also to know the latter. Rather, I say that if the child knows the former, then *on the assumption that he has and can apply at least a moderate amount of reasoning ability to what he knows so as to know other things which follow from it,* then the child can or could know also that there is no evil scientist. That explains the need for the first part of our assumption. We consider next a mystic who thinks he knows, let us *suppose* correctly, that all beings are at one with each other. Let us for the moment also allow that this mystic is correct in thinking that if he were able to reason from this knowledge so as to get new knowledge, that would in fact have prevented him from gaining this mystical knowledge in the first place. We allow for this also with our assumption. For, then, we do *not* say that if the mystic knows this, then he must be able also to know that no scientist is deceiving him in the matter, providing only that he has a moderate reasoning ability and can apply it relevantly. We say that if he knows this, then *on the assumption* that he has such an ability which he can relevantly apply *and that he will not lack any knowledge (he might otherwise have) because of this ability or its exercise*, then he can or could know that there is no such scientist. Both the necessity for and adequacy of our assumption should now, I think, be appreciated. Though the assumption means complexity in our premiss, we may get a simpler wording so long as we are always prepared to bear this complexity in mind. We may call this assumption, 'the assumption of reasoning'. And then, for expository convenience, we may put our first premiss in these fewer words: In respect of anything which might be known or believed about the external world, say, that *p*, if someone *knows* that *p*, then *on the assumption of reasoning*, the person *can or could know* that there is *no* evil scientist, a being other than himself, who is, by means of electrodes, deceiving him into *falsely* believing that *p*. One who has followed the reasoning behind this premiss will quickly realize that the premiss represents an entirely general principle, and in no wise is confined to things which are about the external world. By having those four words there, we just focus concentration on our topic area; the words may be removed without loss of logical power.

Now, if we join this first, quite general premiss with the following, which really does pertain most compellingly only to our topic area, our wanted sceptical conclusion follows straight away: In respect of anything which might be known or believed about the external world, say, that *p*, nobody ever *can or could know* that there is *no* evil scientist, a being other than himself, who is, by means of electrodes, deceiving him into *falsely* believing that *p*, not even on the assumption of reasoning. For these two propositions, or premisses, deductively yield the conclusion: In respect of anything which might be known or believed about the external world, say, that *p*, nobody ever *knows* that *p*. And, this last is of course equivalent to the more simply stated: Nobody ever *knows* anything about the external world. The logical relations here are all quite clear, and every logically possible case appears to be well covered. (The only extra import provided by the words '*or could*' is that needed to allow that the assumption of reasoning must be used in certain cases; it is not there to indicate that there may be possibilities *of* possibilities which need looking into once all the possibilities themselves have been accounted for or eliminated.) This second premiss is quite appealing; it *seems* to be correct, or at least to be essentially correct. There are some other logical loopholes, however, which we must close in order that our argument have any chance of covering all cases validly.

§5. *Some Cartesian Complications*

As it stands, our second premiss *should not* seem compellingly correct. For the difficulty suggested for one's knowing by the evil scientist will not apply in the case of *any* possible person and *anything* which he might know or believe about the external world. Here is one case which is not accommodated clearly and well: Suppose that you do *not* believe that there are rocks. This is not because you know that there are and, so, do not merely believe it. Rather, you may hold no position at all in the matter, or you may *at least believe* that there are *no* rocks, not a one. We may say that in such cases you do not *even believe* that there are rocks. We may suppose further that you *know* this about yourself, that is, that you know that you don't even believe this thing. For such self-knowledge as this is not compellingly eliminated by our brief allusion to the evil scientist. Knowing this, you can reason deductively from what you know as follows: I don't even believe that there are rocks. Now, for all I can know, there may be an evil scientist and he may be deceiving people who, in many cases thinking themselves to know there to be rocks, *do believe* that there are rocks. But, as I don't have any belief in this matter, no such scientist can possibly be deceiving *me* into falsely *believing* that there are rocks. Therefore, by reasoning thus validly from what you *know* in the first place, perhaps you can and now do *know* as well this entailed conclusion: There is *no* evil scientist who is, by means of electrodes, deceiving me into *falsely* believing that there are rocks. Now, even if you are wrong in your conclusion, perhaps because a quite *wholesale* form of scepticism is right after all is said and done, your error is *not* compellingly demonstrated by the classical argument we are now trying to articulate. For that argument is only designed to advance compellingly the idea that we all know nothing of *external* things. How, then, are we to block this easy way out while remaining true to the classical intent and design?

The point for us now is this: While *some* people might not *even* believe that there are rocks, *anyone who knows* that there are must *at least* believe it. Perhaps, it is not required of one who knows this thing that he *believe* this thing. Perhaps, even, this is not required because it *is* required of him *not* to believe that there are rocks but to be in some *higher* or *better* state or position: to *know* that there are rocks. One may here think to oneself: 'What do you mean, do I *believe* that there are rocks? I don't *believe* there are rocks; I *know* that there are.'[6] On the other hand, it is *also* easy to think that believing *is required* by knowing. One may here think to oneself that the previous sentence requires an implicit 'just' or 'only' in front of the 'believe' to make complete sense: 'I don't *just believe* it; I *know* it.' What the precise requirements are here is extremely hard to decide, as many philosophers have experienced even in my presence. But those difficulties are here quite irrelevant. Fortunately, what is not so difficult to decide, and what is relevant, is this: If you know that there are rocks, then you must *at least* believe that there are. Perhaps, this uncontroversial condition holds true because you must believe the thing and more must be true of you in addition to that. Or, perhaps, it is true because you must be in a higher or better state than that of believing. But, whatever the specifics, those words, 'at least believe', must correctly apply to you if you are to know that there are rocks. If you don't *even* believe that there are rocks, then you can't

---

[6] On this view, the relation between knowing and believing is something like that between being a general in the U.S. Army and being a colonel in that Army. Being a general excludes being a colonel; but anyone who is a U.S. general is *at least* a U.S. colonel. This seems the view advocated by H. A. Prichard in *Knowledge and Perception* (Oxford, 1950), pp. 85–91. What I am saying here is that it doesn't matter for the purposes of the main sceptical issues whether this position is right or not. The same applies to any other position about whether knowing does or does not exclude or include believing. Our use of 'at least' signifies the triviality of any debates among these positions.

possibly know that there are. This presents an obvious remedy for our overly lenient second premiss: restrict it to people who *at least* believe that *p*. If we do that, and also add a premiss which says that only those who at least believe that *p* may possibly know that *p*, we close this logical loophole and take our classical argument a step towards being sound.

There are other cases of knowing which our argument should rule out but so far does not. One is the case where someone believes that there is an evil scientist, a being other than himself, or that there are electrodes, or anything else entailed by the description of our contrasting situation. For if you believe such a thing, you may reason deductively as follows: An evil scientist may deceive me about all sorts of things outside my own mind. But one thing *he* can't deceive me into *falsely* believing is *that he exists*. And, one thing he can't use *electrodes* to deceive me into *falsely* believing is *that there are electrodes*. Indeed, whether I believe these things or not, I can and now do *know* that there is no evil scientist who is thus deceiving me into falsely believing any of *them*. In so far as I do *at least believe* these things, and now *know* this other as well, I *might* really *know* that there is an evil scientist out there, at least as far as this argument goes. This now seems quite possible, providing that your knowing that there is a scientist is compatible with your believing that there is.

This suggests the use of other contrast cases. One such case is where someone's brain is filled by nature from the first with drugs or chemicals which keep him continuously in error with regard to all sorts of external matters; but no scientist does anything in this case. In another, no scientist or drug does anything to him, but all his experiences are only randomly related to any external things there may be. And, of course there are so many others. A person who at least believes one of these exotic cases to obtain, if he is to *know* that it does, must be able to *know* that another does not. For example, one who knows that there is an evil scientist playing upon him must be able to know that he does not have, with respect to all external things, only randomly related experiences of such a nature that he *falsely* believes there to be such a scientist. But he can't know that. So, we can now play one contrast case off against another. And, with even two cases, and suitable restrictions, we may perhaps have a powerful if scattered argument for our perfectly general thesis.

§6. *A Unified Statement of the Argument*

Such a scattered formulation is hard to have at hand. We may however avoid it altogether, and may formulate our argument in a unified way. This formulation requires but two premises. Both of these are long-winded, even with our abbreviation, 'the assumption of reasoning'. The need for such long premisses may now be appreciated, but it would not without our having gone through the Cartesian turnings of the previous sections. Having done that, I will now lay out the fullest unified version of our classical argument that I will trouble to give. The first premiss here is, more or less, just an extended version of the original:

(1) In respect of anything which might be known or believed (about the external world), say, that *p*, *if* someone *knows* that *p*, *then*, on the assumption of reasoning, the person *can or could know*, first, that he *at least* believes that *p* and, furthermore, that there is *no* evil scientist, a being other than himself, who is, by means of electrodes, deceiving him into *falsely* believing that *p*, and, here finally, that his own experiences and mental states are *not* randomly related to any external things there may be *but of* such a nature that he *falsely* believes that *p*.

Now, each of these three things, which the consequent, or then-part, of the premiss says the knower also must be able to know, can be deduced to follow from his knowing that *p* by routes familiar from previous discussion. And, if each of these things can thus be known, so can their conjunction. For that conjunction, having but three parts and none of any great length or complexity, presents no barrier to one of even moderately good reasoning ability, unless of course such a barrier to knowing is already introduced in one or more of the conjuncts themselves. Accordingly, it does not matter whether one takes the consequent conjunctively or as declaring only that three separate things must each be possible there to know. In any case, this premiss is hardly controversial; on the contrary, it seems quite impossible to deny. The second and only remaining premiss, then, is this:

(2) In respect of anything which might be known or believed about the external world, say, that *p*, no one *can or could know*, first, that he *at least* believes that *p* and, furthermore, that there is *no* evil scientist, a being other than himself, who is, by means of electrodes, deceiving him into *falsely* believing that *p* and, here finally, that his own experiences and mental states are *not* only randomly related to any external things there may be *but of* such a nature that he *falsely* believes that *p*, not even on the assumption of reasoning.

It is this premiss which makes the *substantive* point of the argument. Discounting exotic logical difficulties, that point is made equally well by denying that the second thing, or by denying that the last thing, can or could ever be known. (One may here allow that a person can, without too much trouble, know that he *at least* believes that *p*. In any case, that is not where this argument is compelling.) Further arguments, about the soundness of this argument, will revolve around these two things. If one must be accepted, then so must the other, not because they are connected, but because the considerations in favour or against either one will be essentially the same as those for or against the other. To keep things vivid, I would resolve the issue around the former of these two: whether anyone can (or could) ever *know* that there is *no* evil scientist. That is indeed what I would examine right away but for the logical difficulties which a quick formulation has been seen to entail. (From section 8 onward, for the sake of both convenience and vividness, I generally will write as though the only issue in this argument is whether one can know this exotic thing about the external evil scientist.) These two premisses jointly entail our sceptical conclusion:

(3) In respect of anything which might be known or believed about the external world, say, that *p*, no one ever *knows* that *p*.

But, while this conclusion does indeed follow, there are still cases which escape our second, substantive premiss.

§7. *How Further Complications place Limits on this Argument*

Certain conditional propositions escape our second premiss. They do so in such a way that no further complication of that premiss can rule out all of them. Yet, they represent cases where one might know things *about* the external world, each being the third sort of case we specified for our thesis at the outset (in section 1). As far as *this form of argument* goes, nothing is done to rule out compellingly the possibility of knowing these things.

To begin, we may take the following conditional proposition: *If* there is *no* evil scientist deceiving me about anything *and* my experiences are *not* randomly related to any external things there may be, *then* there are rocks. This is *about* the external world in that it asserts that the existence of a certain sort of concrete external thing, rocks, is associated with certain contingent conditions. And also, this conditional is something which, as far as this form of argument goes, I might *know*. I will take the conditional in its weakest sense, as a *material conditional*. That means that it will be, or will express something, true provided that its antecedent, the if-clause, expresses something false. Now even material conditionals, weak as they are, may be *about* the external world, as this one is. A valid sceptical argument should rule out one's having such conditional knowledge of the external world. But, can't I *know* such a material conditional to be true, *whether or not* I may know the truth of *other* sorts of conditionals which pertain to external things?

First, I may suppose that there is an evil scientist deceiving me about various things. In that case, the antecedent of the conditional is false (by the falsity of its first conjunct), and the conditional as a whole is true. So, the evil scientist can't possibly be deceiving me into *falsely* believing this conditional proposition; *that* I *know*. Now, suppose that my experiences are only randomly related to any external world. Then, the antecedent will again be false (this time by the falsity of its second conjunct), and the conditional as a whole will again be true. So, no such randomly related experiences can deceive me into *falsely* believing this conditional; *this* I also can *know*. Thus, the contrast cases so far adduced, concerning evil scientists and randomly related experiences, do nothing to rule out the possibility of my *knowing* this conditional thing. And we may suppose that I do at least believe it. *Mightn't* I then *know* it; at least as far as this argument goes?

How are we to rule of the possibility of this rather exotic little piece of conditional knowledge about the external world? We may put in a new contrast case, say, one of deceiving drugs, or whatever. But, then a new conditional emerges, this time with *three* conjuncts in the antecedent, one for the drugs and the other two as before. This can keep going: It may be an incorporeal witch who deceives me about various things, and so on, and so on. This may appear to be a stand-off. But I think that things are a bit worse than that for our classical argument. For the purpose of that argument is *compellingly to yield* its sceptical conclusion. And, whatever other things may be said about it, 'Won't more than a moderate reasoning ability be needed to extract the infinite consequences now needed from the proposition that one knows that *p*?', the argument, in relation to *every* logically relevant case, is no longer a *compelling* one. Nor does it seem that we should *ever* have thought it to have *that* much power. What, then, are we to make of this form of argument?[7]

Well, first, it does seem compellingly to show something about all the positive things people *most ordinarily* suppose themselves to know about the external world. It shows that *these* things, e.g. that there are rocks, are never known by anyone, nor can they ever be. Moreover, it appears that the only sorts of things which might escape the argument may be treated rather lightly in most discussions. For it seems quite implausible that any of these exotic things *are* ever known if these simpler ones *can never be*. Accordingly, while I am mindful of the difficulty we have unearthed, I will proceed to treat it rather lightly in most discussions. I will, indeed, generally write as though our argument does compellingly yield a conclusion as strong as our stated thesis. And, I will pretend, in section 11 and following, that we may also argue for such sweeping conclusions in related topic areas, unless, of course, other difficulties develop there.

[7] This conditional case is due to Gilbert Harman. John Taurek points out a simpler case involving disjunction: we can have someone at least believe that either there is an evil scientist or his experiences are randomly related to any external things. Scientists and randomly related experiences can't rule out this knowledge; if either obtains, the whole of the disjunction is true. And further disjuncts can always be added. Taurek's case has the advantage of simplicity, Harman's that of presenting something which looks like ordinary knowledge—and knowing something about *rocks* to boot.

Now, in a way, other philosophers, almost all of them I would suppose, have probably treated these attempts at care on my part as something of a game. For the exotic cases that concern me seem hardly the main problem to them. They would, I believe, think that this classical argument doesn't even begin to work soundly. Not only won't it touch exotic knowledge, it can't even say anything compelling about the simplest, most ordinary cases of knowing about the external world, e.g. our knowing that there are rocks. This is their prevailing thought and attitude. And this is surely where the real issues lie between sceptics and the 'commonsensical' majority.

§8. *On Trying to Reverse this Argument: Exotic Cases and Feelings of Irrationality*

Our sceptical conclusion would not be welcome to many philosophers. Indeed, most philosophers would be inclined to try to reverse the argument, perhaps in the manner made popular by G. E. Moore.[8] They would not, I think, wish to deny the first premiss, which in any case seems quite unobjectionable, at least in essential thrust. But even in its early formulation, they would be most happy to deny the second premiss, which is the more substantive one.

The Moorean attempt to reverse our argument will proceed like this: According to your argument, nobody ever *knows* that there are rocks. But, I *do* know that there are rocks. This is something concerning the external world, and I do know it. Hence, somebody *does know* something about the external world. Mindful of our first premiss, the reversal continues: I can reason at least moderately well and thereby come to know things which I see to be entailed by things I already know. Before reflecting on classical arguments such as this, I may have never realized or even had the idea that from there being rocks it follows that there is *no* evil scientist who is deceiving me into *falsely* believing there to be rocks. But, having been presented with such arguments, I of course *now know* that this last *follows* from what I know. And so, while I might not have known

---

[8] See several of Moore's most famous papers. But most especially, I suggest, see his 'Four Forms of Scepticism', in his *Philosophical Papers* (New York, 1959), p. 226.

before that there is no such scientist, at least I *now* do know that there is no evil scientist who is deceiving me into falsely believing that there are rocks. So far has the sceptical argument failed to challenge my knowledge successfully that it seems actually to have occasioned an increase in what I know about things.

While the robust character of this reply has a definite appeal, it also seems quite daring. Indeed, the more one thinks on it, the more it seems to be somewhat foolhardly and even dogmatic. One cannot help but think that for all this philosopher really can *know*, he might have all his experience artificially induced by electrodes, these being operated by a terribly evil scientist who, having an idea of what his 'protégé' is saying to himself, chuckles accordingly. One thinks as well that for all *one can know oneself*, there really is no Moore or any other thinker with whose works one has actually had any contact. One's belief that one has may, for all one really can *know*, be due to experiences induced by just such a chuckling operator. For all one can *know*, then, there may not really be any rocks. Positive assertions to the contrary, even on one's own part, seem quite out of place and even dogmatic.

Suppose that you yourself have just positively made an attempt to reverse; you try to be a Moore. Now, we may suppose that electrodes are removed, that your experiences are now brought about through your perception of actual surroundings, and you are, so to speak, forced to encounter your deceptive tormentor. Wouldn't you be made to feel quite *foolish*, even *embarrassed*, by your claims to *know*? Indeed, you would seem to be exposed quite clearly as having been, not only wrong, but rather irrational and even dogmatic. And *if* there *aren't* ever any experiences of electrodes and so on, *that* happy fact can't mean that you are any *less* irrational and dogmatic in saying or thinking that you know. In thinking that you *know*, you will be equally and notably irrational and dogmatic. And, for at least *that* reason, in thinking yourself to *know* there is no such scientist, you will be *wrong* in *either* case. So, it appears that one doesn't ever really *know* that there is no such scientist doing this thing.

Now, if you think or say to yourself that you are *certain* or *sure* that there is no scientist doing this, you may be doubly right, but even that does not seem to make matters much better for you. You may be right on *one* count because you may, I will suppose, *be* certain that there is no such scientist, and so be right *in what* you *think*. And in the second place, there may be no evil scientist deceiving you, so that you may be right *in that of which you are certain*. But, even if doubly right here, it seems just as dogmatic and irrational for you ever sincerely to profess this certainty. Thus it seems that, even if you *are* certain of the thing, and even if there *is no* scientist, you *shouldn't be certain* of it. It seems that you are *wrong*, then, and *not* right on a third count, namely, *in being certain* of the thing. It seems much better, perhaps perfectly all right, if you are instead only *confident* that there is no such scientist. It seems perfectly all right for you to *believe* there to be no evil scientist doing this. If you say, not only that you believe it, but that you have some *reason* to believe this thing, what you say *may* seem somewhat suspect, at least on reasoned reflection, but it doesn't have any obvious tint of dogmatism or irrationality to it. Finally, you may simply *assert*, perhaps to yourself, *that there is no evil scientist who is deceiving me into falsely believing that there are rocks.* Perhaps strangely, this seems at least pretty nearly as foolhardy and dogmatic as asserting, or as thinking, *that you know the thing.*[9]

These are, I suggest, our intuitions in these matters. All of them cry out for explanation, and any sceptic should be interested in explaining them. By the same token, so should any other philosopher. The difference between the two here is only this: these intuitions favour a sceptic's case. As nothing in scepticism seems to prevent any explanation here, the task of giving this account is an opportunity for a sceptic. On the other hand, the philosopher of 'common sense', who tries to reverse our classical argument, now has some very damaging evidence stacked against his attempt. Quite plainly, there is *no* intuition here to favour *his* case, to hold out the opportunity for *him* to give a favourable explanation. Rather, there are here only feelings which cut the other way, and he must try to dispel, and to 'explain away', these distinctive and intuitive feelings.

This idea, that claims to *know* about external things are at

---

[9] I discuss the notion of *asserting* in detail in Chapter VI.

least somewhat foolhardy and dogmatic, applies in all possible situations, even the most exotic cases. Suppose, for example, that you actually *do* have a sequence of experience which seems to indicate that an evil scientist was deceiving you into falsely believing that there are rocks. You seem to be confronting an exotic scientist who shows you electrodes, points out places of insertion on your skull or shell, and explains in detail how the whole thing works. And you seem to see no rocks outside the window of this scientist's laboratory. The scientist assures you that there really are no such things as rocks, that he only created an impression of such things by stimulating certain groups of cells in your brain. After enough of this sort of thing dominates your experiences, you *might* suppose that you *know* that there *is* an evil scientist who deceived you in the past, but he now does not. And, you may also come to suppose that you *know* that there were *never any* rocks at all. But, *should* you think you *know*? These latter experiences might *themselves* find no basis in reality, for all you really might *know*. For all you can *know*, it may be that all the time your experiences are induced by electrodes which are operated by *no* scientist, and it may be that there are no scientists at all, and plenty of rocks. Whether or not this is the case, you may always have new experience to the effect that it is. Is the new experience part of an encounter with *reality*, or is it *too* only part of an induced stream, or perhaps even a random sequence of experience? No matter how involved the going gets, it may always get still more involved. And each new turn may make any previously developed claim to *know* seem quite irrational and dogmatic, if not downright embarrassing. No matter what turns one's experience takes, the statement that one *knows* there to be no scientist *may* be wrong for the reason that there is a scientist. But, it *will always* be wrong, it seems, for the reason of dogmatism and irrationality, however this last is to be explained.

I think that these reflections make a strong intuitive case for the idea that, no matter what coherent situation one considers, no one there will ever *know* that there is no evil scientist who is deceiving him into falsely believing that there are rocks. And, this makes it very compelling indeed, I suggest, that no one *can* or ever *could know* this thing. While I am *not* absolutely *certain* that our argument can't be reversed, the more I think about it the more this does indeed seem so. Perhaps, these are matters where there can easily be too much thinking and reflection, and where thought tends to lead one into error. Perhaps, only an *unthinking* acceptance of habitual ways is the safeguard of truth. But, I find that idea itself hard to accept. I hope that other philosophers will feel this way too. At any rate, they all have some intuitions now to face squarely: In any situation, robust attempts to reverse our argument *seem*, at least, only to turn up intuitions which support the argument itself.

§9. *Ordinary Cases and these same Feelings*

Largely because it is so exotic and bizarre, the case of a deceiving scientist lets one feel acutely the apparent irrationality in thinking oneself to *know*. But, the exotic cases have no monopoly on generating feelings of irrationality.

If you are planning a philosophical book and trying to estimate the energy you will spend on each of the several chapters, you might think that you *know* that it will not take much to write the *third* chapter. For the argument *there* may seem *already* so *clearly* outlined in your head. But, experience may later seem to show that this argument is far from clear. And much time and effort may become absorbed with no clear fruits to show for it. In that case, you will, I suggest, feel somewhat embarrassed and foolish, even if there is no other person to whom your idea that you *knew* was ever communicated. If you just *believed*, or even if you were quite *confident* that this chapter would not take much effort to write, then, I suggest, you would not feel nearly so foolish or embarrassed, oftentimes not at all.

Again, you may think you *know* that a certain city is the capital of a certain state, and you may feel quite content in this thought while watching another looking the matter up in the library. You will feel quite foolish, however, if the person announces the result to be *another* city, and if subsequent experience seems to show that announcement to be right. This will occur, I suggest, even if you are just an anonymous, disinterested bystander who happens to hear the question posed and the answer later announced. This is true even if the reference was a newspaper, *The Times*, and the capital was changed only yesterday. But, these feelings will be very much less apparent, or will not occur at all, if you only feel very confident, at the outset, that the city is thus-and-such, which later is not announced. You might of course feel that you shouldn't be quite so confident of such things, or that you should watch out in the future. But you probably *wouldn't* feel, I suggest, that you were *irrational* to be confident of that thing at that time. Much less would you feel that you were *dogmatic* in so being.

Finally, if you *positively* *asserted* something to another in a conversation, as though reporting a *known fact*, later contrary experiences might well cause you to feel that you had overstepped the bounds of good sense and rationality. The feeling is that you have manifested a trait of a dogmatic personality. If you happen to be right, your extremely positive approach is not likely to be questioned. In case subsequent events seem to indicate you are wrong about the matter, then you come in for a severe judgement, whether or not this judgement is ever made out loud. This is a rather familiar social experience. (As I say this, even in trying to make my style a little less cautious, to be readable, I leave myself open to just such a judgement by putting the matter in such a positive, unqualified way.) I suggest that such feelings *ought* to be far *more* familiar, occurring even where you are *right* about the matter. They *should not* just occur where you are in fact wrong about things. Accordingly, we should avoid making these claims in *any* case, whether we be right or whether wrong in the matter, e.g. of which city is the capital of that state.

It is hard for us to think that there is any important similarity between such common cases as these and the case of someone thinking himself to *know* that *there are rocks*. Exotic contrast cases, like the case of the evil scientist, help one to appreciate that these cases are really essentially the same. By means of contrast cases, we encourage thinking of all sorts of new sequences of experience, sequences which people would never begin to imagine in the normal course of affairs. How would you react to such developments as *these*, no matter *how* exotic or unlikely? It appears that the proper reaction is to feel as irrational about claiming knowledge of rocks as you felt before, where, e.g., one was apparently caught in thought by the library reference to the state's capital. Who would have thought so, before thinking of contrast cases? Those cases help you see, I suggest, that in *either* case, no matter whether you are in fact right in the matter or whether wrong, thinking that you *know* manifests an attitude of dogmatism. Bizarre experiential sequences help show that there is no essential difference between any two external matters: the apparently most certain ones, like that of rocks, and the ones where thinking about *knowing* appears, even without the most exotic sceptical aids, *not* the way to think.

But that is not the last word here. While it needs some explaining, the last word is roughly this: *Because* one is (and must be) dogmatic in one's claim to know external things, one is therefore *wrong* in these claims, and in one's thoughts to the same effect. It is the aim of the next section to sharpen this up a bit, and to begin the explanation needed.

§10. *The Explanatory Power of the Attitude of Certainty*

I now begin my attempt to explain the effectiveness of this classical argument for scepticism. Accordingly, I will try to uncover the reason that no one ever *knows* that there are rocks. And, if I have been right in the discussion just preceding, it is the *same* reason also as that which explains one's feelings of irrationality in certain situations of everyday life. It will explain, for example, why one feels irrational when certain thoughts seem to turn out to be incorrect, e.g. one's thought that one *knows* that a certain city is the capital of a certain state. What, then, is this common explanatory factor?

A main hypothesis of my work is this: that an excessively severe attitude, or approach, or frame of mind, is entailed in one's being absolutely *certain* of something, and that speakers of English, at least (perhaps only implicitly), accept the idea that this is so. The attitude is at least roughly this: No matter what any experience may *seem* to show or suggest as to whether or not something is so, I will now *reject as misleading* any experience which seems to show or suggest that the thing is *not* so. Roughly, at least, this is the attitude one must have towards the matter if one is to be absolutely *certain* that the thing is so. Thus, I call this the *attitude of (absolute) certainty*, and it is, I suppose, more or less equivalent to a certain *approach*, which I then call *the approach of (absolute) certainty*, and to a certain *frame of mind*, and so on.

If someone is absolutely *certain* that at a certain time he feels tired, perhaps because he looks at his watch while noting how he feels, then he must have at least roughly this attitude: Any experience which seems to show or suggest that I don't or didn't feel tired at that time will now be treated by me like this: Without any further thought or consideration, I will simply reject it as misleading in the matter. This is *not* a prediction one makes about oneself, nor a belief about the future. One may think it quite likely that one will not reject the evidence as misleading. But, then, one will think something which entails that it is quite likely that one will *not* be absolutely certain then. One may now be certain, and have the attitude of certainty, even while one correctly believes that soon one will become less than absolutely certain. What we focus on is *the attitude involved*.

Our characterization of this attitude seems to need some refining. Perhaps one may be absolutely certain of something but not care much, even then, whether or not one is right in the matter. We may imagine this to hold of the case, just described before, where right now I am certain that I feel tired at 3.16. (It is now 3.16 as my watch-face shows, and I do now feel tired.) But, I may not and probably will not, care much if at all about being right in *this* matter, i.e. about my feeling tired at 3.16. I may then *allow* myself to forget immediately that at 3.16 I feel tired. If I was in a *frame of mind to allow* this, then perhaps it is not true that my attitude is that I will reject any new contrary experience as misleading in the matter. Still, I may at the same time be absolutely certain that at 3.16 I feel tired.

Perhaps even if I continue to remember this thing, because I hate to forget anything, I may not care whether I am steeled against contrary appearances in the matter. Perhaps, because I don't care, I am not so steeled and remain somewhat open to new evidence about whether at 3.16 I feel (or felt?) tired. Even though for want of the proper motivation I again lack the severe attitude, it seems that I may still be absolutely certain that I feel (or felt?) tired at 3.16.

Now, I am not certain that these descriptions, offered as

coherent, are actually coherent ones. Accordingly, I am not sure that the descriptions just offered require us to reformulate our description of the key attitude. But they seem to be coherent, and thus to do so. In any case, fortunately enough, we may describe the attitude needed for certainty with the relevant motivation built in with a new clause, which we conveniently place up front: *In so far as I care about being right in the matter*, I will now reject as misleading any experience which seems to show or suggest that the thing is not so. The revision is unimportant to our further discussion, the reason being that this attitude is no less dogmatic for the addition of this qualification. Indeed, one may reflect that in the case of the state capital, one's feeling of irrationality would, if anything, be *heightened* to the extent that one cared about being right. Because it has no material effect, I will omit this new clause in what follows; the clause makes the exposition more cumbersome, and anyone can easily supply it should he want the logical insurance it seems to provide.[10]

This attitude concerns any logically possible experience, not just any experience one thinks has any real possibility or chance of turning up. Thus, you may feel certain that God will not tell you that you didn't feel tired at that time, and feel certain also that no experience to that effect will ever turn up. But if your attitude is that, even caring most about being right, you would be *less* certain that you were tired *if* God told you that you weren't, then you *don't* have this attitude. Also, it is pretty plain, I think, that you will *not* be absolutely *certain* that you felt tired then. You *might still* be absolutely certain that God won't tell you this, but *if you are*, you will be *more certain* of that than you are that you felt tired then. That is enough to show that you will *not* be absolutely certain *that you felt tired then*.

Even if this extremely severe attitude is entailed by one's being absolutely certain of something, how is it to explain the effectiveness of our sceptical argument? That argument explicitly concerns *knowing*; it says nothing explicitly about being

---

[10] These possible difficulties were raised by Gilbert Harman and by Thomas Nagel. The accommodating clause to cover them is adopted from some remarks from Saul Kripke. I will discuss further questions about characterizing this attitude in Chapter III.

certain. To make the connection, I put forward the following hypothesis, which is complementary to the one so recently advanced: If one *knows* that something is so, say, that *p*, then it follows that it is (perfectly) *all right* for one to be absolutely *certain* that *p*, and this is accepted (perhaps only implicitly) by the speakers of English at least. Combining the two hypotheses, we get this further idea, which we may also suppose to be accepted (implicitly) by speakers of English (and perhaps others): If one *knows* that *p*, then it is (perfectly) all right for one to have the following attitude: nothing whatsoever will be counted as any reason to think that it is not or may not be true that *p*, and anything which may seem to show or suggest that will be rejected immediately as only misleading in the matter. Accordingly, if one *knows* something, one is in a state, position, or situation, which justifies (or is supposed to justify) an extremely severe negative attitude, an absolute one.

Now, in *many* cases, one will think this attitude to be *excessively* severe and, for that reason, dogmatic and irrational. In such cases, one will think that the person does not *know* the thing, that if he *thinks* he knows, he must be wrong. For in *these* cases, one thinks, *nothing* could justify *this* attitude. It is quite easy to think this about the case of a person believing himself to *know* that there is no evil scientist. For in the case of the scientist, it is easy to think of experiences which surely *seem* to show that such a scientist exists, or existed at the time. These experiences seem ones which *should not* be rejected out of hand, no matter what one's state, position or situation. Rather, they *should* have at least *some* dampening effect on one's certainty or confidence, both in fact and according to one's attitude. This allows these hypotheses to explain the compelling power of our argument.

We want to explain also why our thought that we *know* a certain state's capital can so easily arouse feelings of irrationality in everyday life. This is also done well by these hypotheses of ours. For on the hypotheses it is entailed by a man's thought that he knows, in a way which is not beyond his implicit understanding, that it is quite all right for him to have the *attitude of certainty* in the matter of whether this city is the capital of this state. He thinks something which entails something so severe as this: He is *justified* in having the attitude that *no*

matter what experience turns up next, he will give *no* consideration towards possibly lessening his certainty that that city is
that capital. And, this entailment is not beyond his grasp. Once
the library reference is announced, he feels that he should not
and cannot adhere to this attitude, that the attitude was really
ràther irrational and dogmatic in the first place. In ways like
this, we may explain why feelings of irrationality emerge
clearly and easily in ordinary cases.

Finally, we want to explain, in terms of our hypotheses, why
it is comparatively difficult to arouse any of these feelings in
the case of someone thinking that he knows that there are rocks.
At the same time, we want to explain why our classical argument seems effective against even so resistant a case as that.
The explanation of each is part of the same story. First, what
the person thinks is something which entails that it is, in the
case of there being rocks, perfectly all right for him to have the
attitude of certainty in the matter: no matter what might next
seem to turn up, especially in so far as he cares about being
right in the matter, he will not give any serious consideration
to anything that seems to show or suggest that there aren't
rocks (i.e. that there isn't even one rock). And, this entailment
being tacitly accepted by him, we may take him to be accepting as well the thought that it *is* perfectly all right for him to
have this attitude in this matter. In this case, unlike the others,
it is quite hard to see how anything *could* seriously call into
question, or even make one seriously think twice about, the
idea *that there are rocks*. Given that we live in the world we do,
and have had the experiences we have had, which we surely
do seem to be given, how could there conceivably be *no rocks?*
What would possibly serve to show that, or to suggest it in any
way deserving of serious consideration? Nothing turns up in
ordinary contexts, or in everyday life, to answer these questions.
Accordingly, feelings of irrationality and embarrassment don't
ordinarily arise here. One is hard put to have any idea that
there may be any dogmatism implicit in thinking oneself to
know *this* thing.

By means of its first premiss, the classical argument provides us with the idea that dogmatism is not easily isolated.
That is the power of the contrast cases employed therein. The
premiss has its effect, then, by giving us the idea, the correct

idea, that any dogmatism implicit in the thought that one *knows* these exotic cases *not* to obtain is *also* implicit, though of course less obviously so, in the idea that one *knows* that there are rocks. What the second premiss implies is that, in the exotic cases, that is quite enough dogmatism for one *not* to be justified in having the attitude of certainty. Thus it implies that it is quite enough for one *not* to *know* the exotic case not to obtain. Accordingly, what the two premisses say or imply together is this: there is quite enough dogmatism and irrationality even in the case of there being rocks for one never to know in that case either. By bringing one through steps of reasoning which show how dogmatism permeates the simple as much as the exotic, the classical argument succeeds in arousing feelings of irrationality which undermine the thought that one *knows* that there are rocks. After going through the argument, one can answer the questions which just before seemed to defy any answer. What could seem to show there to be no rocks? We have only to look to the sequences of possible experience we characterized before, in section 8. For example, one may have experiences as of a voice correctly predicting bizarre experiences next in store for one, of this voice seeming to explain in detail how it induced these bizarre experiences by means of certain electrodes, and of how it did the same before with experiences seeming to show there to be many rocks. In this way, our hypotheses explain why we *initially* treat the case of there being rocks quite *differently* from the other two cases. And, they also explain our treating it *later*, after having gone through the classical argument, in just the *same* sceptical way. Accordingly, our hypotheses have explained all we have wanted from them.

A further point now quickly comes to mind. If these hypotheses are right, as they seem to be, they may explain a good deal more. The attitude of certainty may be out of place in other matters as well, in particular, in the matter of whether exotic conditionals are true: *If* I am *not* being deceived by a scientist and my experiences are *not* randomly related to external things, *then* there are rocks. Shouldn't certain experiences, like those already described, sometimes make one less certain of the truth of such propositions also? It certainly seems so. On our hypotheses, then, one doesn't know them either. Thus, while our classical argument has not itself got us all the way there, our case for scepticism about knowledge of the external world may now be considered quite complete. In closing this section, I will make one last set of remarks. This relates to our wanting to explain our intuition, more tutored than the others, that *if* one doesn't know these things, e.g. that there are rocks, then it is *necessarily* true that one doesn't. This is explained by two things. First, the fact that speakers of English all accept these ideas about knowing is itself best explained on the idea that the sentences expressing them are *analytic* (however that is to be further explicated than just saying 'true in virtue of meaning'). So, those ideas represent necessary truths. Second, any *normative* proposition, in so far as it is complete and universal in scope, seems necessarily true if true at all. For example, if it is perfectly all right to neglect people who suffer needlessly, then it is *necessarily* true that this is all right. If it is all right *only in certain cases*, then what we have just said is *false*, and what *is* true, and *necessarily* true, is that it is all right *in those cases*. So, that is another reason for thinking that our sceptical conclusion is necessarily true. Further support for each of these paths of explanation, which are not incompatible ones, will emerge in the chapters to follow. In the remaining sections of the present chapter, I will try to see how much further we can compellingly extend our scepticism in ways afforded us by our classical form of sceptical argument.

§11. *The Retreat to Reasonable Believing: A Complex of Arguments and Problems*

When one despairs of ever *knowing* about certain things, then in so far as one believes things about those things, it is quite natural for one to aspire to be *reasonable* in one's beliefs about them. One can hardly stop believing various things about the external world. And it seems that in reasonable believing about such matters, one has a natural line of retreat should one accept our argument about knowing: 'Even if I can't ever *know* anything about things outside my own mind, I can very well be reasonable in *believing* various things concerning external matters, for example, that I have two hands, that there are other people and, our by now familiar favourite, that there are rocks. Unlike the situation with *knowing*, this will represent no extreme position on my part. Indeed, I might admit that I may always be wrong in believing these things, but I may still be reasonable in believing them, error or no error.'

But almost as soon as these thoughts occur, it is natural also to think that the same *sort* of considerations which bring one to scepticism about knowing these things, will bring grief as well to the idea that one really is *reasonable* in believing any such things. The simplest argument here is this: 'If I can't know *anything* concerning any external world there may be, then how can I have *any reason* at all for *believing* anything about any such world? It really seems that without this knowledge I can't. And, as we have already concluded, I *can't* know anything about any external world. Therefore, it seems, I can't really *have any reason* for believing any such thing either.'

How can we support this argument? We may take some steps in this way: Suppose I know that it now appears to me that there is a triangular object some distance before me. I may *take* this to be a *reason* for thinking that there is such an object there. But the appearance may be due only to an evil scientist's electrode operations. All of my experience, while it makes it *seem* that a rich external world has existed around me, and now does exist, may in fact have no real relation to this world I believe in. It may just as well be the product of that scientist. Or equally well, it may have no external cause at all. If I can't *know* the *general character* of the source of my experiences, neither they nor anything else can furnish me with any reason at all for believing one way or another about any external world there may be. For though something may *seem* to be a reason for believing some particular external thing, without *knowing* enough to discriminate amongst various possible origins, I *can't have any assurance* that it actually *is* a reason for believing it. And if I *can't ever have any assurance* to this effect, then it seems that it really *isn't* any *reason* for me to believe the thing, my having no more reason for that belief than for the opposite. With this support, the simple argument often has seemed to me to be correct.

If this simple argument has any error, it will be, I suggest, only in this premiss: If I can't *know anything* about the external world, then I can't have any *reason* for believing anything about it. That is the premiss we have tried to support. Now, that premiss *is* quite appealing, and *if* it is not true, it should be false for reasons which are quite unobvious. Still, at least certain cases seem to upset it, which I will call *consequential*, or *pragmatic*, or *non-epistemic* cases. The normal sort of reason for you to believe that there are rocks is something like this: that on many occasions it has appeared to you that some rocks were before you some distance away, or again, that on many occasions people have seemed to you to have been referring to rocks as things existing outside of anyone's mind, and so on. These might be called *evidential*, or *epistemic* reasons, the reasons being in way of evidence for the truth of what is believed, or being much like evidence for it. That is the sort of reason in which epistemology has taken an interest. And, if no one could ever *know* anything about the external world, *it might well follow* that no one could ever have any reason of *this* sort for believing anything about it. Pragmatic reasons work quite differently; nothing much like evidential relations is their primary concern. Here is one example of a pragmatic reason, representative of any case: Even without knowing anything about the external world, I *might know*, say, that it is in my own nature for me to be happier if I believe that there are rocks than if I do not. On the basis of this knowledge (allowed if not required by our classical argument), I might believe that there are rocks. Why, then, could I not have at least one reason for believing this external thing? And, why couldn't that reason be enough to make me reasonable in believing this, given of course that there is no reason here for me *not* to believe it?

It seems that no answer can be given and that, indeed, I do have just such a reason for believing this thing, namely, that I am happier if I believe it than if I do not. Accordingly, I may be quite reasonable in believing that there are rocks, *even if* I know *nothing* of any external world. Once one becomes aware of these pragmatic cases, one may well distrust our simple argument. One may even think that *any* feelings which were aroused by this argument are not trustworthy, but illusory. I don't think that this reaction is correct. Indeed, I think that the argument's sceptical conclusion is true, and that intuitions aroused by the argument for that conclusion are some support for thinking it true, for thinking that we can't be reasonable in beliefs about the external world. For the time being, I just note these intuitions, and make the plea that they *may* be more than just notable illusions. I plan to pursue these matters further in Chapter V, where a general examination of reasonableness and justification will be the topic.

In this same spirit of noting, we may note another line of argument which is also quite natural for resisting this retreat to reasonable believing. The idea here is *not* to get an argument for the new conclusion *from the conclusion already accepted about knowing*. Rather it is to get the new conclusion *from an argument parallel to the one for the conclusion about knowing*. In other words, the idea is that a *classical argument about* reasonable believing will yield scepticism here as well. This argument is easy to formulate now. We just replace 'knows' by 'is reasonable in believing', and then make whatever further changes are required as a consequence of that. The reasoning behind the new premisses will be the same as that for the premisses with knowing, and the resultant argument will be at least very nearly as compelling. Of course, the limitations of the argument will remain, as given before in section 7, but they are so slight that they hardly detract at all from our sceptical conclusion about reasonable believing. The key idea here is that, since any of your experiences may be due to a scientist's operations, they can never give you any reason for believing that there is no scientist deceiving you into falsely believing that there are rocks. So, you can't have any reason for believing that exotic thing and, accordingly, can't be reasonable in believing it. But, if you are reasonable in believing that there are rocks, the first premiss will read, then, on the assumption of reasoning, you *can* be reasonable in believing that there is no such scientist. Therefore, by this parallel argument, you *aren't* reasonable in believing that there are rocks, and the same goes for any other external matter.

Pragmatic reasons upset this classical argument, however, even at the point of its first premiss. According to that premiss, if one is reasonable in believing something, one *can* be reasonable in believing certain things which follow logically from it, presumably because one has at least as much reason in favour of the latter. This *may well be right if* all the reasons here are evidential, as we may now do well to note. But, it does *not* hold for pragmatic reasons. For example, I may know, as before, that I will be happier believing that there are rocks. But, I may not know, and it may not even be true, that I will be happier believing some exotic entailment of this than if I do not believe such an entailed thing. Indeed I may even *know* that *I will be happier* if I have *no* beliefs at all on any of these exotic matters. I may know, or so we may suppose, that any belief on my part to the effect that an evil scientist is, *or that one is not*, doing anything to me may disturb me. In such a case I may have a reason for believing that there are rocks, but I may also have no reason for believing that no evil scientist is deceiving me into falsely believing that there are rocks. In this case, it may well be quite impossible for me to be *reasonable* in believing the latter thing, should I actually believe it. As with our simple argument before, pragmatic reasons appear quite upsetting for this argument of our classical form.

Even so, going through this classical argument also arouses feelings in favour of its sceptical conclusion. And, they should be explained. We shall try to do this also in Chapter V, the chapter where we will treat in fuller detail the issues of scepticism and the conditions of reasonableness. But enough of these issues for now; we must return to look at the classical argument in other contexts concerning *knowing*.

§12. *An Argument concerning Other Times*

The classical argument so far presented has always *allowed*, at least implicitly, that the person *might know* that his experiences and mental states exhibited a certain pattern *over time*: He might know, for example, that he is now experiencing (something) blue and not red, and that at a previous time he experienced (something) red and not blue. Perhaps, as we have suggested, he had this experiential sequence because an evil scientist first stimulated him to experience only red and now is stimulating him to experience only blue. Perhaps, as we have also suggested, these experiences are causally related to no external things at all, neither scientists, nor electrodes, nor whatever. On the other hand, they might even be enjoyed in normal, conscious, visual perception, the person first seeing only red objects and now seeing only blue ones. What we have argued is that, whichever of these may obtain, he won't *know* that it does.

We have also so far allowed that the person *might know* that his experiences and mental states, occurring over time, were *causally related* to each other. He might know, for example, that his now experiencing blue is the causal result of his having experienced red at that earlier time. Anyone with a marked sceptical bent, however, would not wish to allow such knowledge for long. Can sceptics appeal to a compelling argument of our classical form?

Anyone acquainted with Russell's writing in *The Analysis of Mind* should soon agree that nothing could suit a sceptic better where time is concerned.[11] In the relevant passages, Russell concerns himself with memory and, more generally, the past. But application of the same general idea to the future is quite clear and obvious. Thus this Russellian way of thinking works for any time, with the outstanding exception of *the present moment*.

Following Russell, we have the idea that the earth, or even the entire universe (of concrete entities at least) just came into existence a moment ago. This includes people, including myself of course, as well as the rest of the world. In particular, it includes one's own *ostensible* memory beliefs and experiences, that is, beliefs to the effect that one remembers this or that, and experiences which seem to one to pertain to certain past events, in certain apparently familiar ways. This might be because one has a brain configured just like that of someone who has experienced many things, or just like some such brain *would be* in a world which did not just come to exist. Additionally, anything which one might perceive in one's surroundings would be just like what one would expect from a gradually developed world. There might be 'aged' people as well as 'young' ones, 'old' yellow newspapers as well as 'today's' white ones, fossils in the rocks at certain levels, and so on. So even if one could know about external things, that would be of no avail.

Nor would it be of any avail *even if* one could begin to know things about the newly developing past, by living into the future. For knowledge of a recent past interval would be of no aid in getting back to times before the supposed coming into existence. But, then, of course, one *can't* suppose that one may

[11] Russell places the limit of the past at five minutes ago, but I will not be so generous. In Bertrand Russell's *The Analysis of Mind* (New York, 1921), pp. 159–60.

gain any knowledge of this recent, newly developed past period either. For the same supposition may be made about *any* moment; what is *now* the present, and now, and now. Those are essentially Russell's ideas on these matters, or at least a version of them filtered through a sceptic about knowledge.

Russell's hypothesis about the world presents a vivid contrast case to our 'common sense' beliefs about, or presumed knowledge of, any past times. As regards any future time, we may contrast our common sense views with the following case: The entire world (of concrete entities at least) might cease to exist as of the very next moment. By combining this with Russell's idea about the past, we get the idea of an entire world (of concrete entities at least) existing only for a moment, right *now*. How can anyone ever *know* that this Super Russell case does not obtain?

This Super Russell case parallels closely enough the case of the 'randomly related' experience in the argument about the external world. (For an exact parallel, we just say that the man's experiences may be only randomly related to any past or future things *there may be*, making the case open on the possibilities.) If you at least believe in the (less open) Super Russell case, at least believe that the world only exists for this moment, might you not *know* this? To know this would be too much for any true sceptic regarding our (alleged) knowledge of other times. We want, then, another contrast case, such that it also seems clearly impossible to know about. That case can parallel the case of the evil scientist in the argument about the external world. We need such a case, *incompatible with* the world's existing for only a moment *as well as with* 'common sense' beliefs, in order to move towards a perfectly general, valid argument about other times, one that covers all logically possible situations. What, then, will satisfy this need here?

We may again call on an evil scientist. This time he need not be using any electrodes, or be now actively engaged in deceiving you in any way (though he may too, and will if you like to combine your sceptical arguments into a 'simultaneous assault'). The description of the scientist now is this: He has created you, complete with your ostensible memory beliefs and experiences. And, for good measure, he will immediately destroy you, so that in the next moment you no longer exist. To complete this timely contrast case, the other things in the world's 'history' can be as crazy as you like, providing the chosen description is self-consistent and also that it contradicts the Super Russell case description. In terms of these exotic contrast cases, it is very easy to construct a classical argument for the conclusion that no one ever *knows* anything about any other time. This argument is at least very nearly as compelling as our offered argument about the external world (though, in Chapter III, I will say some things which indicate that it should not be *quite as* compelling). The limitations of the previous argument of course will apply here as well. Again, this means that a *slightly less strong* conclusion is yielded than the proper thesis of scepticism regarding knowledge of other times. Again as well, the difference is so slight that I will proceed generally to ignore it in what follows.

The intuitions aroused by this argument, and intensified in reflection on an attempt to reverse it, also parallel what happened with the external world. The explanation here too may best be given, I suggest, in terms of our hypotheses. Thus it is in terms of the dogmatism implicit in the attitude of certainty, which this classical argument now helps us to see to be always there with claims to know anything about other times, or even with thoughts to the same effect. So, the external world and other times join in supporting these hypotheses about knowing and being absolutely certain.

Now, it is traditional, and of some interest I think, to state what follows from our two conclusions taken together, and then to try to see what remains left for us possibly to know about. For it appears that this exercise will take us near the limits within which our classical arguments work in a compelling way. Within these limits at least, the attitude of certainty seems clearly to be always dogmatic. As is not surprising, the sceptical thesis about other times and that regarding the external world combine to form a position which denies almost all of our commonly assumed knowledge of things. I call this position *epistemic solipsism of the present moment*. According to this position, as far as *knowing* goes, if one is interested in contingent truths about concrete entities, one is confined to one's present moment existence, experience, and immediate mental states. In addition to that, the position *allows* one's knowing various necessary truths, and also some contingent things about some abstract entities, if such there be, e.g. *the colour red* is now being experienced by me. But as concerns anything which would normally seem to be of *interest*, it will *not* be known, now or ever, by anyone at all.

§13. *How much Alleged Knowledge can this Form of Argument Compellingly Exclude?*

Discounting the cases raised by exotic conditionals and similar logical difficulties, this classical form of argument excludes all the alleged knowledge denied by solipsism of the present moment. Can this form of argument compellingly exclude still more cases, or is the force that it can generate for scepticism limited to this admittedly huge domain? While the argument can be quite easily given *formal* parallels in other areas, those parallels rarely appear very convincing. The reasons differ in different cases. The worst cases for the argument go wrong for *logical* reasons. The other hard cases seem to go wrong for what we may call *phenomenological* reasons.

Certain propositions present logical difficulties for this form of argument, rendering it self-defeating, question-begging, circular, or otherwise inoperative. These difficulties share something in common with the limiting problems we encountered in trying to formulate a perfectly general argument about the external world. Even more than there, we are in tune with the spirit of Descartes if we call these *Cartesian propositions*.

We may consider first the famous Cartesian proposition 'I exist'. Can you *know* that there is *no* evil scientist who, by means of electrodes, is deceiving you into *falsely* believing that you yourself exist right now? You will think that you *can* know this. You may think, first, that you can reason to this proposition from the premiss that you exist right now. This is correct. And, second, you may think that this last is something which one knows with absolute certainty. What could call *that* knowledge into question? An evil scientist? It seems that you can reason against such a possibility: I couldn't be deceived by an evil scientist about *anything* unless *I exist* in the first place. That I exist is a condition for him to deceive me at all. So, he can't deceive me into *falsely* believing that *I exist*.

If one allows that the proposition that one thinks is entailed by the proposition that one at least believes something, then this other famous Cartesian proposition appears similarly immune from this form of sceptical argument. And, in any case, the proposition that one at least believes something does itself appear immune. For if you didn't at least believe something, no scientist, however evil or good, could possibly be deceiving you into falsely *believing anything.* Somewhat different logical reasons make other propositions immune. The proposition that one can reason cannot be called into question by this argument, or so it appears. For if you cannot reason, then you have no business being convinced by any argument at all. Thus, you should, in particular, feel under no constraint of rationality to accept a classical argument to the effect that you may not know that you can now reason.

Many other propositions do *not* seem to have a close *logical* relation to the very idea of one's being properly convinced by a classical argument. But, at any time one *feels most compelled to accept them,* being then 'struck by one's experience', they seem so absolutely certain and sure that there appears no hope for any deceiving scientist. These are the difficult *phenomenological* cases. The proposition 'I am in pain' is one which we feel most compelled to accept when in rather intense pain. Of course, by logic, when you *are* in such pain, no evil scientist can be deceiving you into falsely believing that you are in pain. But, beyond this, it seems that when in rather intense pain, you couldn't possibly fail to believe, or even to know, that you are. The first is a logical impossibility, the latter perhaps a phenomenological one—but as much an impossibility for all that. Thus, it seems that when you are in rather intense pain, you must *know* that you are in pain, and that at such a time no evil scientist can block or prevent you from knowing it. Something like this seems also to go on as regards propositions concerning the meaning of your words, the content of your beliefs, and the presence of things answering to those contents: 'By "red", I mean *that* colour,' 'I believe that there are red things,' '*That* thing is red.' It seems that, at certain times, you *can't fail to know* these propositions to be true. A classical argument seems powerless against this apparent fact.

With respect to certain necessary truths, those often thought to be intuitively known, no convincing classical argument seems available either. How is an evil scientist to prevent you from knowing that one and one are two? It appears that if you did not, at the very least, *correctly* believe that one and one are two, you could not understand any premiss of any argument in which that belief is under discussion. Therefore, no argument which relies on the idea that you might *incorrectly* believe this thing will appear at all compelling. ('Incorrectly or falsely believe *what*?' you might ask.) This same reasoning applies to simple analytic propositions, like the proposition that any bachelor there may be is unmarried.

No such reasoning would seem to apply, however, to those necessary propositions whose acceptance is generally based on reasoning or calculation, like the proposition that $45 + 56 = 101$. Some of these, I suggest, are also analytic propositions, expressed by analytic sentences, like 'My mother's father's son's daughter is my cousin or sister' (if that one is figured out correctly here!). For in these cases, it is quite clear that one can understand the content without having even a fair idea as to whether or not the proposition expressed is true. In these matters, one thinks, an evil scientist just might be deceiving one into false belief; one can't *know* that none is doing so. Thus, a classical argument seems *forceful* for excluding alleged *knowledge* of these things. And, doesn't the attitude of certainty seem out of place here; and feelings of dogmatism and irrationality often to lurk close by? The limits of the argument seem to be the limits of its getting our implicitly accepted hypotheses to connect with our thoughts on what we know.

While our classical form of argument will not demand acceptance in every matter, it convincingly excludes virtually all alleged knowledge of any interest. The remainder, as familiar to epistemologists as it seems untouched by our argument, may yet be ruled out by *other* sceptical arguments. For us to be happiest with those other arguments we would like to see some connection between them and the intuitively effective arguments of the classical form. My own thought is that a connection is available, and that the main connecting link is their common reliance on the dogmatism in the attitude of certainty. Before trying to expose this connection, I want to find a basis for my thought in some general features of our language. I turn, then, to examine contemporary English which, as it happens, is the only language in which I can think.

II

A Language with Absolute Terms

F E W philosophers now take scepticism seriously. With philosophers, even the most powerful of traditional sceptical arguments has little force to tempt them nowadays. Our classical form of argument is hardly an exception in these positive times. And the robust approach of Moore is not the only way of quickly rebutting arguments for scepticism. Without stretching the point too much, we might even say that nowadays philosophers think scepticism important only as a formal challenge to which positive accounts of 'our common sense knowledge' are the satisfying responses.[1] Consequently, I have quite a lot of work to do before philosophers will feel ready to give any sceptical arguments or intuitions a fair and patient examination.

I write these words at a time when the greatest concentration of philosophical intelligence appears concerned with language, more particularly, with natural languages, and most particularly, with contemporary English.[2] In order to gain credence for the idea that a quite sweeping sceptical thesis is correct, then, I will look for a basis for that idea in our language, that is, in contemporary English. This will be one main theme for the rest of this book, though what is perhaps the

[1] Among G. E. Moore's most influential papers against scepticism are 'A Defense of Common Sense', 'Four Forms of Scepticism', and 'Certainty'. These papers are now available in Moore's *Philosophical Papers* (New York, 1962). Other recent representatives of similar anti-sceptical persuasion include A. J. Ayer's *The Problem of Knowledge* (Baltimore, 1956), Roderick Chisholm's *Perceiving* (Ithaca, N.Y., 1957), papers in Norman Malcolm's *Knowledge and Certainty* (Englewood Cliffs, N.J., 1964), and so on down the roll of the most influential recent writers on the subject. My own earlier attempts may be classed here as well, most especially my paper, 'Our Knowledge of the Material World', *Studies in the Theory of Knowledge*, American Philosophical Quarterly Monograph No. 4 (1970).

[2] To have this point brought home forcefully, one need only read the tables of contents of such collections as these: *Semantics and the Philosophy of Language*, ed. Leonard Linsky (Urbana, Ill., 1952), *Philosophy and Ordinary Langage*, *ed.* Charles E. Caton (Urbana, Ill., 1963), *Words and Objections*, ed. Donald Davidson and Jaakko Hintikka (Dorcrecht, 1969), *Semantics of Natural Language*, ed. Donald Davidson and Gilbert Harman (Dordrecht, 1972), and so on.

largest part of finding this basis will be done within the confines of the present chapter. Within these same confines, I will also present a relatively independent and quite new sceptical argument. This argument is quite directly based on the relevant linguistic materials to be exposed. Its conclusion is not quite as strong as *universal* scepticism, but it is quite strong nevertheless. In response to a philosophical environment which is so hostile to scepticism, I will speak of myself throughout this chapter as *defending* this sceptical thesis. But I am trying to advance it just the same.

The scepticism that I will defend is of course a negative thesis concerning what we do or do not know. While I am at base a sceptic also about reasonable believing (as in Chapter I, section 11 and especially in Chapter V), at this point I will allow that there is much that many of us correctly and reasonably believe. But much more than that is needed for us to know even a fair amount. Here, I will not argue that nobody knows anything about anything, though that would be quite consistent with the sceptical thesis for which I will argue. The somewhat less radical thesis which I will defend is this one: Every human being knows at most hardly anything to be so. More specifically, I will argue that hardly anyone knows that forty-five and fifty-six are equal to one-hundred-and-one, if anyone at all. On this sceptical thesis, no one will know the thesis to be true. But this is all right. For I only want here to argue that it may be reasonable for us to suppose the thesis to be true, not that we should ever know it to be true. I want to move us towards favouring this thesis.

Even with these softening remarks, resistance to this sceptical thesis is almost bound to be massive. For there is now something which goes far beyond any concentration of intelligence on our language. I write at a time when, among philosophers, there is an almost universal faith that, so far as expressing truths goes, all or almost all is well with the language that we speak.[3] Against this common, perhaps optimistic assumption, I shall illustrate how our language habits might serve us well in practical ways, even while they involve us in saying what is not true. And this often does occur, I will maintain, when our

---

[3] This is represented in almost all of the material in the works cited in the previous two footnotes to this chapter.

positive assertions contain terms with special features of a certain kind, terms which I call *absolute* (*limit*) *terms*.

English is a language with absolute terms. Among these terms, 'flat' and 'certain' are *basic* ones. Due to these terms' characteristic features, and because the world is not so simple as it might be, we do not speak truly, at least as a rule, when we say of a real object, 'That has a top which is flat,' or when we say of a real person, 'He is certain that it is raining.' And just as basic absolute terms generally fail to apply to the world, so other absolute terms, which are at least partially defined by the basic ones, will fail to apply as well. Thus, we also speak falsely when we say of a real object or person: 'That is a cube' or 'He knows that it is raining.' For, an object is a cube only if it has surfaces which are flat, and, as I shall argue, a person knows something to be so, only if he is certain of it.

If a condition of something's being *flat* is, as I shall argue, that nothing could ever possibly be even the least bit flatter, we would be in a strong position to advance the thesis, in the most ordinary meaning of the words, that *at most hardly any* physical objects are *flat*. (If there is only one flat object per billion galaxies, but an infinite number of galaxies and so an infinite number of flat objects, each surrounded by billions of objects which are not flat, this will satisfy the most ordinary meaning, I think, of 'at most hardly any of those (infinite) objects are flat'.) Now, in the case of any or almost any physical object, you can find another which is flatter. Of course, the flattest object you might ever find *may* itself *not* be flat, or the few tied for flattest *may* themselves actually *not* be flat. At the same time, it or they may be flat. If it is or they are, then it is still true that hardly any are flat, and so, that at most hardly any are flat. If it is not or they are not, it will also be true that *at most* hardly any physical objects are flat. In either case, then, it will be true that at most hardly any physical objects are flat.

Similarly, if a condition of someone's being *certain* of something is, as I shall similarly argue, that no one could ever possibly be any more certain of anything than he is of that, we would be in a strong position to advance the thesis that, in the case of every human being, there is at most hardly anything of which he is certain. This thesis may be true, then, because no one is ever certain of anything, or it may be true because no one is certain of more than a very few things.

This is the strategy of my defence. But before I apply it, or look for its linguistic basis, I must address some worries about what our thesis entails or requires. For these worries will now be natural for almost any sophisticated philosopher.

§1. *Sophisticated Worries about what Scepticism requires*

The reason that contemporary sophisticated philosophers do not take scepticism seriously can be stated broadly and simply: They think that scepticism implies certain things which are, upon a bit of reflection, quite impossible to accept. These unacceptable implications concern the functioning of our language.

Concerning our language and how it functions, the most obvious requirement of scepticism is that some common terms of our language will involve us in error systematically. These will be such terms as 'know' and 'knowledge', which may be called the 'terms of knowledge'. If scepticism is right, then while we go around saying 'I know', 'He knows', and so on, and while we believe what we say to be true, all the while what we say and believe will actually be false. If our beliefs to the effect that we know things are so consistently false, then the terms of knowledge lead us into error systematically. But if these beliefs really are false, shouldn't we have experiences which force the realization of their falsity upon us, and indeed abandon these beliefs? Consequently, shouldn't our experiences get us to stop thinking in these terms which thus systematically involve us in error? So, as we continue to think in the terms of knowledge and to believe ourselves to know all sorts of things, this would seem to show that the beliefs are not false ones and the terms are responsible for no systematic error. Isn't it only reasonable, then, to reject a view which requires that such helpful common terms as 'know' and 'knowledge' lead us into error systematically?

So go some worrisome thoughts which might lead us to dismiss scepticism out of hand. But it seems to me that there is no real need for our false beliefs to clash with our experiences in any easily noticeable way. Suppose, for instance, that you falsely believe that a certain region of space is a *vacuum*. Suppose that, contrary to your belief, the region does contain some gaseous

stuff, though only the slightest trace. Now, for practical purposes, we may suppose that, so far as gaseous contents go, it is
not important whether that region really is a vacuum or
whether it contains whatever gaseous stuff it does contain.
Once this is supposed, then it is reasonable to suppose as well,
that, for practical purposes, it makes no important difference
whether you falsely believe that the region is a vacuum or truly
believe this last thing, namely, that, for practical purposes,
it is not important whether the region is a vacuum or whether
it contains that much gaseous stuff.

We may notice that this supposed truth is entailed by what
you believe but does not entail it. In other words, a region's
being a vacuum entails that, for practical purposes, there is no
important difference between whether the region is a vacuum
or whether it contains whatever gaseous stuff it does contain.
For, if the region *is* a vacuum whatever gas it contains is nil,
and so there is no difference *at all*, for any sort of purpose,
between the region's being a vacuum and its having that much
gaseous stuff. But, the entailment does not go the other way,
and this is where we may take a special interest. For, while a
region may not be a vacuum, it may contain so little gaseous
stuff that, so far as gaseous contents go, for practical purposes,
there is no important difference between the region's being a
vacuum and its containing whatever gaseous stuff it does contain. So, if this entailed truth lies behind the believed falsehood,
your false belief, though false, may not be harmful. Indeed,
generally, it may even be helpful for you to have this false
belief rather than having none and rather than having almost
any other beliefs about the matter that you might have. On
this pattern, we may have many false beliefs about regions
being vacuums even while these beliefs will suffer no important
clash with the experiences of life.

Where finer distinctions are necessary to our activities, we
may make them even if our key terms have less to do with the
job than might be supposed. Thus, the standards for something's
being a vacuum are higher for the purposes of certain laboratory
research than for the commercial preservation of peanuts.
Someone in a peanut factory may declare that vacuums have
been established in certain cans. He will not be understood to
believe, or to intend to convey the idea that, those cans are as

empty as can be. Rather, his intended and presumably accepted point will be that the interior of those cans, surrounding the nuts, is in each case near enough to being a vacuum for the purposes at hand (whether or not for other purposes more or less practical). Even if he does not fully understand what it is to be a vacuum, that it is to be a *perfect* vacuum, we who do understand it can report his intended point as we have done: His intent is to convey the idea that, for those purposes, there is no important difference between the insides of those cans and a space which really is a perfect vacuum. The meaning of 'vacuum', *along with contextual factors*, lets him make his point succinctly, whether or not he appreciates the meaning of the word as fully as we are forcing ourselves now to do.

The meaning of 'vacuum' remains the same whether on the canner's lips or in a laboratory report. As regards being a vacuum, is there no difference between the regions the canner picks out and those referred to in the lab report? Of course there is a difference: The regions in the laboratory are much closer to being real vacuums than those in the peanut cans. But, that difference, while important to the research, is not important to keeping the peanuts fit for eating in several months.

More to our central topic, suppose that, as scepticism might have it, you falsely believe you *know* that there are elephants. As before, there is a true thing which is entailed by what you falsely believe, and which we should notice. The true thing here, which you presumably do not believe, is this: That you are in an intellectual (or 'epistemic') position with respect to the matter of whether there are elephants which is such that, for practical purposes, it makes no difference whether you *know* there are elephants or whether you are in that intellectual position with respect to the matter that you actually are in. This latter, true thing is entailed by the false thing you believe, namely, that you know that there are elephants. For, if you do know, then, with respect to the matter of the elephants, there is no difference at all, for any purpose of any sort, between your knowing and your being in the position you actually are in. On the other hand, the entailment does not go the other way, and, again, this is where our pattern allows a false belief to be helpful. For, even if you do not really know, still, it may be that, for practical purposes, you are in a position with respect to the matter (of the elephants) which is not importantly different from knowing. If this is so, then it may be better, practically speaking, for you to believe falsely that you know than to have no belief at all here. Thus, not only with beliefs to the effect that specified regions are vacuums, but also with beliefs to the effect that we know certain things, it may be that there are very many of them which, though false, it is useful and thus quite good for us to have. In both cases, the beliefs will not noticeably clash with the experiences of life.

As with regions more or less like vacuums, sometimes finer discriminations are needed in practical situations as regards people's positions which are more or less like knowing. In making a sworn statement, if you answer affirmatively a question as to whether you know a certain thing, you had better be at least very close to knowing the thing, no matter how difficult, or even impossible, knowing the thing may be. In casual conversation, so long as you are right about the thing itself, and it is not an accident that you are right, you will be near enough to knowing the thing for the purposes there to be satisfied.[4] When making the sworn statement, though, not only had this better obtain, but you had better satisfy some further conditions which will bring you, at the least, quite a bit nearer to *knowing* the thing. The contexts make it clear enough what is wanted and, thus, what is or is not an appropriate thing there to say. There is no reason to suppose that the meaning of 'know' changes from the courtroom to the living room and back again; no more than for supposing that 'vacuum' changes from the laboratory to the cannery. Without noting something else, then, we have no powerful reason for dismissing the thesis of scepticism. Noting the smooth functioning of the 'terms of knowledge', even across many varied contexts, gives us no such reason.

There is, however, a second worry which will tend to keep

[4] I made too much of this, trying to argue that only a somewhat stronger condition was logically sufficient for knowing, in my paper, 'An Analysis of Factual Knowledge', *Journal of Philosophy*, vol. lxv, No. 6 (1968). The analysis there offered was this (with new emphasis here): For any sentential value of p, (at a time t) a man knows that p if and only if (at t) it is not *at all* accidental that the man is right about its being the case that p. Noting the words 'at all', I now take this to be a rather strong necessary condition for knowing, and no more. For one thing, as I shall argue, knowing requires being certain, and I can't see that the fulfilment of this condition requires that.

sophisticates far from embracing scepticism, and this worry is, I think, rather more profound than the first. Consequently, I shall devote most of the remainder of this chapter to treating this second worry. The worry to which I shall be so devoted is this: That, if scepticism is right, then the terms of knowledge, unlike other terms of our language, will never or hardly ever be used to make simple, positive assertions that are true. In other words, scepticism will require the terms of knowledge to be isolated freaks of our language. But, even with familiar, persuasive arguments for scepticism, it is implausible to think that our language is plagued by an isolated little group of useful but semantically troublesome freaks. So, by being so hard on knowledge (and vacuums) alone, scepticism seems implausible once one reflects on the exclusiveness of its persecution.

§2. *Absolute Terms and Relative Terms*

Against the worry that scepticism will require the terms of knowledge to be isolated freaks, I shall argue that, on the contrary, a variety of other terms are similarly troublesome. As scepticism becomes more plausible with an examination of the terms of knowledge, so other originally surprising theses become more plausible once their key terms are critically examined. When all of the key terms are understood to have essential features in common, the truth of any of these theses need not be felt as such a surprise.

The terms of knowledge, along with many other troublesome terms, belong to a class of terms that is quite pervasive in our language. I call these terms *absolute terms*. The term 'flat', in its central, literal meaning, is an absolute term. (With other meanings, however closely related, perhaps as in 'His voice is flat' and 'The beer is flat', I have no direct interest.) To say that something is flat is, so far as content goes, no different from saying that it is absolutely, or perfectly flat. To say that a surface is flat is to say that some things or properties *which are matters of degree* are *not* instanced in the surface *to any degree at all*. Thus, something which is flat is not all bumpy, and not at all curved. Bumpiness and curvature are matters of degree. When we say of a surface that it is bumpy, or that it is curved, we use the *relative terms* 'bumpy' and 'curved' to talk about the surface. Thus, many absolute terms and relative terms go together, in at least one important way, while other terms, like 'unmarried', have only the most distant connections with terms of either of these two sorts.

Semantically, we may say that our absolute terms indicate, or purport to denote, an absolute *limit*. This limit is approached to the extent that the relevant relative property or properties are absent in the thing to which one might sensibly apply the absolute term, or its correlative relatives.[5] Thus, 'flat' purports to denote a limit, flatness, which more or less curved and bumpy things approach to the extent that they are not bumpy, and are not curved, and so on. Accordingly, the absolute terms to which I refer might best be called 'absolute *limit* terms', but I will not use the word 'limit' much explicitly.

I am not at all sure that whenever we have an absolute term there are relative terms which neatly define it at least partially. For example, both 'empty' and 'full' intuitively seem to mark absolute limits: If something is full (of stuff), then, it seems, it is absolutely and completely full (of stuff); if something is empty (of stuff), then, it appears, it is absolutely and perfectly empty (of stuff). But what relative terms (adjectives) can be used even partially to define these? When we say that something is empty, that is to say that it contains *nothing* whatsoever (perhaps, of the sorts of things or stuffs it might conceivably contain). Perhaps there is a relative property of containing things or stuff: how much stuff is contained will be the same, more or less, as to what extent something has this property. But it does not seem that there is any relative term (adjective) ready neatly to denote this property, ready neatly to help in defining 'empty'. Similar thoughts appear to hold for 'full', the absolute term which appears to mean the opposite. But whether or not 'full' and 'empty' pair up with relative terms which may be used neatly to define them (at least in a partial way), there will remain an intuitive semantic difference between them and 'flat', on the one hand, and such terms as 'bumpy', 'rich', and 'large' on the other. At the same time, of

---

[5] To make this generalization good, perhaps I must use the term 'property' in a somewhat extended sense. Thus, I will speak of a property of containing stuff, which pretty empty things lack to a pretty great degree, and which empty things lack entirely.

course, many, perhaps most, relative terms do not seem to help in defining any absolute term. For example, if 'rich' and 'large' don't fail to do so, at least their opposites, 'poor' and 'small', seem to find no correlative absolute to help define.

The key limit terms are all *adjectives*, as are their relative counterparts; 'flat' is an adjective, so is 'bumpy'. There seems to be a syntactic feature, or set of features, which is common to these absolute adjectives and also to relative terms, but which does not seem to be found with any other terms. This feature is that each of these terms may be modified by a great variety of terms that serve to indicate (matters of) degree. Thus, for example, we find 'The table is *pretty* bumpy', and 'The table is *pretty* flat', but not, except as a figure of speech or a joke, 'The lawyer is *pretty* unmarried'. Among those absolute terms which admit such qualification appear all those absolute terms which are *basic* ones. A basic absolute term is an absolute term which is not (naturally) defined in terms of some other absolute term, not even partially so. I think that 'straight' is such a term, and that 'flat' is as well. But, in its central, spatial meaning, 'cube' quite clearly is not a basic absolute term even though it is an absolute term. (Perhaps another meaning of 'cube', a related one, is its numerical meaning: 'Twenty-seven is the cube of three.') For 'cube' means, at least, '. . . which has edges that are *straight* and surfaces which are *flat*'; and 'straight' and 'flat' are absolute terms. While 'cube' does not admit of qualification of degree, 'flat' and 'straight' do admit of such qualification; this has to do with the fact that the latter are both adjectives while 'cube' is a noun. Thus, all relative terms and all *basic* absolute terms admit of a large battery of constructions of degree. While this is another way in which these two sorts of terms go together, we must ask: How may we distinguish terms of the one sort from those of the other?

But is there anything to distinguish here? For, if absolute terms admit of degree constructions, why think that any of these terms is not a relative term, why think that they do not all purport to predicate things or properties which are, as they now look to be, matters of degree. If we may say that a table is pretty flat, then why not think flatness a matter of degree? Isn't this essentially the same as our saying of a table that it is pretty bumpy, with bumpiness being a matter of degree? So,

perhaps, 'flat', like 'bumpy' and like all terms that take degree
constructions, is, fittingly, a relative term. But basic absolute
terms may be distinguished from relatives even where degree
constructions conspire to make things look otherwise.

To advance the wanted distinction, we may look to a procedure for paraphrase. Now, we must grant that it is common for
us to say of a surface that it is pretty, or very, or extremely flat.
And, it is also common for us to say that, in saying such things
of surfaces, we are saying *how* flat the surfaces are. What we
say here seems of a piece with our saying of a surface that it is
pretty, or very, or extremely bumpy, and our then saying that,
in doing this, we are saying *how* bumpy the surface is. But even
intuitively, we may notice a difference here. For, only with our
talk with 'flat' do we have the idea that these locutions are only
convenient means for saying how closely a surface approximates
or, how close it comes to being, a surface which is (absolutely)
flat. This seems true *whether or not* there actually are any
(physical) surfaces which indeed are flat. Thus, it is intuitively
plausible, and far from being a nonsensical interpretation, to
paraphrase things so that our result with our 'flat' locutions is
this: What we have said of a surface is that it is pretty *nearly*
flat, or very *nearly* flat, or extremely *close to being* flat, and, in
doing that, we have said, not simply how flat the surface is, but,
rather, how *close* the surface is *to being* flat. This form of paraphrase gives a plausible interpretation of our talk of flatness
while allowing the term 'flat' to lose its appearance of being a
relative term. (The only true relative terms here are 'close'
and 'near'.) How will this form of paraphrase work with
'bumpy', where, presumably, a genuine relative term occurs in
our locutions?

What do we say when we say of a surface that it is pretty
bumpy, or very bumpy, or extremely so? Of course, it at least
appears that we say *how* bumpy the surface is. The paraphrase has it that what we are saying is that the surface is
pretty *nearly* bumpy, or very *nearly* bumpy, or extremely *close
to being* bumpy. In other words, according to the paraphrase,
we are saying how *close* the surface is *to being* bumpy. But anything of this sort is, quite obviously, a terribly poor interpretation of what we are saying about the surface. Unfortunately
for the paraphrase, if we say that a surface is very bumpy it is

entailed by what we say that the surface is bumpy, while if we say that the surface is very close to being bumpy it is entailed that the surface is *not* bumpy.[6] Thus, unlike with 'flat', our paraphrase cannot apply with 'bumpy'. Consequently, by means of our paraphrase we may distinguish between 'flat' and 'bumpy', and thus between basic absolute terms and relative ones.

Another way of noticing how our paraphrase lends support to the distinction between absolute and relative terms is this: The initial data is that such terms as 'very' standardly serve to indicate that there is a great deal of something. But they serve with opposite effect when they modify terms like 'flat', terms which I have called basic absolute terms. That is, when we say, for example, that something is (really) very flat, then, so far as flatness is concerned, we seem to say *less* of the thing than when we say simply, that it is (really) flat. The 'augmenting' function of 'very' is turned on its head. It is as if we said that the thing is very *nearly* flat, and so, by implication, that it is *not* flat (but only very nearly so). Perhaps what we said with 'very' *means* that. Once the paraphrase is exploited, the term 'very' may be understood to have its standard augmenting function. At the same time, 'very' functions without conflict with 'bumpy', another mark of this being a relative term. Happily, the term 'very' is far from being unique here: we get the same results with other 'augmenting modifiers': 'extremely', 'especially', and so on.

For our paraphrastic procedure to be comprehensive, it must work with contexts containing explicitly comparative locutions. Indeed, with these contexts, we have a common form of talk where the appearance of relativeness is most striking of all. What shall we think of our saying, for example, that one surface is not *as* flat as another, where things strikingly look to be a matter of degree? It seems that we must allow that in such suggested comparison, the surface which is said to be the *flatter* of the two may be, so far as logic goes, (absolutely) flat.

---

[6] To see what sense, if any, may attach to 'very nearly bumpy' we must think of some such context as this: A flat object is about to be pressed by a heavy, bumpy one. After contact, but not now, the flat object will be bumpy. Now, then, it may be very nearly bumpy. Even this case may not be well described by 'very nearly bumpy' or 'very near to being bumpy'. Perhaps all that we can *properly* say of this flat object is that it is very near, or very close, to *becoming* bumpy.

Thus, we should *not* paraphrase this comparative context as 'The one surface is not as *nearly* flat as the other.' For, this form of paraphrase would imply that the second surface is not flat. And so, it gives us a poor interpretation of the original, which has no such implication. But, then, a paraphrase with no bad implications is not far removed. Instead of simply inserting our 'nearly' or our 'close to being', we may allow for the possibility of absolute flatness by putting things in a way which is only somewhat more complex. For, we may paraphrase our original by saying: The first surface is either *not flat though the second is* or else it is not as *nearly* flat as the second. Similarly, where we say that one surface is flatter than another, we may paraphrase things like this: The first surface is either *flat though the second is not* or else it is *closer to being* flat than the second. But, in contrast to all this, with comparisons of bumpiness, no paraphrase is available. To say that one surface is not as bumpy as another is *not* to say that the first surface is either not bumpy, though the second is, *or else not as nearly bumpy as* the second one.

In one way, at least, the comparative constructions appear to provide a more sensitive test than the modifying adverbs. For the two most 'obvious' absolute terms, going by semantic intuitions, do not take the modifying adverbs smoothly. Thus, the sentence ?'His waltzing was very perfect' is mildly deviant. And, the sentence ??'His loyalty is pretty absolute" is more than mildly so. If these can be relied on at all, though, they seem to mean just 'His waltzing was very *nearly* perfect' and 'His loyalty is pretty *close to being* absolute.' Unlike with adverbs, comparative constructions with these terms are without deviance: 'His waltzing was more perfect than that of any other man in Vienna' and 'His loyalty was more absolute than that of his commander.' The first means just what our paraphrase says it should, and so does the second. Thus, discounting the deviance with adverbs, these two terms also belong to our class of absolute limit terms.[7] And, it is in this way that comparative constructions provide a more sensitive syntactico-semantic test than adverbs do.

Our noting the availability of degree constructions allows us to class together relative terms and basic absolute terms, as against any other terms. And, by noting that only with the

[7] These points are due to Michael Slote.

absolute terms do our constructions admit of our paraphrase, we may distinguish between the relative terms and the basic absolute terms. In that these terms may be quite clearly distinguished, even on syntactico-semantic grounds, we may restate more clearly some semantic ideas on which we relied to introduce our terminology (and which remain the main ground of it). Thus, to draw the connection between terms of the two sorts we may say this: Basic absolute terms, and so other absolute terms as well, generally may be defined, at least partially, by means of certain relative terms. The defining conditions presented by means of the relative terms are negative ones; they say that what the relative terms purport to denote is *not* present *at all*, or *in the least*, where the absolute term correctly applies; in that sense, the *limit* has been reached. Thus, these negative conditions are logically necessary ones for the correct application of the absolute terms. For example, something is flat, in the central, literal, spatial sense of 'flat', only if it is *not at all*, or *not in the least*, curved or bumpy. And similarly, something is a cube, in the central, spatial sense of 'cube', only if it has surfaces which are not at all, or not in the least, bumpy or curved. In noting these demanding negative requirements, we may begin to suspect that a variety of absolute terms, if not all of them, might well be quite troublesome to apply, perhaps even failing consistently in application to real things and beings.

This test of paraphrase separates out, quite well at least, the basic absolute terms. But terms which fail this test need not be relative terms, not even if they grammatically take a full battery of degree constructions. For a term which grammatically looks to be a relative may actually be a *defined* absolute term. The term will, we may admit, then have certain relative features, or relative dimensions, in its conditions of application. But if it has a single necessary condition which is absolute, it will experience the difficulties in which absolute terms may be suspected of being involved. To anticipate our later work (in section 5 and in Chapter IV), we may notice the sentence 'Mary is *happy* that there are rocks.' The adjective 'happy' here looks to be a relative term. For if Mary is very happy that there are rocks, that does not mean that she is very nearly happy that there are. Yet, it appears that, because it contains 'happy' and not, say, 'hopeful', what this sentence expresses entails what is expressed by 'Mary is *certain* that there are rocks.' It is inconsistent to say, 'Mary is *happy* that there are rocks, but she *isn't certain* that there are.' And, to anticipate our work further (in section 3), 'certain' does appear to be an absolute term, even a basic one, even as it occurs in our entailed sentence. For *if* Mary is *very* certain that there are rocks, *then* she is *very close to being absolutely* certain that there are. Thus, at least as it occurs in our chosen sentence, 'happy' now seems to function as an absolute term, to be sure, a defined one rather than a basic one. It does not seem to function semantically like the innocuous relative term it syntactically looks to be. Now, if whenever anyone or anything is happy there is an implication to someone or something being certain, then 'happy' will always really function semantically as, and so be, an absolute term (a defined one). If there is such an implication with *only certain sorts* of sentences, then (assuming 'certain' to be a basic absolute term) *in those sentences* 'happy' will serve as, and so we may say that it *there* is, a defined absolute term. In that case, in the *remaining* sentences, assuming that there is no implication to any *other* absolute condition, 'happy' will serve as, and so *there* will be, a relative term. In short, our procedure for paraphrase does more to establish a basic absolute term as absolute than it does to establish a relative term as relative. This is a sign, I suggest, that we have a language which, through its meaning relations, is indeed well stocked with absolute terms.

In a final general remark about these terms, I should like to support my choice of terminology for them. A reason that I call terms of the one sort 'absolute' is that, at least in the case of the basic ones, a term may always be modified, grammatically, with the term 'absolutely'. And, indeed, this modification fits so well that it is, I think, always redundant as far as content goes. (Its function appears to be mainly that of emphasis.) Thus, something is flat if and only if it is absolutely flat. In contrast, the term 'absolutely' only questionably gives a standard, grammatical modification for any of our relative terms: To say that something is (?) absolutely bumpy is, at best, to say that it is absolutely true that it is bumpy. On the other hand, each of the relative terms takes 'relatively' quite smoothly as a grammatical modifier. (And, though it is far from being clear, it is at least arguable, I think, that this modifier is redundant for these terms. Thus, it is at least arguable that something is bumpy if and only if it is relatively bumpy.) In any event, with absolute terms, while 'relatively' is grammatically quite all right as a modifier, the construction thus obtained must be understood in terms of our paraphrase. Thus as before, something is relatively flat if and only if it is relatively close to being (absolutely) flat, and so, only if it is not flat. In this terminology, and in line with our linguistic tests, I think that the first term of each of the following pairs is a relative term while the second is an absolute one. And, most importantly, our semantic intuitions coincide: 'wet' and 'dry', 'crooked' and 'straight', 'important' and 'crucial', 'incomplete' and 'complete', 'useful' and 'useless', and so on. I think that both 'empty' and 'full' are absolute terms, while 'good' and 'bad', 'rich' and 'poor', and 'large' and 'small' are all relative terms. Finally, in the sense of limits, and also by the syntactic marks given by our· tests, each of the following is *neither* an absolute term *nor* a relative one: 'married' and 'unmarried', and 'living' and 'deceased'. This, though, in other plausible senses, including some very closely related ones, some or all of this last group might be called 'absolute'.

§3. *On Certainty and Certain Related Things*

Certain terms of our language are standardly followed by propositional clauses, and in the case of many of them, if not all, it is plausible to think that wherever they occur they *must* be followed by such clauses on pain of otherwise occuring in no sentence, or else in a sentence which is elliptical or incomplete. We may call terms which take these clauses, *propositional terms*, and we may then ask: Are some propositional terms absolute ones, while others are relative terms? If there are some which are absolute, there should be some propositional terms which are *basic absolute* terms. Those terms will be adjectives, even though the most common thoughts about propositional terms look towards their being verbs. Of course, many *defined* absolute terms may be propositional terms which are verbs, and the verb 'know' may be particularly prominent among them. Indeed, that thought is important to the strategy of my defence.

But, then, first things should be looked at first. Accordingly, we now look to certain adjectives which are propositional terms, or, if we may call 'know' a *propositional verb*, to certain *propositional adjectives*.

By means of our paraphrastic tests, as well as by our semantic intuitions, I will argue that 'certain' is an absolute term, while various contrasting adjectives, 'confident', 'doubtful', and 'uncertain' are all relative terms. (This begins my following up on points made in the next to last paragraph of the preceding section.)

With regard to being certain, there are two ideas which are important: first, the idea of *something's* being certain, where that which is certain is *not* certain *of* anything, and, second, the idea of *a being's* being certain, where that which is certain *is* certain *of* something. A paradigm context for the first idea is the context 'It is certain that it is raining' where the term 'it' has no apparent reference. I will call such contexts *impersonal* contexts and the idea of certainty which they serve to express, thus, the impersonal idea of certainty. In contrast, a paradigm context for the second idea is this one: 'He is certain that it is raining,' where, of course, the term 'he' purports to refer as clearly as one might like. In the latter context, which we may call the *personal* context, we express the personal idea of certainty. This last may be allowed, I think, even though in ordinary conversations we might speak of dogs as being certain; presumably, we will there treat dogs the way we typically treat persons.

Though there are these two important sorts of context, I think that 'certain' must mean the same in both. (In the sentence 'A certain toadstool was plucked one day', 'certain' *may* mean something else. Whether it does or not, I will not be concerned with that context or with any other which does not easily connect with the two I have mentioned.) In both of our contexts we must be struck by the thought that the presence of certainty amounts to the complete absence of doubt. This thought leads me to say that 'It is certain that p' means, within the bounds of nuance, 'It is not at all doubtful that p', or 'There is no doubt at all but that p.' The idea of personal certainty may then be defined accordingly; we relate what is said in the impersonal form to the mind of the person, or subject, who is said to be certain of something. Thus, 'He is certain that *p*' means, within the bounds of nuance, '*In his mind*, it is not at all doubtful that *p*,' or '*In his mind*, there is no doubt at all but that *p*.' Where a man is certain of something, then, concerning that thing, all doubt is absent in that man's mind. With these definitions available, we may now say this: Connected negative definitions of certainty suggest that, in its central, literal meaning, 'certain' is an absolute term.

But we should also like some syntactico-semantic evidence for thinking that 'certain' is an absolute term. To be consistent, we turn to our procedure for paraphrase. I will exhibit the evidence for personal contexts and then say a word about impersonal ones. In any event, we want contrasting results for 'certain' as against some related relative terms. One term which now suggests itself for contrast is, of course, 'doubtful'. Another is, of course, 'uncertain'. And we will get the desired results with these terms. But it is, I think, more interesting to consider the term 'confident'.

In quick discussions of these matters, one might speak indifferently of a man's being confident of something and of his being certain of it. But on reflection there is a difference between confidence and certainty. Indeed, when I say that I am certain, I tell you that I am *not* just confident of it but *more than* that. And if I say that I am confident that so-and-so, I tell you that I am *not so much as* certain of the thing. Thus, there is an important difference between the two. At least part of this difference is, I suggest, reflected by our procedure for paraphrase.

We may begin to apply our procedure by resolving the problem of augmenting modifiers. Paradoxically, when I say that I am (really) very certain of something, I say *less* of myself, so far as certainty is concerned, than I do when I say, simply, that I am (really) certain of the thing. How may we resolve this paradox? Our paraphrase explains things as before: In the first case, what I am really saying is that I am very *nearly* certain, and so, in effect, that I am not actually certain. But, in the second case, I say that I actually am. Further, we may notice that, in contrast, in the case of 'confident' and 'uncertain', and 'doubtful' as well, no problem with augmenting arises in the first place. For when I say that I am very confident of something, I say *more* of myself, so far as confidence is concerned, than I do when I simply say that I am confident of the thing. And, again, our paraphrastic procedure yields us the lack of any problems here. For the augmented statement cannot be sensibly interpreted as saying that I am very nearly confident of the thing. Indeed, with any modifier weaker than 'absolutely', our paraphrase works well with 'certain' but produces only poor interpretations with 'confident' and other contrasting terms. For example, what might it mean to say that he was rather close to being confident of the thing? Would this be to say that he was rather confident of the thing? Surely not.

Turning to comparative constructions, our paraphrase separates things just as we should expect. For example, from 'He is more certain that p than he is that q' we get 'He is either certain that p while not certain that q, or else he is more nearly certain that p than he is that q'. But from 'He is more confident that p than he is that q' we do *not* get 'He is either confident that p while not confident that q, or else he is more nearly confident that p than he is that q'. For, whatever the last clause might mean, he may well already be confident of both things. Further comparative constructions are similarly distinguished when subject to our paraphrase. And no matter what locutions we try, the separation is as convincing with impersonal contexts as it is with personal ones, so long as there are contexts which are comparable. Of course, 'confident' has no impersonal contexts; we cannot say 'It is confident that p', where the 'it' has no purported reference. But, where comparable contexts do exist, as with 'doubtful' and perhaps 'uncertain', further evidence is available. Thus, we may reasonably assert that 'certain' is an absolute limit term, indeed a basic one, while 'confident', 'doubtful', and 'uncertain' are relative terms.

§4. *The Doubtful Applicability of some Absolute Terms*

If my account of absolute terms is essentially correct, then in the case of many of these terms it appears that fairly reasonable suppositions about the world make it quite doubtful that the terms properly apply. (In certain contexts, generally where what we are talking about divides into discrete units, the presence of an absolute term need cause no doubts. Thus, considering the absolute term 'complete', the truth of 'His set of steins is now complete' may be allowed without hesitation, but the truth of 'His explanation is now complete' may well be doubted. It is with the latter, more interesting contexts, I think, that we shall be concerned in what follows.) For example, while we *say of* many surfaces of physical things that they are flat, a rather reasonable interpretation of what we presumably observe makes it quite doubtful that these surfaces actually *are* flat. When we look at a rather smooth block of stone through a powerful microscope, the observed surface appears to be rife with irregularities. And, this irregular appearance seems best explained, not by its being taken as an illusory optical phenomenon but, by our taking it to be a finer, more revealing look of a surface which is, in fact, rife with smallish bumps and crevices. Further, we account for bumps and crevices by supposing that the stone is composed of much smaller things, molecules and so on, which are in such a combination that, while a fairly large and sturdy stone is the upshot, no stone with a flat surface is found to obtain.

Indeed, what follows from my account of 'flat' is this: that, as a matter of logical necessity, if a surface is flat at a certain time, then there never is any surface which is flatter than it is at that time. For on our paraphrase, if the second surface is flatter than the first, then, either the second surface is flat while the first is not, or else the second is more nearly flat than the first, neither surface being flat. So, if there is such a second, flatter surface, then the first surface is not flat after all, contrary to our supposition. Thus, there cannot be any second, flatter surface. Or in other words, if it is logically possible that there be a surface which is flatter than a given one, then that given surface is not really a flat one. Now, in the case of the observed surface of the stone, owing to the nature of the stone's irregular composition, the surface is *not* one such that it is logically impossible that there be a flatter one. (For example, we might veridically observe a surface through a microscope of the same power which did not appear to have any bumps or crevices.) Thus, it is only reasonable to suppose that the surface of this stone is not really flat.

Our understanding of the stone's composition, that it is composed of molecules in a certain way, and so on, makes it reasonable for us to suppose as well that any similarly sized or larger surfaces will fail to be flat just as the observed surface fails to be flat. At the same time, it would be perhaps a bit rash to suppose that much smaller surfaces would fail to be flat as well. Beneath the level of our observation perhaps there are small areas of the stone's surface which are flat. If so, then perhaps there are small objects that have surfaces which are flat, like this area of the stone's surface: for instance, chipping off a small part of the stone might yield such a small object. So, perhaps there are physical objects with surfaces which are flat and, perhaps it is not now reasonable for us to assume that there are *no* such objects. But, even if this strong assumption is not now reasonable, one thing which does seem quite reasonable for us to assume is this: we should at least suspend judgement on the matter of whether there are *any* physical objects with flat surfaces. That there are such objects is something it is not now reasonable for us to believe. At the same time, it does seem reasonable to believe that (in comparison with all) at most hardly any physical objects have surfaces which actually are *flat*.

It is at least somewhat doubtful, then, that 'flat' ever applies to actual physical objects, or to their surfaces. And the thought must strike us that if 'flat' has no such application, this must be due in part to the fact that 'flat' is an absolute term. We may then do well to be a bit doubtful about the applicability of any other given absolute term and, in particular, about the applicability of the term 'certain'. As in the case of 'flat', our paraphrase highlights the absolute character of 'certain': As a matter of logical necessity, if someone is certain of something then there never is anything of which he or anyone else is more certain. On our paraphrase, if the person or some other is more certain of any other thing, then either he or the other is certain of the other thing while he is *not* certain of the first, or else he or the other is more nearly certain of the other thing than he is of the first. Thus, if it is logically possible that there be something of which any person might be more certain than he now is of a given thing, then he is not actually certain of that given thing.

Owing to these considerations, it is reasonable to suppose, I think, that hardly anyone, if anyone at all, is certain that forty-five and fifty-six are one hundred and one. For it is reasonable to suppose that hardly anyone, if anyone at all, is so certain of that particular calculation that it is impossible for there to be any of which he or anyone else might yet be more certain. But this is not surprising; for, hardly anyone *feels* certain, or feels himself to be certain, that those two numbers have that sum. What, then, about something of which people commonly do feel absolutely certain; say, of the existence of automobiles?

Is it reasonable for us now actually to believe that many people are *certain* that there are automobiles? If it is, then it is now reasonable for us to believe as well that for each of them it is not possible for there to be anything of which he or anyone else might be more certain than he now is of there being automobiles. In particular, we must then believe of these people that it is impossible for anyone ever to be more certain of his own existence than all of them now are of the existence of automobiles. While these people *might* all actually be as certain of the automobiles as this, just as each of them presumably feels himself to be, I think it somewhat rash for us actually to believe that they *are* all so certain. But, more than this, it seems reasonable for us to believe that not many people are actually certain that there are automobiles and, indeed, even that very few actually are. Thinking one matter over after the next, and comparing it with *how* certain someone *might* be of his *own present existence*, the reasonable thing to conclude seems this: in the case of each human being, there is at most hardly anything of which he really is *certain*.

§5. *Meaning and Use*

Many philosophers, I suppose, will think that my account ot terms like 'flat' and 'certain' flies in the face of how people in fact ordinarily use these words. But, I don't think that this need be correct. True enough, people *call* all sorts of things 'flat'. They use the word to pick out surfaces which compare poorly with those needed for certain precision machinery. They use it even to refer to certain prairies where, even discounting the curvature of the earth, which one really should not discount, there are dips and rises of inches and feet. This surely does say something about the normal use of these terms, and no account can afford to deny it.

It doesn't follow from these undoubted facts of use, however, that the normal use of 'flat' is to class together objects in terms of a property they all have in common, namely, that of flatness. That loads the question against my account. It may be, rather, that the normal use is, in each case, to indicate that the object in question is close enough to being flat, for the kind of thing it is, for the purposes which may be presumed in the case, and relative to other factors the context may provide. That is the way my account would have it, and it is far from clear, I suggest, that this is not correct. All parties may agree that we normally use the term to call things 'flat', and even to say of things that they are flat. But any *more revealing* description of normal use is, at the very worst for us, contentious at this point.

The same sorts of remarks apply to normal uses other than those involved in the saying of something true or false. We may look at the asking of questions and will do so, though we might just as easily look at the giving of orders, the making of promises, and so on. If someone normally utters, 'Is that flat?', we may all agree that he is asking of that whether it is flat. But, in addition to this, why can't the normal use here also be to ask for information concerning that which will serve to indicate whether it is close enough to being flat, for things of its contextually understood kind, for purposes understood to be at hand, and so on? On my account, we do the second unwittingly in doing the first, the unwitting character of the whole enterprise perhaps allowing it all to go on. In any case, on my account of 'flat', if we didn't here use the word normally to do the second, there could be little point to its use which the term itself could help properly to describe.

There is, then, no solid case from use against us here. Indeed, the opposite seems to be happening. For it appears that to get even a moderately revealing description of the use of 'flat', as with any other meaningful term, we first have to get a reasonably clear account of what the term really means. Only then can we have any confidence with regard to such a description that it is correct, or that it is badly incorrect. And our account of the meaning of 'flat' and 'certain' is, I suggest, the most nearly, if not the only, clear account of their meaning which we have available.

Now I suppose that those who would oppose our account on grounds of use are likely to be moved to such thoughts by an idea which is really very simple. The idea is this: People can usually give a correct and revealing description of the normal use of very ordinary terms, of terms like 'flat' and 'certain'. But why should anything even much like this be thought correct? On my account, which is at least moderately plausible, this is not correct, but false. And I have never seen any reason to suppose that we are so easily wise, or that matters of use are so simple, that anything else must be accepted instead.

A good theory of use is at least as far from available as an adequate theory of meaning. In the absence of general theories to check things against, we can only suppose this: whatever theory proves adequate to its domain will explain why the apparent facts about use, or about meaning, are indeed facts. And, it appears that we have turned up facts about the meaning, and even the use, of 'flat' and 'certain'. Most likely, then, any good theory of these words' meaning, and of their use, will contain and explain the idea that these are indeed absolute terms.[8]

§6. Understanding, Learning, and Paradigm Cases

There are often further thoughts behind the idea that our ordinary use of common terms (whatever that really is) somehow ensures that the terms usually, often, or sometimes correctly apply. Perhaps the most appealing of these ideas, and surely one which has enjoyed great popularity, is the notion that certain central or paradigm cases must govern the use of any of these terms. These are cases of things, beings, situations, etc. which by ostension, or by stipulation, or whatever, must satisfy the meaning of a term. The idea is that these cases must thereby serve to help determine the term's meaning.[9]

[8] In writing this section, I profited greatly from comments from Michael Slote.

[9] A rather famous espousal of this view occurs in L. Susan Stebbing's *Philosophy and the Physicists* (New York, 1958), and is reprinted in *Philosophy of Science*, ed. Arthur Danto and Sidney Morgenbesser (Cleveland, Ohio, 1960), p. 73: '. . . What are we to understand by "solidity"? . . . we can understand "solidity" only if we can truly say that the plank is solid. For "solid" just is the word we use to describe a certain respect in which a plank of wood resembles a block of marble, a piece of paper, and a cricket ball, and in which each of these differs from . . . the holes in a net. . . . If the plank is nonsolid, then where can we find an example to show us what "solid" means?'

Behind this reassuring thought, which at the outset would not seem to compel even a moderately sceptical thinker, lie some ideas about what is necessary to understand, and to learn, the meaning of 'simple' terms of our language.

By 'simple' terms, I mean those which seem close to our experience, or to what we might or do experience, or experience in some direct or immediate way. Among these terms would be counted, I suppose, 'red' and 'pain', and also 'bumpy' and 'flat'. Perhaps 'certain' would be among the most favoured terms here; at any rate it is better placed than, say, 'magnetic'. But, what applies most clearly and directly to these 'simple' terms also is supposed to apply, in some less direct way, I suppose, to other terms, including 'army', if not 'magnetic' (why not 'magnetic' too?). Now, the first idea here seems to be this: In order to understand these terms, you must learn them, or learn their meanings. And, the second idea is then this: In order to learn that, one must become acquainted with, or experience, or somehow be connected with some paradigm cases, some things or situations in the world to which the terms actually do apply. The upshot of the two ideas together is that in order to understand these terms one must somehow be connected with these paradigm cases. Accordingly one's very understanding of the terms guarantees the existence of such cases; it ensures the *correct application* of the understood terms. But, *neither* of these ideas represents a necessary condition, even if the condition *happens to hold* at least as a rule. Much less does their composite conclusion yield any necessary condition. (Of course, I do not mean to say that learning is not, as a matter of fact, important or even crucial to *my own* understanding of 'red' or 'pain'. Nor do I say that I would ever understand these terms without in fact having had the proper experience. Least of all do I want to deny that there are experiences of red, red objects, or pains. Indeed, I am quite confident that I have in fact experienced each of these.) Arguing to show that these are not valid conditions will, I think, make us quite safe from the grip of 'paradigm cases'. This will help let our doubts flourish about absolute terms, like 'flat' and 'certain', as flourish they should.

First, we look at the idea that understanding requires learning. Now, with the possible exception of certain terms, like 'cat' and 'heat', whose character seems to resemble that of proper names,[10] the understanding you have of a word is essentially just a function of the state of the basis of your mind: of your brain if you are a human being, of your organic systems if you are an organism, or whatever. If you just came into existence *à la* Russell, along with the things outside of you, you might still understand (almost) any ordinary word, even words as 'simple' as 'red' and 'pain', much less 'flat'. But you would not have been taught these words at all, much less would you have been taught them from paradigm cases. If no one else were around at *any* time either, then *no one* would *ever* be a teacher or learner of these words, but you would *still* understand them. Further, if you also were always hooked up to electrodes, being stimulated by an 'accidentally arrived' computer from your first moment on, you would never have the opportunity to apply 'red' to any physical object, and so for 'flat'. Further, still, if you were never stimulated to have experience as of red things, or as of flat things, and were instead stimulated to have only other experiences, you would *still* understand these terms, so long as your starting state was just as your state now in fact is, and so long as nothing was done to change it much. You would understand these words just as well even if there never were any red things or flat things in the entire history of the world, and also no experiences as of any such things in all the world's history. Whatever connections there may be between understanding meaning, on the one hand, and, on the other, experiencing and learning, it is not that the latter are conditions of the former, much less that learning from paradigm cases is.[11]

Nor does learning meaning logically require there to be paradigm cases. If you just come into existence with a brain just like a small infant has, you could learn the meaning of 'flat', and of 'red', by stimulations through our electrodes. No actually flat or red things are logically required. All that is required is a suitable series of changes in the state of your

---

[10] In this connection, see Saul Kripke's 'Naming and Necessity', in Harman and Davidson, *Semantics of Natural Language*, pp. 314 ff.

[11] I discuss these ideas in greater detail, usually to good effect, I think, in 'On Experience and the Development of the Understanding', *American Philosophical Quarterly*, vol. iii, No. 1 (1966).

brain, or of your body. First, the series must be such that it counts as, or provides a physical basis of, learning. In that pleasure centres may be stimulated at the appropriate times to reward 'proper' internal acceptances or expectations, such learning seems entirely possible. (If pleasure centres didn't exist, philosophers would have to invent them.) And, second, the series must end in a state which counts as, or provides a physical basis of, understanding. Presumably, your current state will do fine here, and as that might be arrived at in the indicated way, it is possible for one to learn the meaning of 'red' without there being any red things, and so for 'flat'. Perhaps for this learning one must have certain experiences *as of* red things or *as of* flat ones; but these experiences will not themselves be flat or red: everything coloured may be either green or yellow; and everything with a shape may be rather bumpy.

Just as learning is not required for understanding, so sceptically objectionable paradigm cases are not required for learning. It is true *a fortiori*, then, that such paradigm cases need not even exist, much less govern the use of any terms; one may still understand the 'simplest' terms as fully and as well as anyone ever might do.

While the foregoing cases are admittedly bizarre, the point which emerges from them is intuitive and perhaps even a commonplace: the *most* that is needed for you to learn the meaning of a term is that, at certain times, it should *seem* to you that certain things satisfy that term, or that meaning. As far as logic goes, the most needed for you to learn the meaning of 'flat' is that at some time(s) it should seem to you that there are certain things which are flat, which are, that is, not *at all* bumpy, not *at all* curved, and so on. This may obtain because whatever bumpiness there is is not perceptible to you then. Or it may obtain because you are not called on to notice whatever little bumpiness may be perceptibly there.[12] Indeed, it is not even clear that this much is required. With 'flat', you might have the idea that there was a slight but real deficiency in the case, and that a teacher, or a disinterested talker, likely *meant* to have picked out a case which did *not* have this little bumpiness in it. In demanding paradigm cases to back learning and understanding, we seem to offer little insight indeed into the

---

[12] These points are due to James Rachels.

notions of learning, understanding, meaning, or language. Rather, we seem only to speak ill of people's abilities to imagine, and, worse yet, ill of the ingenuity they might exercise, however tacitly, in learning things.

§7. *How Better to Focus on Actual Meaning*

The drift of this chapter so far has been, I hope, helpful in getting us to focus on what some of our words really do mean. I take it that we will agree that if one approaches the key sentences I've exhibited in *one* way, everything I say seems to make good sense. But it is very easy and natural to approach these sentences in *quite another* way. In this *other* way, at least very much of what I have said seems and sounds just plain wrong. Accordingly, it is quite easy for someone who finds my remarks uncongenial to oppose me forcefully. Here is a forceful thing he might naturally now say to us.

According to your account, he notes, 'flat' means the same as 'absolutely flat'. Thus, the simplest hypothesis for you is that sentences of the form 'x is flat' always are equivalent in meaning to ones of the corresponding form 'x is absolutely flat', at least when 'x' is not meant to pick out some old beer, etc. This creates something of a problem for you: When people say things like 'That is flat; the other is flatter', your account would have them saying something which is *inconsistent*, something which must always be false. But, the sentence doesn't *sound* inconsistent. And, indeed, it really does seem that sentences of this sort are often used to say things which are true. How are you to account for such blatant discrepancy?

In that people are, at the very least, not aware of my account while normally using absolute terms, they do not demand much from these words in their everyday speaking or hearing. If one person says that a certain thing is flat and another then says that another thing is flatter, we would not take the second person to be contradicting the first. And, if one person himself says that this is flat but that other is flatter, we do not take him to be contradicting himself or to have uttered anything inconsistent. We do not demand him to put his words through our paraphrase so that a consistent thought will be properly expressed; nor do we make any demand on ourselves to do so. But, on our account, what this person *says* actually is inconsistent. We just allow the inconsistency to slip by unnoticed. And, in the course of quick business, we take his words to function as relative terms.

Taking in sentences quickly, with no special attention given to them or any of their constituents, that is one way to approach sentences, including our key ones. It is when they are approached in this way that our key sentences sound consistent, and their key adjectives look to be relative. Another way of approaching sentences is to take them more slowly, emphasizing what might seem to be key constituents and attending to whatever meaning this emphasis might seem to bring forth. With words which have meaning, the emphasis of a word, by stress, italics, modifiers, or whatever, has the primary function of getting us to focus on that word, and generally its meaning(s) if it has at least one. Secondary functions will derive from this. For example, if you say 'Bring me the mug' and someone brings you the jug, you may well say, 'I said "Bring me the *mug*!" ' If you said that, and he brought you the cup, you might also well say, 'I said bring me the *mug*!" ' In each case you try to get the person to bring you the thing you have in mind, the mug we may suppose, by getting him to understand what you are referring to. And, you do that, in the most normal circumstances, by getting him to understand the terms whose meaning helps to make the reference. By emphasizing '*mug*', you get the person, you hope, to attend to the actual meaning of your words, and thus to understand what it is you want him to bring you.

In English, stress is the main way to emphasize chosen words. In speech, stress generally means loudness, sometimes slowing down; it can even be done by speaking in low tones or a single whispered word. In writing, underlining and italics provide the main conventions for stress. Certain modifiers can also be very useful for emphasis, especially when placed right in front of the term on which attention is to be focused. Adjectives can precede nouns for this purpose; adverbs may similarly precede adjectives. Thus, 'He is a real scholar' has 'scholar' emphasized, and 'He is really scholarly' makes us focus on 'scholarly'. Figures of speech can trade on this emphasis, deriving extra punch from the attention to meaning (which meaning is not satisfied by things): 'He is a real devil'.

Emphasis does not change the meaning of words or sentences to which it is applied.[13] Thus, the sentence 'He killed her' means the same as 'He *killed* her.' The first will express what is true if and only if the second does. There are here really only two slightly different forms of inscription of the same sentence. The first form will be used in most discourses; the emphatic form will be used, e.g. if someone thinks he *kissed* her, or that he only hurt her. When names are used, and so meaning is not (much) a factor, emphasis will direct attention by bringing to the fore *which* name is involved. Thus, if someone sends a message to John, you might say 'I told you to send it to *Don*.' Assuming that context allows everyone to understand that there is only one Don involved, emphasis helps you make your point, though this time not by getting people to focus on meaning. In any case, the importance of emphasis does *not* derive from any effect on issues of meaning or truth. Quite the contrary, its importance in our language derives from its having no such effect.[14] Shouldn't we have *some* device(s) to attract attention to a term which work in a way that does not effect the term's meaning, or the meaning of sentences of which that term is a part? Shouldn't we have a device for every term, and every sentence, that is, a device whose application is wholly general? If different devices were neutral with respect to different sentences, and thus differentially effect the meanings of different ones, in learning our language, we'd have to learn a great deal more; our language would be less efficient and more difficult. It seems to me that emphasis, especially with the device of stress, does just this desired and expected job.

Against the idea that emphasis is neutral as regards issues of meaning and truth, one might think that emphasis promotes

[13] This is true for stress anyway, discounting syllabic emphasis. With modifiers, the situation may be more complex. I have some inclination to suppose that 'He is a real scholar' means, very nearly at least, 'In reality, he is a scholar.' And this *may* entail 'There is something in which he is a scholar, namely, reality.' But, then, 'He is a scholar' *may* entail that too! I find these ideas very confusing. But, then, the issues involved here are marginal for the present discussion.

[14] On the level of vocabulary—of which word is being used—there may be an effect of stress on the meaning of a word, and thus on the sentence(s) in which the word is used there. This happens with different syllables of the same word stressed, resulting in different pronunciations of the word, each conveying a different meaning: a coach writing ambiguously of a polite but inept quarterback just after the latter was traded, 'He gave me no offence.' I neglect this sort of stress in making my negative generalization; it is quite clearly unimportant, I suggest, to any reliance on stress which we shall ever place. For one thing, it has nothing to do with emphasis.

certain contrasts in ways that matter to meaning, and so to truth. For example, Fred Dretske thinks this happens with sentences that contain certain 'operators'.[15] According to Dretske, the sentence:

The reason Clyde *married* Bertha was to qualify for the inheritance,

means something different from the (same or different?) sentence:

The reason Clyde married *Bertha* was to qualify for the inheritance,

so that the first may express something true while the second (or the same but in a second instance?) may not. The idea is that Clyde may be a bachelor heir who, while a confirmed bachelor, must marry to collect on his inheritance. That is specified in the will. He happens to select Bertha because she is away on business, in Turkey or somewhere, almost all year; a marriage to *her* will hardly effect Clyde's bachelor life-style. Were it not for the will, Clyde would have just kept on dating: Bertha one month a year, and other women at other times. This situation is supposed to provide a context in which our sentence with the first emphasis expresses something true, but with the second only something which is false.

Not to discriminate too harshly against the latter emphasis, the context is supposed to allow it too to give expression to something true, but of course this time with another completing clause used:

The reason Clyde married *Bertha* was to effect his life-style as little as possible while being married.

At the same time, this completing clause gives us something *false* for the former emphasis to help express:

The reason Clyde *married* Bertha was to effect his life-style as little as possible while being married.

[15] Fred I. Dretske, 'Contrastive Statements', *Philosophical Review*, vol. lxxxi, No. 4 (1972). In describing his examples I make slight alternations. But no substantial points are, I think, thus effected. Actually, the only alleged changes in meaning which Dretske's remarks make even plausible look to be syntactically based, while the only changes which could speak against our (future) employment of emphasis should be based lexically. But, for good measure, I shall argue that there are no meaning changes here of any sort.

This is supposed to show, of course, that emphasis can change the meaning of an unemphasized sentence, so much so that the sentence may express something true with one emphasis but false with another. One immediately thinks: with *which* emphasized sentence is the *unemphasized* sentence equivalent in meaning, or at least in conditions of truth? With neither? With both? Still, Dretske's example does make a certain appeal for the idea of differences in meaning here.

This appeal is best resisted. Other accounts can be given of the phenomena. And, more importantly, entirely general considerations serve to rule out any account in terms of meaning differences, or any differences in conditions of truth. First, we may better explain in other terms what is going on in such examples. In this case of Clyde and Bertha, what seems to be the reason Clyde married Bertha is this: to qualify for the inheritance while effecting his life-style as little as possible. Perhaps the reason Clyde settled on Bertha to marry was that she would effect his life-style less than any other wife he might ever have. Those *are* different reasons, but then they are clearly reasons *for* different *things*. What the different emphases do, I suggest, is just this. They indicate what the speaker or writer represents as the thing to focus on. That gives the idea that that thing is the *important* thing in the context. Here, the context is the stating of a certain reason, of the reason Clyde married Bertha. The speaker indicates that the important feature of the event or action in question, of Clyde's marrying Bertha, is that marrying went on, when he says that Clyde *married* Bertha. What may then be taken as the *important part or feature* of the reason is then, sensibly enough, offered: to qualify for the inheritance. Unfortunately, it is falsely offered as *the* reason, the whole reason, that the event occurred. But it is not that, no matter what the speaker represents as most worth attending to.

Now of course I don't expect that everyone will be influenced much by what I have just said. But, at the very least, it should help to prepare us for the following argument, which appears to me to be as conclusive as it is homely and simple. Suppose that Dretske says:

The reason Clyde *married* Bertha was to qualify for the inheritance.

He may be trying to get me to understand something, so that I will no longer think that Clyde should have just kept on dating, Bertha or anyone else he chose. But you might not have heard us very well, or not heard Dretske well anyway. So, you might interject, saying, for example:

> I don't believe it. Eartha told me last week that she'd never marry anyone.

I suppose that Dretske might then say, and well he might:

> I didn't say anything about Eartha. I said that the reason Clyde married *Bertha* was to qualify for the inheritance.

Now, as I said before, Dretske would in neither case, with the one stress or the other, be giving the real reason Clyde did what he did here. But, of course, that is not the present point. The point now is simply this. He would be right in using the *new* emphasis to put forward *the thing he said before*, and to put it forth *as the thing he said before*. With any sort of saying which is relevant to our topics, to meaning and to truth, he said the same thing both times as concerns Clyde's doings, namely, that the reason Clyde married Bertha was to qualify for the inheritance. Of course, with *some* sort of saying, he said different things. But that is only the sort in which a stutterer also says something different when he says:

> The r-r-reason Clyde m-m-married Bertha was to qualify for th-th-the inheritance.

So, emphasis does not alter the content of what is said. The reason for this is that it doesn't alter the meaning of the (un-emphasized) sentence which standardly serves to express what is said. This argument is of course entirely general. Different variations scotch various efforts to show that emphasis ever makes any significant semantic difference. Unsurprisingly, then, what emphasis does is just to emphasize. It helps get us to focus on what might be thought important to think about.

When we apply our devices of emphasis to the sentence we would normally let pass:

> That is flat; that other is flatter.

we do seem to bring an inconsistency to light:

That is *flat*; that other is *flatter*.

True enough, this inconsistency would not be so strongly felt were we not now acquainted with my account. But, if we do feel an inconsistency now, that should not, I suggest, be held against the account. Rather, the account articulates and places more clearly in our thought the inconsistency emphasis helps bring to light. Even without our account, the emphasis promotes some feeling of inconsistency. This feeling must in any case be explained, as our account does, or else explained away. Why is there no such feeling with a comparable relative sentence:

That is *bumpy*; that other is *bumpier*?

Our account gives a simple answer.

While it is hard not to have noticed it already, we may now explicitly point out how much we used emphasis in presenting our classical arguments. It was not for nothing that we so consistently emphasized '*know*', in the premises as well as in the conclusions. In doing that, we made ourselves concentrate on what 'know' means, and so on what may really be involved in *knowing* something. It seems, then, that the demanding meaning of 'know' got us to accept the arguments, as well it should if the arguments are essentially sound. If this emphasis hurt our arguments, rather than helped them, then we might have something to suspect. As it is, however, the only thing which seems suspicious there is knowing itself.

§8. *A Method, a Principle, and some Auxiliary Aids to getting Proper Focus*

Devices of emphasis help us to attend to the actual meanings of our words and, to the extent that these devices are allowed to work properly, they help us feel any inconsistencies those words may express. But even when the devices are employed, inconsistent sentences may be presented which all but defy a proper focus of our attention. One way this can happen is for one expression to be emphasized much more than another to which it is to be contextually compared. The imbalance works against a proper focus, and against the proper comparison which might be made were attention focused better. An example is given in the sentence:

That is *flat*; that other is definitely, really *flatter*.

In encountering this sentence, most of our attention is focused on the second clause, on what is going on with the thing said to be *flatter*. We don't think so much on the first part, even though there is *some* emphasis there. Not giving an equal weight to each clause, we are not so likely to feel, or to feel strongly, any inconsistency there may be between them.

Balance may be restored by adding more emphasis to the term with less, or by taking some away from the one with more. If the latter course is taken, we eventually return to:

That is *flat*; that other is *flatter*.

which restores a (stronger) feeling of inconsistency. If the former course is taken, we get a longer sentence like:

That is really absolutely *flat*; that other is definitely, really *flatter*.

This also does something to restore the (stronger) feeling. But, it may not be *quite as* effective. If it is not, the reason for the lesser effect is, I suggest, hardly mysterious. The longer sentence is a bit harder to understand; it is a bit harder to keep track of. To some extent, our energy may be employed just in that, and we may be less likely to appreciate any contradiction there to be discerned. Accordingly, the latter, shortening course is preferable.

Apart from considerations of balance, considerations of length and energy speak against our unbalanced sentence as a good testing ground for meaning and truth. And, moreover, the problem for our attention is *compounded* in that sentence because the emphatic words modifying 'flatter' serve to *separate* the two words, 'flat' and 'flatter', which one should most closely attend to and compare. For this reason, this sentence is less good for arousing feelings of inconsistency than the following inversion, with the modifiers no longer separating the two words most important to compare:

This is definitely, really *flatter*, but that is *flat*.

Admittedly this last is not a very pleasant sentence; it is even a bit awkward. But then, its working more effectively towards inconsistency is all the more striking. In any case, good sense itself says that for any logical decision on words whose meanings one is to compare, there should be as little as possible to take one away from making the comparison, and a fair and balanced comparison at that.

If one likes names for things, one might call the strategy I propose, 'The Method of Opposed Terms'. Can something be flat, but another be flatter? Can something be flat but not absolutely flat? Oppose the terms:

That is flat; that other is flatter.
That is flat; but it is not absolutely flat.

In applying this method, it is important to use the Principle of Emphasis:

That is *flat*; that other is *flatter*.
That is *flat*; but it is *not* absolutely *flat*.

But, in applying *that* principle it is important to adhere to the Principle of Balance. Thus, on the plausible assumption that 'absolutely' functions as an emphatic device in the second sentence here, we place a balancing 'really' before the first occurrence of 'flat':

That is really *flat*, but it is *not* absolutely *flat*.

And, in any case one should adhere to the Principle of Shortness, which abhors:

While it is clearly true to say that it is the case that that is really *flat*, it is also true that it is *not* in fact the case that it is absolutely *flat*.

More particularly, we should adhere to the Principle of Close Juxtaposition (of Opposed Terms), which also abhors this sentence.

I think that this Method and these Principles are little more than good sense applied to the problem of getting at the actual meaning of our words. When good sense is followed, the opponent who says that our account defies the meaning of our words seems on shaky ground at best. If he is not advocating loose talk, he seems to want only a quite facile approach to getting at that meaning.

§9. *Does Knowing Require Being Certain?*

One tradition in philosophy holds that knowing requires being certain: as a matter of logical necessity, a man knows something only if he is certain of the thing. In this tradition, certainty is not taken lightly: rather, it is equated with absolute certainty. Even that most famous contemporary defender of common sense, G. E. Moore, is willing to equate knowing something with knowing the thing with absolute certainty.[16] I am rather inclined to agree with this traditional view, and it is now my purpose to argue for it.

To a philosopher like Moore, I would have nothing left to say in my defence of scepticism. But recently some philosophers have contended that, not certainty, but only belief is required for knowing.[17] And some philosophers have held that not even so much as belief is required for a man to know that something is so.[18] Thus, I must argue for this traditional view of knowing. But, then, what has led philosophers to progress further and further away from the traditional, strong assertion that knowing something requires being certain of the thing?

My diagnosis of the situation is this: In everyday affairs we often speak loosely, charitably, and casually; we tend to let what we say pass as being true. I want to suggest that it is by being wrongly serious about this casual talk that philosophers (myself included) have come to think it rather easy to know things to be so. In particular, they have come to think that certainty is not needed. Thus typical in the contemporary literature is this sort of exchange: An examiner asks a student when a certain battle was fought. The student fumbles about and, eventually, unconfidently says what is true: The Battle of Hastings was fought in 1066. It is supposed, quite properly, that this correct answer is a result of the student's reading. The examiner, being an ordinary mortal, and so unconfident of many things

---

[16] See Moore's cited papers, especially 'Certainty', p. 232.

[17] I accepted a view *at least* as weak as this when, not professionally sceptical, I wrote 'Experience and Factual Knowledge', *Journal of Philosophy*, vol. lxiv, No. 5 (1967). And, I accepted a weaker view in the later papers already cited in this chapter.

[18] This view is well advanced by Colin Radford in 'Knowledge by Examples', *Analysis*, No. 27 (October 1966). I endorsed such a view in 'An Analysis of Factual Knowledge' and in 'Our Knowledge of the Material World'.

himself, allows that the student knows the answer; he judges that the student knows that the Battle of Hastings was fought in 1066. Surely, it is suggested, the examiner is correct in his judgement even though this student clearly isn't certain of the thing; therefore, knowing does not require being certain. But is the examiner really correct in asserting that the student knows the date of this battle? Do such exchanges give us any good reason to think that knowing does not require certainty?

My recommendation is of course this: we should try to focus on just those words most directly employed in expressing the concepts whose conditions are our object of inquiry. To this purpose, we should employ our Method of Opposed Terms, and our Principle of Emphasis, introduced in sections 7 and 8. We remember from those sections the devices we can use to apply them. We may apply them by prefacing emphatic terms, like 'really' and 'actually', to the term(s) most in question (here, the term 'know' and, less directly, the term to be opposed, 'certain'). Thus, instead of looking at something so apparently innocent as 'He knows that the Battle of Hastings was fought in 1066,' we may encounter the apparently more relevant 'He (really) *knows* that the Battle of Hastings was fought in 1066.' Now, we begin to be quite uncertain, I suggest, that the fumbling student knows the thing.

In sections 7 and 8, we discussed and supported the principle we just employed; it is the key to successfully employing our Method of Opposed Terms. I would like, however, to further our confidence in the principle and the method by employing them to help settle a minor difficulty about the meaning of definite descriptions, of expressions of the form 'the so-and-so'. About these expressions, it is a tradition to hold that they require uniqueness, or unique satisfaction, for their proper application. Thus, just as it is traditional to hold that a man knows something only if he is certain of it, so it is also traditional to hold that there is something which is the chair with seventeen legs only if there is exactly one chair with just that many legs. But, again, by being wrongly serious about our casual everyday talk, philosophers may come to deny the traditional view. They may do this by being serious in the wrong way, I think, about the following sort of ordinary exchange. Suppose an examiner asks a student, 'Who is the father of Nelson Rockefeller, the one-time Governor of New York State?' The student replies, 'Nelson Rockefeller is the son of John D. Rockefeller, Jr.' No doubt, the examiner will allow that, by implication, the student got the right answer; he will judge that what the student said is true even though the examiner is correctly confident that the elder Rockefeller sired other sons. Just so, one might well argue that definite descriptions, like 'the son of x', do not require uniqueness. But against this argument from the everyday flow of talk, let us insist that we focus on the relevant conception by employing our standard means for emphasizing the most directly relevant term. Thus while we might feel nothing contradictory, at first, in saying 'Nelson Rockefeller is the son of John D. Rockefeller, Jr., and so is David Rockefeller,' we must confess that even initially we would have quite different feelings about our saying 'Nelson Rockefeller is *the* son of John D. Rockefeller, Jr., and so is David Rockefeller.' With the latter, where emphasis is brought to bear, we cannot help but feel that what is asserted is inconsistent. And, with this, we feel differently about the original remark, rightly taking it to be essentially the same assertion and so inconsistent as well. Thus, it seems that when we focus on things properly, we should suppose that definite descriptions do require uniqueness.

Let us now apply our Principle of Emphasis, and our Method of Opposed Terms, to the question of knowing. Here, while we might feel nothing contradictory, at first, in saying 'He knows that it is raining, but he isn't certain of it,' we should feel differently about our saying 'He really *knows* that it is raining, but he isn't certain of it.' And, if anything, this feeling of contradiction is only enhanced when we further emphasize, 'He really *knows* that it is raining, but he *isn't* absolutely *certain* of it.' Thus it is proper to suppose that what we said at first is actually inconsistent, and so, that knowing does require being certain.

We may confirm our idea of how strong is this requirement by unearthing some related inconsistencies. First, we may try, in parallel with our sentence with 'flat' and 'flatter', this sentence:

He is absolutely *certain* it is a Cadillac, but he's really *more certain* it's an automobile.

ICS—D

This is, I submit, quite an apparent inconsistency. And, then, we may try to contrast the latter clause with an assertion of his *knowing* the thing:

He actually *knows* it's a Cadillac, but he's really *more certain* it's an automobile.

And this, I suggest, also forces a contradiction upon us. Accordingly, our evidence for thinking that knowing requires being certain is support for a requirement that really is quite strong indeed.

Having supported this traditional contention, we may say some things about the (admittedly rather unimportant) difficulty of whether or not knowing excludes or includes believing, which we discussed before in Chapter I, section 5. On the assumption that knowing requires being certain, our conflicting intuitions should obtain as they did before. And they do. On the one hand, one sometimes wants to say 'I don't *believe* it, I'm *certain* of it.' Other times, one feels that a 'just' or 'only' must be implicit before the 'believe' for complete sense here; one then feels that being *certain*, like *knowing*, actually requires one to believe. So our traditional contention, that knowing requires being certain, appears in no danger at all from any good account of the relation between knowing and believing. Indeed, the truth of this contention makes that whole question pale into relative insignificance.

There remains the interesting question, of course, of why the ordinary tendency to be liberal with 'know' is *greater than* our tendency to be liberal with 'certain' in common conversations. It is this fact, I suggest, which is the only relevant thing brought out by stories like that of the examined student. But though this fact yields nothing for the logical relation between knowing and being certain, it is a fact. And it should be explained. Here is a partial explanation of it: first, 'certain' is an adjective with a whole systematic battery of modifiers. This gives one a systematic way of falling back with 'certain', of retreating with it. If you say that he is certain, and you're challenged, you can say 'Well, he's pretty certain of it' or perhaps more usefully, 'Well, he's more certain of it than he was of that, and that turned out right, didn't it?' In contrast, there is comparatively little room for retreat with 'know'. There is no real retreat with

?'Well, he knows it pretty well that they left', and so on. So far as alternative constructions with the word 'know' can go, we are encouraged to think of knowing as an all-or-none thing. Are we to be so uncharitable as to deny the term 'know' to people quite entirely? This leads to a related strand of explanation. For, secondly, there is much more to knowing than just being certain: the thing must be the truth; one is in a position where one is justified in thinking as one does—or at least where one *would* be justified if one did believe the thing; it is not an accident that one is right; the foregoing conditions are themselves actually connected in some appropriate way; and so on. Perhaps we even accept, at least tacitly, that much more than all of this is required by knowing. But, at least these things are generally supposed to obtain. If one then denies knowing, just because the subject is not certain, one may risk or fear misleading others into thinking that other conditions fail as well, e.g. that maybe it *is* an accident that the subject is right. So, one does not readily deny knowing, especially with such meagre resources with 'know' to fall back on. This explanation is far from complete, but it does, I think, represent a reasonable start. But, *however* the explanation should run, the dominant point remains this: at the end of any story or discourse, if the final line is 'He really *knows* it, but he *isn't* absolutely *certain* of it', then a contradiction has been uttered at the story's end.

§10. *Closing our Defence and Opening a New Argument*

For my defence of scepticism, it now remains only to combine the result we have just reached with that at which we arrived in previous sections. Now, I have argued that each of two propositions is correct:

(1) In the case of every human being, there is at most hardly anything of which he is certain.
(2) As a matter of necessity, in the case of every human being, the person knows something to be so only if he is certain of it.

But I think I have done more than just that. For the strength of the arguments given for each of these two propositions is, I think, sufficient for a similar force to attach to propositions

which are quite obvious consequences the two of them together. One such consequential proposition is this:

(3) In the case of every human being, there is at most hardly
anything which the person knows to be so.

This is the sceptical thesis for which, at the beginning of this
chapter, we set out to argue.

Now that we have seen what lies behind this sceptical thesis,
and behind parallel theses concerning what is or is not flat, or a
vacuum, etc., we might pause to try to assess what it is that the
theses contradict. Where flatness is the issue, it might be
doubted that we really *believed* of the things we call 'flat' that
any of them, or more than hardly any of them, *were* flat: one
might say, 'I never really *believed* that prairie was *flat*; I see
that now clearly enough!' Perhaps we may have believed some
such things in early childhood, but perhaps not once we became
at all sophisticated about things. After all, does this sort of
argument about flatness make one think that one must change
one's beliefs about many things we call 'flat'?[19]

I am not sure what the answer to this question is. How to tell
what someone believes about things can perhaps be a difficult
logical question. And, it *may* be that the answer in the case of
flatness *is* that we have very few, if any, beliefs to the effect that
things are flat. If so, then our remarks that such beliefs need not
clash with experience (in section 1 of this chapter) will be un-
necessary in the case of flatness. But parallel remarks about our
statements, or about what we say, will still be important to
observe. For no matter how demanding the meaning of 'flat'
may be, it does seem that we often say of things that they are
flat. Accordingly even if we do not believe they are, and make
no attempt to get others to think we believe it, we do say that
things are flat. And so, if our account has been correct, we
systematically say what is false in saying such things. But, saying
what is false here need cause no harm; nor need it ever run up
against experiences which startle us into correction. Further
questions arise, though none, I think, which at all endanger our
account: If you never really believed that the top of your desk
was flat did you at least think that you believed it? If not, then
why did you say that it was flat, on this occasion and that one?

[19] These difficulties were raised by John Taurek.

In the case of 'certain', and especially of 'know', it seems clearer that we do, or just recently did, believe the simple positive things: that I am certain of this; that I know that. Bringing out the absolute features of these terms doesn't do much to make us think that we *never* really believed *these* things. There is a difference, it seems, between the cases here, on the one hand, and those of 'flat' and 'vacuum', where an attention to meaning does make one want to disavow that one had the positive beliefs in the first place. Why this difference appears I cannot explain, and I leave it as a further question to do so. In any case, at least for 'know' and 'certain', it is once again important to observe and remark on how false *beliefs* need not noticeably clash with the experiences of everyday life. Of course, further questions may again arise: *If* you never even *believed* that you knew this or that, isn't that extremely surprising? And, if so still, why did you say, in cases where you were later convinced you didn't know, 'Well, at least I *believed* I knew it?'

I have argued that, because we are certain of at most hardly anything, we know at most hardly anything to be so. My offering the argument I did will strike many philosophers as peculiar, even many who have some sympathy with scepticism. For it is natural to think that, except for the requirement of the truth of what is known, the requirement of 'attitude', in this case of personal certainty, is the *least* problematic requirement of knowing. Much more difficult to fulfil, one would think, would be requirements about one's justification, about one's grounds, and so on. And, in a way at least, I am inclined to agree with these thoughts. Why, then, have I chosen to defend scepticism by picking on what seems to be, excepting 'the requirement of truth', just about the easiest requirement of knowledge?

My reason derives from our classical arguments, and from the hypotheses we advanced to explain the intuitions those arguments arouse. Those hypotheses concern someone's being *certain* of something, not just his believing it, or his being confident of the thing. True enough, one of the hypotheses is normative, and so their import together is normative. But, then, they talk about when it is all right for one to be *certain*, when one is justified in *that*, and in having the attitudes involved in *certainty*. They go far beyond saying what is needed for mere belief or confidence to be all right, for one to be justified in those less demanding things and in the less demanding attitudes (whatever those exactly are) which they involve.

Accordingly, we have spent some time giving an account of being certain, and of the most direct way in which being certain relates to knowing. And, we have been able to obtain a rather strong sceptical result from that account in a way that is very direct indeed. That is one reason I put forward this sceptical argument, and did so at this point in our essay.

Our hypotheses for explaining our classical arguments are always near the forefront of my mind. Perhaps the more striking and controversial of our hypotheses is the one which sets out the attitude involved in someone's being certain of something: In so far as I care about being right here, nothing whatsoever will be allowed by me as any reason to be less certain in my position, no matter how much it may seem to show or suggest the opposite to be so. This is a very severely exclusionary attitude; indeed, one that is *absolutely so*. It would be much more compelling to think that such an attitude as this might be involved in being certain, and be logically related to knowing, if one could argue that, for their meaning, the terms 'certain' and 'know' were themselves absolute in relevant respects. This has perhaps been the main motivation behind this entire chapter. Without its meaning to, so to speak, this motivating idea has led easily to the direct sceptical argument around which the chapter has been written.

In remarking on this defence of scepticism, I close with an admission of cautious avoidance of controversy, and for balance, a promise to become involved shortly in more controversial matters. Now, as is almost notorious, questions involving normative conceptions tend to be more controversial than those which do not. By staying away from these conceptions, we have been able to argue for a strong sceptical thesis in a way which is not so controversial. But by thus placing ourselves beyond whatever controversy normative matters may involve, we have lost out on three things.

First, we have not argued for any sceptical conclusion as a *necessary* truth. Of course, nothing in our argument *excludes* our sceptical conclusion from being necessary. But nothing does positively argue either for its being necessarily true that each human being knows at most hardly anything to be so. (We may notice that if it is necessarily true that in the case of *every being* there is *nothing* which he knows to be so, it will follow that our weaker conclusion is also necessarily true.) Second, as the normative requirements intuitively seem the most difficult to satisfy, we might expect to be able to increase the *scope* of our scepticism by using an argument which focuses on them. Hence, we might expect thus to be able to argue that no one knows *anything* to be so, not even that he himself exists or that one and one are two. And, we might also expect to argue, on normative grounds, that no being, not even a God, if there is one, knows even that he himself exists. And, third, beyond the necessity and the greater scope afforded by a normative argument, the intuitively felt difficulty of knowing's normative requirements bodes well for the *compelling power* of an argument with them in focus. We may especially expect this if we may keep our normative argument simple and direct. With these three ends in mind, then, I now proceed to offer just such a direct argument for scepticism. For the work of the present chapter, we may now have some hope, perhaps even some confidence, that this argument's ideas will be firmly based in a language that is quite demanding, a language with absolute terms.

III

An Argument for Universal Ignorance

THIS is a good point for me to present an argument for the universal form of scepticism about knowledge. In Chapter I, I tried to arouse our intuitions for scepticism by means of classical arguments, the most effective means initially to promote arousal. And, I tried to explain this effectiveness, in a way favourable to scepticism, in terms of two companion hypotheses about our concepts of knowledge and of certainty. The classical arguments make indirect use of these hypotheses; the argument I shall now present makes more direct use of them. This new argument is quite a direct argument for scepticism.

Each of the two premises of this new argument is put forward as necessarily true. If these premises may be accepted as such, then their conclusion, the thesis that nobody knows anything to be so, will also be a necessary proposition. This accords with philosophers' tutored intuitions about this thesis, as we remarked in Chapter I, section 10. We do not think that if no one knows anything, that it is just an unfortunate feature of the way the human condition happens to be. Accordingly, this will be a positive feature of our argument.[1] Each of our two

---

[1] The idea of a certain proposition's being necessarily true is, however vague and difficult, quite different from any ideas concerning the epistemic status of the proposition. Among the latter are notions like that of a proposition's being *a priori*, in one way or another, of its being certain, or knowable for certain, and so on. A sceptic about knowledge will, in virtue in his position, deny the applicability only of (some of) the latter notions. He may hesitantly, as I do, hold that a certain proposition is necessarily true, not for a minute supposing that he *knows* even that it is true at all. If he is a quite radical sceptic, as I am in Chapter V, he will not suppose that he even has any *reason* to think the proposition true, much less any to think it to be necessarily true. To do justice to this idea of strict necessity requires much space, and a great deal more than I can here afford: Saying that the proposition holds true for all possible worlds, or any possible situation, is only a beginning. If one thinks little of this idea of necessity, one can look at my work here in the following way, and the support for scepticism will be the same: Philosophers often have the *idea* that universal scepticism about knowledge is, *if* true, *necessarily* true. They also often have the *idea* that *if* a universal, purely normative proposition is true, *it* is *necessarily* true. I want only to explain the former idea in

premisses will be normative in character; they will each concern when it is at least all right for someone to be certain of something. I think that their necessary truth derives, at least in part, from this characteristic. We may look at these propositions to help make the point: If someone promises to do something, then it is at least all right for him to do that thing, providing that no overriding (consideration or) considerations make(s) it not all right. I take it that this proposition is, if true at all, necessarily true, and that its necessary truth then derives, at least in part, from its normative character. So, I think that the normative character of our premisses will be a further positive feature of our argument.

I will speak of this argument as an argument for universal *ignorance*. Now this may require me to use the word 'ignorance' in a way which contradicts its actual meaning. It may be, for example, that for anyone to be ignorant of anything, and so to manifest ignorance, it must be possible for at least some being to know something to be so. If this is indeed the case, then in arguing that knowledge is impossible, I will serve to show as well that there can be no ignorance. In that case, attending to what 'ignorance' means, one will hardly want to call this an argument for ignorance. While I see no reason to accept such an idea about ignorance, I do not want to argue the point here. For, from our point of view, if worse comes to worst, and ignorance does require knowledge, then 'ignorance' will be too *weak* a term to express our radical negative conclusion about knowledge. What we are arguing for, no matter what the argument is called, is the thesis that no one ever knows anything to be so.

Bearing in mind that this is the conclusion to be yielded, we may, if their meanings make us, use 'ignorance' and 'ignorant' as convenient and dramatic terms of art. Flying in the face of meaning or not, then, I will say that a being is *ignorant* as to whether something is so if and only if the being does *not know* that it is so and also does *not know* that it is not so; that is, just in the case the being does not know whether or not the thing is so. And I will say that the sceptical conclusion we now seek to

---

terms of its connection with the latter, more general idea, however inadequate the ideas themselves or, for that matter, however inadequate may be any idea involving a notion of strict necessity.

yield may be put like this: Everybody is always *ignorant of everything*. Perhaps this requires us to be yet more artful with our language than I have so far feared. But that means no real trouble for any sceptic either. And, intending to establish our conclusion as a necessary truth, I will say, finally, that this argument means to show that ignorance is necessary, or inevitable, as well as universal, or complete, or total. Perhaps if I put things in this dramatic way, other people, and not just other philosophers, will be more inclined to take seriously whatever defects in the idea of knowing our argument may force us to admit.

Our argument is meant to connect with our efforts for scepticism in both of our preceding chapters. As I have said, the argument will rely on the correctness of the two hypotheses we used to explain the power of our classical arguments. In this way, our argument for ignorance will connect with these classical arguments, and with our efforts in Chapter 1. In that it relies on our two explanatory hypotheses, our argument, in particular, will rely on the first of these. This means that it relies on the idea that a severe, absolute attitude is involved in someone's being certain. This is where we begin to connect our argument with our efforts in Chapter II. We further this connection when we advance an analysis of knowing to support our argument for ignorance.

The connection with our ideas about absolute terms is meant to be considerable. Once our argument is presented, and once various considerations have been adduced in its behalf, I aim to find a linguistic basis for the ideas that make it work. I will try to find an absolute term, no, several absolute terms, which can readily provide an analysis of knowing. This analysis is to reveal knowing to be the absolute limit of a series of justifying states, or positions, or conditions. Thus, contrary to what Chapter II may have seemed to suggest, in relevant contexts, 'know' can be defined completely, rather than just partially, by means of a suitable absolute adjective. When the implications of this analysis are explored, we may come reasonably near to completing our explanation of those important intuitions our classical arguments first aroused. But any of that comes near this chapter's end; first, we must advance our argument for universal ignorance.

§1. *A Preliminary Statement of the Argument*

I begin by giving a statement of the argument which, while correct in all essentials, does not account for certain complications. On this statement, the argument is exceedingly simple and straightforward. It has but two premisses and each of them makes no exceptions whatsoever. The first of these is the proposition:

(1) If someone *knows* something to be so, then it is all right for the person to be absolutely *certain* that it is so.

For example, if it is true that Mary *knows* that there was a general called 'Napoleon', then it is (perfectly) all right for her to be absolutely *certain* that there was. And, if René really *knows* that he exists, then it is (perfectly) all right for René to be absolutely certain that he does. This is (the first part of) our second explanatory hypothesis.

Our second and final premiss, then, is this categorical proposition:

(2) It is never all right for anyone to be absolutely *certain* that anything is so.

This connects with (the first part of) our first hypothesis. According to this premiss, it is not all right for Mary to be absolutely certain that there was a general called 'Napoleon', nor is it even all right for René to be absolutely certain that he exists. No matter what their situations, these people should not be absolutely certain of these things. When one understands what is involved in being absolutely certain of something, one will presumably understand why it is never all right to be absolutely certain.

These two premisses together entail our conclusion of universal scepticism:

(3) Nobody ever *knows* that anything is so.

In particular, Mary does not really *know* that there was a general called 'Napoleon', nor does René really *know* that he exists.

Upon reading the first premiss, some will think it wrong for a reason which, if anything, can only help in getting this sort of

argument to yield scepticism effectively. The thought is that
if one *knows* that something is so, then one *ought* to be absolutely certain of it. But the thought continues, if one *ought* to be
certain, it follows that it is *not* true that it is *all right* for one to
be certain; it is *more than that*. Accordingly, this reasoning concludes, our first premiss is incorrect, and so our statement of
the argument. Now, I am not at all sure that this thinking is
correct. It is similar to the thought, encountered before, that
knowing something to be so excludes *believing* it. Certain things
incline me to the exclusionary idea in both cases; other feelings
incline me to think that there is no excluding. Perhaps, a 'just'
is needed in both cases for complete explicit sense: 'It's not
just all right for him to do it, he *ought* to,' 'He doesn't *just*
believe it, he knows it.' By the same token, I cannot be very
confident that the exclusionary position is wrong in either case.
Consequently, I am not as confident as I'd like that my
premisses are proper.

The reason I chose 'all right' rather than 'ought' or 'should'
for my premisses is simple: unlike this exclusionary objector,
others may think that while knowing does not require so much
as that one ought to be certain, it does entail that it is all right
for one to be certain. Seeing nothing clearly wrong with this
'milder' position, I wish to accommodate it. Thus, I chose 'all
right'. For I think that a very strong second premiss can be
supported anyway, so that scepticism can be arrived at even
with this accommodation. To continue to accommodate the
milder position, while at the same time accommodating the
exclusionary objection to 'all right' as we have employed it, we
may employ a locution we used before, when treating 'know'
and 'believe'. There we said that, whatever else is true of their
relationship, we can be quite confident that if someone knows
something to be so, then he *at least* believes it. Now, we can say
that, whatever else is true of the present relationship, if someone ought to be certain of something, it is *at least* all right for
him to be certain of it. Accordingly, we may now, most
accommodatingly, put our first premiss this way: If someone
knows that something is so, then it is at least all right for him
to be absolutely certain of it. And, then, we can get our second
premiss to match up with it by putting in an 'even', like this:
It is never even all right for anyone to be absolutely certain

that anything is so. From here on in, I will omit these qualifying, accommodating words, 'at least' and 'even'. For, as
will become plain enough, none of the supporting arguments
depend importantly on their presence. And their continued
repetition would make my essay more tedious For those who
want them, however, these words may always be inserted in
quite obvious positions.

Thus qualified or not, the first of these premisses is hardly
novel unless novelty may be gained in any slight change in the
words one chooses. Words to the same effect are prominent in
the philosophical literature; one might mention Moore, Ayer,
and Malcolm as a few significant examples.[2] To my own way of
thinking any such words are in need of some small qualification
to get things right. But the essential idea of this premiss can
hardly be faulted without doing violence to the concept of
knowing.

The second premiss is, I think, also in need of a small qualification, one which matches that needed for the first. But even
with a qualification, it is difficult to find such a proposition put
forward in the literature. Indeed, the philosophers we just
mentioned seem all too typical in denying it, at least by implication. It is this premiss which is most crucial, and I will argue
that denying it amounts to embracing real dogmatism. Now,
the opposite of scepticism is often called *dogmatism*; it is also
often called *common sense*. Given the truth of the first premiss,
it is for this reason that dogmatism is indeed the alternative to
scepticism. That, of course, is the import of our two companion
hypotheses, as well as of our two premisses here.

The force of these remarks will be better appreciated, I think,
when we understand more fully what the premisses really
amount to. That will also help us appreciate how the premisses
must be qualified in order that the argument may actually be
sound. For unlike our classical form of the argument, this
direct argument really can handle every logically possible case
or situation. Accordingly, I will now discuss each of the
premisses in turn, beginning with the first.

[2] G. E. Moore, 'Certainty' in *Philosophical Papers* (New York, 1962), p. 223,
A. J. Ayer, *The Problem of Knowledge* (Baltimore, 1956), pp. 33–5, and Norman
Malcolm, 'Knowledge and Belief' in *Knowledge and Certainty* (Englewood Cliffs,
N.J., 1963), pp. 67–8.

§2. *The First Premiss: The Idea that if one Knows it is all right for one to be Certain*

We often have the idea that someone is certain of something but he shouldn't be. Perhaps from his expressive behaviour, perhaps from something else, we *take* it that he is certain of something—whether or not he really is certain of it. We ask him, if we are so inclined, 'How can you be *certain* of that?' In asking this question, we manage to imply that it might not be all right for him to be certain and imply, further, that this is because he might not really *know* the thing. If the man could show us that he does know, then we should withdraw the question and, perhaps, even apologize for implying what we did by raising it. But, then, how do we manage to imply so much by just asking this question in the first place? Neither 'know' nor any cognate expression ever crosses our lips in the asking. We are able to imply so much, I suggest, because we all accept the idea that, at least generally, if one does know something then it is all right for one to be certain of it—but if one doesn't then it isn't. This suggests that there is some analytic connection between knowing, on the one hand, and, on the other, its being all right to be certain.

The very particular idea that knowing *entails* its being all right to be certain is suggested, further, by the fact that knowing entails, at least, that one *is* certain. As we saw in section 9 of the preceding chapter, that this is a fact is made quite plain by the inconsistency expressed by sentences like 'He really *knew* that it was raining, but he *wasn't* absolutely *certain* that it was.' Such a sentence can express no truth: if he wasn't certain, then he didn't know. We get further confirmation from considering related sentences. To anticipate again our work in Chapter IV, the sentences 'He was *sad that* it was raining, but he *didn't know* it was' and 'He was really *sad that* it was raining, but he *wasn't* absolutely *certain* it was' are likewise inconsistent. Their inconsistency means an entailment from being sad that p to knowing that p, in the first case, and to being certain that p in the second. The same experience is felt with a statement to the effect that someone *regretted that* he did something, and with the denials that he *knew* he did, and that he was *certain* of it. This can be best explained, it would seem, by an entailment from knowing to being absolutely certain. The entailment from knowing to being certain is pretty convincingly clinched, I think, by appreciating the equivalence between someone's knowing something and his knowing it for certain, or with absolute certainty. To be sure, we may describe cases which we would more naturally react to with the words 'He knew it' than 'He knew it for certain.' One such case is that of the examined student (considered in Chapter II, section 9). Another concerns a man who, looking for his cuff-links, unerringly goes to the very spot where they are while doubts go through his mind. Does he know that they are in that spot? We readily say 'Yes'. But our readiness to say that these people know might only indicate loose usage of 'know' by us, while we are more strict in our use when the words 'certain' and 'certainty' enter the picture. That this is much the more plausible hypothesis than thinking there to be an inequivalence here is evidenced by the inconsistency of the relevant sentences: 'He *knew* it, but he *didn't* know it *for certain*,' 'He really *knew* it, but he *didn't* know it *with absolute certainty*,' 'He knew it was there, but he didn't *really know* it', and so on. No truth can be found in these words no matter when they might be uttered. Even if they are put forth at the end of stories like that of the cuff-link finder, where we are inclined at first to say he knows, we realize that they must express what is false. Accordingly, we are forced to be unswayed by our tendency to loose usage and to admit the equivalence between knowing with absolute certainty and just plain knowing to be so. Admitting this equivalence, we can be quite confident that knowing does indeed entail being absolutely certain. This reinforces further the arguments and conclusions of the chapter just preceding.

Now, our intuitive thought about knowledge or knowing is that it is something good, of value, which ought to be sought and prized when attained. But if knowing always entails being certain, and the latter may so often be bad, as our questions often imply, how might it be that knowing is so often good? The situation here is very unlike others that are only superficially alike, e.g. the case of helping someone in trouble, which entails someone's being in trouble. These latter cases involve the righting of a wrong, or the improvement of a situation which starts off bad. But our idea is not that being certain is bad, or generally bad, like being in trouble. Rather, it is bad *unless* one knows, but if one does know then there's nothing wrong at all with being certain; there need be nothing wrong with it in the first place. This is the reason that there is no conflict between the supposed value of knowing and its entailing that one is absolutely certain.

All of these ideas suggest the universal and unqualified proposition that if one knows, it is always all right for one to be certain. And, quite surely, at least something like this must be right. But a qualification must be made if we are to arrive at a statement which is actually correct. Everyday life provides cases where it is bad that one knows, and these are also cases where it is bad for one to be certain even if one does in fact know. For example, one shouldn't know too much about the private lives of others. If one's neighbour sleeps in the nude and doesn't want others to know it, it may well be no good thing for one to know that he sleeps this way. In such a case as this, even if one knows that the neighbour sleeps in the nude, it is neither all right for one to know it nor all right for one to be absolutely certain that he does. A more unrealistic case but in some ways a clearer one is as follows. Here one's being certain of a particular thing is so bad that it is quite clear that one should not be certain of it even if one in fact knows the thing. We may suppose, for example, that a powerful god makes it quite plain that he will bring fruitful times for the multitude just in case a particular individual is *not certain* of a particular thing; just in case Max is not certain that frogs are animals. Otherwise, years of pain are all that lie in store. Even if Max knows that frogs are animals it is not all right for him to be certain of this thing. If this means tampering with himself so that he no longer knows it, then Max had better go to a hypnotist or whatever. The price is too high and the knowledge too trivial. As in more realistic cases, a man's knowing something is not enough to entail that it is all right for him to be certain of it.

Cases like these, both ordinary and bizarre, show that our first premiss must be qualified if we are to have any sound argument. They also show that a qualification is needed for Ayer's dictum that if one knows something one has the right to be sure of it, and for any other proposition which involves our basic idea, e.g. the proposition that if one knows something, then one is justified in being certain of the thing. There is no doubt much truth in these propositions, as we have argued and as is evidenced by the inconsistent appearance of sentences to the contrary: 'He *knows* that it's raining, but he *shouldn't* be *sure* of it,' 'He really *knew* they were fools, but it was *wrong* for him to be absolutely *certain* that they were,' and so on. But, this inconsistent appearance, while important to notice, is not due to any actual inconsistency in what is expressed. It is due, rather, to the fact that when one attends to these sentences one is liable to think only of evidential or epistemic considerations. One is not likely to think in terms of cases or possibilities that have little or nothing to do with these considerations. But of course *those* cases are the only ones which might falsify the statement.

The sorts of cases which make us qualify our premiss present considerations which are not entailed by the person's being certain or by his knowing. They involve the contingencies of bad consequences, or similar external factors which must be given their due weight. Thus, the upsetting cases present unusual considerations which *override* any considerations to the effect that one knows. An adequate premiss must take care to allow for these considerations, and we modify (1) to take care of just that:

(1q) If someone *knows* something to be so, then it is all right for the person to be absolutely certain that it is so providing only that no overriding (consideration or) considerations make(s) it not all right.

Such a qualification was to be expected anyway. Few things, if any, are so important that some others might not sometimes take precedence. And anything which might be involved in knowing, unlike avoiding harming or punishing the innocent, is quite surely not so extraordinarily important. Once we make this qualification, however, it seems impossible to deny our first premiss. Indeed, it is no doubt just what this premiss says which is indicated by the words 'for certain' in the sentence 'He knew it for certain.' It is not just the idea that the knower is certain to which these emphatic words here point. Rather, they point to the idea that his *knowing* means that, pending no overriding considerations to the contrary, his being certain of the thing is perfectly all right.

Now it cannot be too strongly emphasized that everything I said is meant to be compatible with the sense which, in any relevant sentence, the ordinary word 'know' actually has. Indeed, it fairly relies on this word's having only one ('strong') sense as it occurs in sentences of the forms 'S knows that p,' 'S knows about X,' and so on. Some philosophers have suggested 'weak' senses of 'know' in which it does not even have an entailment to absolute certainty.[3] But though there is some reason to suppose that 'know' has different meanings in 'John knows that Jim is his friend' and 'John knows Jim,'[4] there appears no reason at all to suppose that 'knows' may mean different things as it occurs in the former sentence. Indeed, reason seems to favour the opposite view. If a genuinely ambiguous sentence has a meaning on which it is inconsistent, there will be one also on which it is consistent. Once the latter meaning is pointed out, this difference is appreciated and felt to be quite striking. Thus, the sentence 'John really *types* many things, but he produces symbols *only orally*' has an obvious meaning on which it is inconsistent. But, it may be pointed out that 'types' has another sense, which it shares (roughly) with 'classifies'. Once this is pointed out, the sentence's consistent reading is appreciated, and the effect is a striking one. No similar phenomenon is ever found with the sentence 'John really *knows* that he types things, but he *isn't* absolutely *certain* that he does.' There may be many *ad hoc* explanations of this fact. But the only plausible explanation is, I think, that 'know' doesn't have a weak sense with no entailment to absolute certainty.[5] With any other sense, one is not really talking about *knowing*.

Now the need for our qualification means that we must

---

[3] For example, see Malcolm, 'Knowledge and Belief', pp. 62ff.

[4] For example, Spanish uses the verb *saber* to translate the first of these sentences and *conocer* to translate the second, and so for various other languages. This evidence is both indirect and inconclusive, but it is *some* evidence anyway.

[5] Perhaps philosophers who seem to see more senses than I do are using 'sense' in a different sense. Or, perhaps more likely, they are inventing a new sense for 'sense', so as to use the word to make important distinctions about the meaning of our expressions. But, without being impertinent, I can only request to see some reason for supposing that, even in such a new sense of 'sense', our verb 'know' has two or more senses.

similarly qualify, and so revise, our second explanatory
hypothesis. What we now hypothesize, to explain our classical
arguments etc., is (1q) and that speakers of English (at least)
all accept (1q). Of course the only part of (1q) which is active
in these explanations is the 'main part'. The 'providing-clause'
is idle in these accounts. But it must be put in for us to be
accurate. For, as we have just seen, we don't accept the main
part without it.

To deny our first premiss, then, is to do violence to the meaning of 'know' and to our concept of knowledge. If our argument
is to be stopped, it must be with the consideration of the second
premiss. In any case, it is with that premiss that the *substantive*
claim of the argument is made: in putting forward that
premiss it is not only with mere questions of logical relations
with which we must contend. Accordingly, we now begin to
enter on the largest and most important part of our discussion.

§3. *The Second Premiss: The Idea that it is never all right to be
Absolutely Certain.*

As I have stated it, the second premiss of our argument is a
triply universal proposition:

(2) It is *never* all right for *anyone* to be absolutely certain that
    anything is so.

It is universal, first, in that it applies to all beings without fear
or favour, the most almighty of gods as well as the humblest of
creatures. Second, it is also universal in that it applies to all
propositions or things (of which one might or might not be
certain). It is to hold no matter how simple and certain a thing
may seem to a being: that one exists right now, that there is an
experience of (phenomenal) blueness, and so on. We want a
premiss which is universal in both of these respects, and I will
argue that we may have one. But there is a third way in which
this premiss is universal, and this aspect of it may be doubted:
it says that no matter what the circumstances, being certain
is not all right. In other words, it says that it is not all right in
any circumstances whatsoever. That is the import of 'never'
here. (If one insists that 'never' can only be used to exclude
times, then we may explicitly place the words 'As a matter of
logical necessity' before our premiss, and then discuss it in those
terms.)

This third point of universality was needed for the second premiss to match up with the first in the original, preliminary statement of our argument. For if there were some circumstances when it is or would be all right to be certain, then, if we just went by our original first premiss, (1), we might know in just those circumstances. Those circumstances might be ones in which things were known. Consequently, we needed to rule out all circumstances in our original second premiss. But, we have found it necessary to alter our first premiss, from (1) to (1q). So, we no longer require a second premiss which, like (2), is universal with respect to circumstances as well as with respect to beings and propositions. Is this universality of circumstances fatal to the truth of (2), so that we *must* reformulate that premiss now that we *may* do so?

As we have been at pains to make clear, no one's being certain of any particular thing is all that important apart from the consequences it might have. Neither is one's knowing something—supposing that one knows—of any such great moment. Just as knowing is not so importantly good that it cannot sometimes be bad, so being certain is not so importantly bad that it might not sometimes be all right and even good. It may be in fact necessary for a researcher to find a cure for a dread disease that that man be absolutely certain that there is a cure to be found. Even if he is dogmatic about the cure's existence, this may prove to be all right, I think, if it increases his chances of discovering a cure. And, suppose that he does find one. As before, a more bizarre case may serve to clarify. We may suppose that this time our powerful god wants Max to be absolutely certain that tulips are animals. This time the god makes it quite plain that the multitude will have fruitful times just in case Max is certain of this thing and that otherwise excruciating pain and suffering will be all. In such a case, Max had better be absolutely certain no matter what negative feature might be inherent in his being so. Even if it takes hypnotism or drugs, Max ought to get himself into the state desired by the eccentric but effective deity. In such circumstances as these, it is perfectly all right for him to be certain that tulips are animals. These cases and others force us to qualify our premiss. The situation is much as before with premiss (1). This time, however, we have overriding considerations which make being certain (perfectly) all right. Accordingly, we must reformulate (2). But, we may do so in a way which gets the result to go appropriately with (1q):

(2q) It is never the case that it is all right for someone to be absolutely *certain* that something is so if no overriding (consideration or) considerations make(s) it all right.

This premiss says that there is something wrong with being certain but allows that this may be outweighed by external factors. These factors have nothing much to do with evidence, or with any other epistemic factors. It is for this qualified proposition that I shall make a case. If it may be accepted, then we may obtain the conclusion of universal scepticism; we may proclaim ignorance as universal and inevitable.

§4. *What Attitude is Involved in one's being Absolutely Certain?*

I will now, at last, begin to argue for the idea that to be absolutely certain of something is, owing to a certain feature of personal certainty, to be *dogmatic* in the matter of whether that thing is so. It is because of this dogmatic feature that there is always *something* wrong with being absolutely certain. In other words, it is because of this feature that our second premiss, (2q), is correct. My argument for the idea that this feature ensures this dogmatism falls naturally into two parts. The first part, which will occupy us in this present section and in section 5 as well, is aimed at specifying the feature. This amounts to supporting (the first part of) our first explanatory hypothesis. Thus, we will argue here that one's being absolutely certain of something involves one in having a certain severely negative *attitude* in the matter of whether that thing is so. As we remember (from Chapter I, section 10), it is, at least roughly, the attitude that *no* new information, evidence, or experience will now be seriously considered by one to be *at all* relevant to any possible change in how certain one should be in the matter; no matter what new experience I may have, I will be no less certain but that *p*. The second part of the argument for this damning idea, which will occupy us in succeeding sections, 6 through 9, is aimed at showing this attitude always to be dogmatic, even in matters which may appear to be absolutely simple and certain. For now, what can we say for the idea that one's being absolutely certain entails one's having such an absolutely severe attitude, or approach, or frame of mind?

The thought that such an absolutely severe attitude should be essential to one's knowing is hardly novel with me. Indeed, philosophers who are quite plainly anti-sceptical proclaim just this attitude as essential to one's knowing. Thus Norman Malcolm, a good representative, thinks himself to know that there is an ink-bottle before him, and describes what he takes to be implicit in this knowledge of his:

> Not only do I not *have* to admit that (those) extraordinary occurrences would be evidence that there is no ink-bottle here; the fact is that I *do not* admit it. There is nothing whatever that could happen in the next moment that would by me be called *evidence* that there is not an ink-bottle here now. No future experience or investigation could prove to me that I am mistaken. . . .
>
> It will appear to some that I have adopted an *unreasonable* attitude toward that statement. There is, however, nothing unreasonable about it.
>
> In saying that I should regard nothing as evidence that there is no ink-bottle here now, I am not *predicting* what I should do if various astonishing things happened. . . .
>
> That assertion describes my *present* attitude towards the statement that here is an ink-bottle. . . .[6]

Now Malcolm, it is true, aligns himself with the idea that there are two (or more) senses of 'know' to be found in sentences like 'John *knows* that there is an ink-bottle before him.' But, while this idea is not correct, it is not essential to his position in these passages. We already have argued, in section 2, that this idea is not correct. That this incorrect idea is not essential to the main thrust of Malcolm's quoted remarks is, I think, equally clear. For he allows that there is at least *a* sense of 'know' where knowing entails one's having the extreme attitude he characterizes. Presumably, that sense, at least, is just the sense where knowing entails being absolutely certain. Now, in that anti-sceptical philosophers think that when one knows the attitude of certainty is not only present but quite all right, their thinking that the attitude is to be characterized in such severe negative terms is some indirect evidence for thinking so. For an attitude which is so severely negative as this might

[6] Malcolm, 'Knowledge and Belief', pp. 67–8.

well *not* be one which is very often justified. The point is that even if one wants to *avoid* scepticism, one may have a concern for the truth about what attitude, regarding possible new experience, is involved in someone's being *certain* and in his *knowing*. This laudable concern seems to make an absolutely severe characterization quite unavoidable.

The attitude of certainty concerns *any* sequence of experience or events (which could consistently be presented to the sentient subject, and which does not prejudge the issue, i.e., is not like 'the experience of realizing that, after all, not-*p*'). Thus, one is certain that there is an ink-bottle before one only if one's attitude is this: No matter how things may seem to appear, *I will not count* as contrary evidence such extraordinary sequences as these:

... when I next reach for this ink-bottle my hand should seem to pass *through* it and I should not feel the contact of any object ... in the next moment the ink-bottle will suddenly vanish from sight ... I should find myself under a tree in the garden with no ink-bottle about ... one or more persons should enter this room and declare that they see no ink-bottle on this desk ... a photograph taken now of the top of the desk should clearly show all of the objects on it except the ink-bottle.[7]

Now, however certain one may be that some or all of these sequences will not occur, that is of course not the same thing as being certain that there is an ink-bottle before one. But, though there may be many differences between the two, perhaps the one which should most clearly be focused on is this: If one is really certain of the ink-bottle, and not just of other things however related, then one's attitude is that *even if one should* seem to find oneself in a contrary garden, one *would disregard* this experience as irrelevant to the question of whether, at the time in question, there is or was an ink-bottle before one. One might resist this characterization, but then, I think, one would lose one's proper focus on what it is of which one is certain.

Here is a line of resistance to our characterization of being certain. Suppose, in contrast, one's attitudes were these: *If strange things seemed to happen, then perhaps I would change*

[7] Ibid., p. 67.

my mind; I just might. But, I am absolutely certain that no strange things will ever happen to speak against there being an ink-bottle. Might not these attitudes be those of a man who was *absolutely* certain *that there is an ink-bottle before him*? Might not he be certain of the ink-bottle, not in or by having a completely exclusionary attitude on that matter itself, but, rather, indirectly, so to speak, in or by having just such an attitude towards the possibility of apparently contrary appearances.[8]

This suggestion, this line of resistance, is an interesting one, but it is neither correct nor of any use even if it were correct. First, let us notice that at least almost invariably when one is even quite close to being absolutely certain of something, one is not nearly so certain that no contrary appearances will turn up. For example, you may be quite sure that I am married. But, you will not be quite so sure that no appearances to the contrary might show up: I may be married but say to you 'No, I'm not really married. Mary and I don't believe in such institutions. We only sent out announcements to see the effect —and, of course, it's easier to have most people believe that you are.' I might, at a certain point, say these things to you and get a few other people to say apparently confirmatory things. All of this, and some more if need be, should and would, I think, incline you to be at least a bit less certain that I am married. Thus, at least with things where one is *quite* certain, the matter seems to be quite the *opposite* of what was suggested: one will not be so certain that nothing strangely contradictory will turn up—but one will reject at least almost any such thing even if it does turn up. We may plausibly project that things work even more strongly in this direction in situations where someone is absolutely certain (if there really are any such).[9]

Let us now take something of which you are as certain as anything, say, that one and one are two. Suppose that you are very sure that your favourite mathematician will never say something false to you about any such simple sum. Imagine that he, or God, tells you and insists that one and one are three, and not two. Or, you may be told that this proposition is *not* true because, according to the *correct* ontology, there are no

[8] Some such line of resistance was suggested to me by Gilbert Harman, and by Michael Lockwood.

[9] I am here indebted to discussion with Saul Kripkle.

numbers at all. If your attitude is that he, or He, is still to be trusted or, at least, that you would no longer be quite so sure of the sum, then you are *not* absolutely certain that one and one are two. If you *are absolutely certain* of this sum, then, I submit, your attitude will be to reject entirely the message from the mathematician or God. In this simple arithmetical matter, you are to give it, perhaps unlike other messages from the same source, no weight at all in your thinking. It seems, then, that this line of resistance is not faithful to the idea of being certain of a particular thing. But would it be of any use in countering scepticism, or the sceptic's charge of dogmatism, even if it were right?

It seems to me that it is *at least as dogmatic* to take the approach that one will count nothing as even appearing to speak against one's position than to take the approach that any such appearances which might show up will be entirely rejected. What about appearances to the effect that some contrary appearances, their precise nature left open as yet, are likely to show up in the future? If one is absolutely certain that the latter sort of appearances won't ever show up, one would, presumably, have the attitude of rejecting entirely the indication of the former appearances. One's attitude of rejection gets pushed farther back from the matter itself. Perhaps according to our line of resistance, this may go on indefinitely. But each retreat, and the consequent new place for rejection, only makes a man look more and more striking in his dogmatism and unreasonableness about the whole affair. Even going back no farther than the second level, so to speak, only a quite foolhardy man would, it seems to me, reject any suggestion that some things might be brought forth to appear to speak against his position. If anything, it is better for him to allow that they may and to be ready to reject them. If *anything*, that would represent a *less* dogmatic approach or attitude. So, even if our line of resistance had presented us with a case of being certain, such an 'indirect' way of being certain would hardly help us to avoid the sceptical charge. That is quite surely no way for being perfectly certain to be perfectly all right.

It is important to stress very hard that a clause like 'I will regard nothing as evidence that there is no ink-bottle now' must be regarded as the expression of a man's *current attitude*, and not as expressing any prediction of what he will do under certain future circumstances.[10] Thus, one may allow that a sentence like the following is indeed consistent: 'He is absolutely *certain* that there are automobiles, but he *may* change his mind should certain evidence come up.' That is because even if his present attitude is that he will not, things may not happen in accordance with his attitude. For example, things might happen to him which *cause* him to become uncertain. Or, his attitude might just evaporate, so to speak, the new evidence then effecting him in the unwanted way; and so on. Such conditions as these give us a consistent interpretation for the foregoing sentence, even if not a very ordinary one. A sentence which will still appear to express an inconsistency, on the other hand, is obtained once we make sure that our severely negative clause is embedded so that it is clear that the man's current attitude is the point. Thus, in contrast with the foregoing, it still seems always inconsistent to say, 'He is absolutely *certain* that there are automobiles, but *his attitude* is that he really *may* change his mind should certain evidence come up.' A proper assessment of the direct linguistic evidence supports the idea that the attitude of certainty is thus absolutely severe.

Even this reference to the attitude may not be enough, however, to ensure that an inconsistency is actually expressed. There is the possibility of what we might call the motivational problem, the problem of the subject being certain of the thing but not caring that much about whether he is right in the matter. We discussed this a bit in Chapter I, section 10, but at least some of that bears going over here. The idea is, again, that you might be certain of a particular thing, say, that there is a lamp-post on the north-east corner of 19th St. and 6th Ave., but you may not care to clutter up your mind with such trivial information (trivial, that is, for your presumed purposes). In such a case, you may not wish to exert any effort to make sure that you will continue to be right about whether there is a

[10] In a footnote on p. 68 of 'Knowledge and Belief', Malcolm says that he doesn't think the word 'attitude' is very satisfactory. He would rather put things, he says there, in terms of some conditional statements about what he would say or think right now if or when he imagines things now as happening, But, actually, this latter suggestion is much the poorer. Bizarre causal networks in him should be compatible with his now being certain. Indeed, Malcom's choice of the word 'attitude' is quite apt and satisfactory.

lamp-post at that particular street location, and you may have a weak attitude in respect of new experiences here, to accord with this lack of desire. The attitude of certainty, however, seems to require a more positive approach on your part towards making such an effort should contrary appearances arise. Thus, it might be concluded, while you *are now certain* there is a lamp-post right there, your attitude is *not* this: no matter what new experiences may show up to suggest that no lamp-post is (or was) there, I will not be any less certain that there is (or was) a lamp-post on the north-east corner of 19th St. and 6th Ave.

As I said when this idea was first introduced, I am not sure that it presents a coherent description of any person's mental states and attitudes. But, again, it may do so. In any event, to accommodate the possibility that it does, we may redescribe the attitude with an appropriate initial clause about caring enough about being right: *Insofar as I care about being right in the matter,* no matter what new experiences may show up to suggest that no lamp-post is (or was) there, I will not be any less certain that there is (or was) a lamp-post on the north-east corner of 19th St. and 6th Ave. If there is no coherent possibility here described, this initial clause may always be dropped in favour of the simpler description. The point for us to bear in mind now is this. The initial clause does nothing to make the described attitude any less dogmatic than it would be without the clause's being applicable. For if a man is not at least a bit open to new experience, his caring about being correct will not save him from the charge of dogmatism.

If one thinks that some such qualifying clause is needed, and if one was previously inclined to accept the idea that an absolutely severe attitude was entailed in being certain, one may now have second thoughts about the whole matter. Here is how those thoughts may run: You can satisfy even the strongest desire to be right about a matter just by believing correctly, by believing what is true. Being *certain* does nothing extra for you here. So why is being certain at all important for this desire, for this motivation? Perhaps our apparently upsetting examples, about the lamp-post and so on, had best be taken as upsetting our whole account of certainty, and not as requiring us only to qualify that account by an appropriate motivational clause.

These thoughts present no direct criticism of our account. But they do ask for a rationale for our motivational clause, for our idea that the concept of personal certainty entails such a severe attitude, and even for our having such a concept in our language. I think we can meet these requests in terms of the following natural considerations. If one cares about being right, one does not just want to be right for the moment. One cares about continuing to be right. Not knowing what may lie in store for one, one wants to have, not just a correct belief, but a belief or some other such attitudinal state which, other things being equal, or in most situations, will withstand the sorts of things which might get one to change one's mind in the matter, or get one to lose the belief or state in some other way. Thus, other things being equal, a stronger belief is better for one's purposes here than a weaker one. The stronger the belief, the less one will accept as evidence sufficient for suitably lessening its strength, and eventually, for abandoning it. The best state for one to be in, then, will be one of absolute certainty. For here, other things being equal, one will be in the least danger of coming to be no longer right. I think that this, or something very like it, lies behind our idea of personal certainty. (I would not be surprised if those who got the idea of certainty into our language, or into an ancestor of it, thought along just such lines.) The way which we would describe cases where other things are not equal bears out the idea that we have now been talking about our actual concept of certainty. Suppose that you believed that an eccentric deity was going to get everyone who was certain that there were automobiles to lose his certainty and, indeed, to stop even being right in the matter. Being a mind-reader, he would of course operate by selective tampering. If you cared most about being right, you might first tamper with yourself so as to avoid selection by him. But our feeling is that this is a special case, where the threats to one's position come from things which must be dealt with separately and specially. No simple state or attitude, like believing or being certain, can be expected to handle such a danger. But, the normal dangers, and most dangers, would best be thwarted by one's being *certain* that there were automobiles. Accordingly, so long as we do not restrict its temporal application too near to the present moment, our clause about caring about being right seems, no *ad hoc* device, but just what we need in describing our attitude of certainty.[11]

Granting that the clause about caring must be added, we have the task of explaining why our sentences without it do sound inconsistent, like the sentence, 'He is absolutely *certain* that there are automobiles, but his *attitude* is that he really *may* change his mind should certain evidence come up.' Perhaps the reason is simply that the sorts of considerations which (at least allegedly) allow a consistent interpretation are themselves so far from our minds when we think of matters of certainty that we would not ordinarily consider them. This would be in line with our explanation of why certain normative sentences *sound* inconsistent even if without qualification they may actually express a thought which is consistent: 'He really *knows* that there are automobiles, but he *shouldn't* be absolutely *certain* of it.' That too *sounds* inconsistent, but without a clause like, 'even if no overriding (consideration or) considerations make(s) it not even all right', the sentence actually will express a consistent idea. Now, the clause with 'even if' rules out certain cases. But these are all cases which don't ordinarily come to mind when thinking of knowledge and certainty. So, the addition of that clause won't have any opportunity to effect the way the sentence sounds to us. The cases involved require so elaborate a description that linguistic intuition has no chance to operate there. Likewise with our present sentences: the clause about caring about being right rules out only bizarre and remote cases; it rules out none which would normally come to mind, or which would fit only simple descriptions. Accordingly, just as the *apparent* inconsistency of the normative sentence with 'knows' provides *some* support for the idea that knowing, if it obtains, is an extraordinarily strong justifying state or condition, so the *apparent* inconsistency of these newer sentences gives *some* support for our simpler description of the attitude. We may say, I think, that the first appearance *equally* supports a premiss about knowing without our 'providing' clause and also one with that clause. Further considerations are needed to decide in favour of the latter, more complex alternative; and they do that. And, we may also say that the latter appearance *equally* supports a description without the

[11] These points owe much to discussion with Michael Slote.

initial 'caring' clause and also one with that clause, thus giving some positive support to each of these. Again, further considerations are needed to decide in favour of one or the other. As I have just suggested, it may well be true that, in the latter case too, the further considerations will decide in favour of the more complex but essentially similar description. The key point here remains this: However the further decisions go, in both of these cases, the direct linguistic evidence gives some good support to a central idea which is much wanted by a sceptic.

§5. *The Attitude of Certainty and the Absoluteness of 'Certain'*

This direct linguistic evidence cannot be enough to satisfy one that being certain, or the attitude in knowing, demands so much as we claim. It is not enough to add the indirect evidence from anti-sceptical authors. And, of course, dispensing with objections cannot really add very much positive. What we want is to fit a severe characterization of this attitude into some more general account of things. Towards this end, I now recall my account of absolute terms. On this account, absolute adjectives like 'flat', 'useless', and 'certain' purport to denote a limiting state or situation to which things may approximate more or less closely. To recapitulate a bit, in the case of these adjectives, the modifier 'absolutely', as well as 'completely' and 'perfectly', is redundant apart from points of emphasis. Various locutions with 'certain' may appear to indicate matters of degree. But they will always admit of a paraphrase where this appearance is dispelled in a favour of a more explicit reference to an absolute limit: 'That's pretty certain' goes into 'That's pretty *close to being absolutely* certain'; 'He is more certain of this than of that' goes into 'He is *absolutely* certain of this but not of that, or else he is *closer to being absolutely* certain of this than of that', and so on. None of this is peculiar to 'certain'; the same happens with locutions containing other absolute adjectives. Sentences with these adjectives also seem to denote matters of degree, but their paraphrases dispel the illusory appearance as well: 'That's the flattest (most useless) thing I've ever seen' goes into 'That's the only *absolutely* flat (useless) thing I've ever seen, or else that's *closer to being absolutely* flat (useless) than anything else I've ever seen.' In the light of these paraphrases, we may repose some confidence in the following formula as indicating an important requirement for something to be x where that is the same as being absolutely x: Something or someone is x (flat, useless, certain, etc.) only in case nothing *could possibly* ever be more x, or x-er, than that thing or person is right now. And here we are speaking of logical possibility, of which situations are consistent and which are not. It is in this strict sense, then, that being certain, and *a fortiori* being absolutely certain, is being at an absolute limit. Now, absolute adjectives typically have contrasting terms which are relative adjectives: 'certain' has 'confident' and 'doubtful', 'flat' has 'bumpy' and 'curved', 'useless' has 'useful' and 'serviceable', and so on. Because matters of degree *are* concerned, there is nothing which is deceptive about the locutions with *these* terms: the sentence 'He is pretty confident' does not go into the somewhat deviant ?'He is pretty close to being absolutely confident'; nor does 'That is very useful' go into ?'That is very close to being absolutely useful.' These relative terms really do denote matters of degree and not any state or situation which is an absolute limit. If something is bumpy, it does *not* follow that nothing could possibly be more bumpy or bumpier. And if someone is confident of something, it does not follow that no one could ever be more confident. Now, a necessary condition for the correct application of an absolute adjective is that certain things, generally denoted by relative adjectives, be entirely absent. Thus, it is a necessary condition of something's being flat that it be *not at all* bumpy, that is, that bumpiness not be present even in the least degree. Also, it is a necessary condition of being flat that the thing be *not at all* curved, or that curvature or curvedness not be present at all. We might expect the same sort of thing to hold in the case of someone's being certain of something, and indeed it does: if someone is certain of something, then that thing is *not at all* doubtful so far as he is concerned, that is, doubt is not present at all in that man with respect to that thing. I have already argued this before, but there are other things which must also be entirely absent if a man is to be certain, though their absence may be included, I suggest, in the absence of all doubt.

One thing which must be entirely absent, and which is, I

think, implicit in the absence of all doubt, is this: any *openness* on the part of the man to consider new experience or information as seriously relevant to the truth or falsity of the thing. In other words, if S is certain that *p*, then it follows that S is *not at all* open to consider any new experience or information as relevant to his thinking or position in the matter of whether *p*. Of course, our saying that the complete absence of openness is a necessary condition of personal certainty by no means commits us to the idea that it is a sufficient condition. Indeed, it is not. Someone may be fixedly attached to a proposition even if he is not certain of it. He might, for example, refuse ever to reconsider his belief in it even though, in any circumstances of choice, there will be other propositions on whose truth he would prefer to base inferences, actions, or to 'risk' goals and goods. Indeed, another necessary condition of being certain of something is, at least roughly this: that one is not at all hesitant or reluctant to risk what he deems valuable or of worth on the truth of that thing. I say, 'at least roughly', because one might have an aversion, moral, aesthetic, religious, or otherwise, to risking anything, or to risking too much, or to risking too much on certain sorts of propositions. Such an aversion might cause one to be somewhat hesitant or reluctant to take the called-for 'risk' despite one's being absolutely certain of the thing involved. But the complete absence of reluctance will still be a condition for certainty, provided that it is suitably connected with the entire outlook of the person in question: In so far as he has no contrary aversions, etc., he is not at all reluctant to 'risk,' etc., on the basis of his position to the effect that *p*.[12] Accordingly, in parallel with our condition of no openness, this condition also will be necessary but not sufficient. One might be entirely willing to 'risk' or base everything on a certain proposition and yet be willing to abandon the proposition or at least risk much less on it, should even rather slight experience to the contrary present itself.

---

[12] A vivid characterization and illustration of this necessary condition of being certain is given by Harry G. Frankfurt in 'Philosophical Certainty', *Philosophical Review*, vol. lxxi, No. 3 (July 1962), sections IV and V. The main difference here between Frankfurt and myself is that he thinks this complete willingness to risk is not implied by a meaning of 'certain' or even 'absolutely certain' but is only a philosopher's idea which deserves a new expression, 'philosophically certain'. My own view of course is that no new expression is needed here.

One may liken these two conditions to the two independently necessary conditions of being flat which we mentioned earlier, namely, being not at all bumpy and being not at all curved. In the case of being flat, we deal with matters which we may picture. So, we may get pictures of the different ways things may meet a necessary condition for flatness and yet fail to be flat. Here, then, is a view of a surface which, while not at all bumpy, is not flat:

The problem with this surface is that it is curved, though perhaps ever so slightly or gently. On the other hand, we may have a surface which is not at all curved (though some technical usages might call it so), but which fails to be flat for failing to be not at all bumpy:

(Of course, things which are not surfaces and which have none may meet both of these necessary conditions while easily failing to be flat. Thus, numbers and treaties are not at all bumpy and not at all curved, but neither are they flat.) In the case of being certain, we do not of course have the aid of pictorial representation. We cannot use our eyes or our mind's eye to see how being not at all open differs from being not at all reluctant to risk. But, we may understand that the logical relation of these two to being certain is just the same as that of our pictorially understood conditions to being flat. (Again, other things, like stones and numbers, may easily fail to be certain of something though they are not at all open and not at all reluctant in the relevant respects. This parallels a number's meeting the necessary conditions but failing to be flat. The parallel holds because in both cases the necessary conditions are just negative ones.)

It should be quite clear from this discussion that we do not identify being certain with being not at all open to new experience, or even to what we call the attitude of certainty. Rather, we only claim that the latter is a *necessary* condition of one's being certain, or a logically *essential* feature of one's personal certainty in a matter. It is in just this way that the attitude described by Malcolm fits into our general account of absolute terms. But, of course, it is in just this way that the absoluteness of the attitude he describes is needed for our sceptical argument.

Later, in sections 10 and 11, we shall present an analysis of knowing which gives further support for the idea that personal certainty is absolute in this needed way. And that evidence will relate this absoluteness quite directly to the notion of knowing itself. But, even at this point, I think we have supported our characterization of the attitude of certainty well enough to take an urgent interest in the consequences of one's having this attitude, thus of one's being certain of something. Towards examining these consequences, we again look to Moore, our paradigm of a philosopher who opposes scepticism. This time we look to actual words from him.

§6. *Why is there Always Something Wrong with Having this Absolute Attitude?*

At the beginning of his excellent paper, 'Certainty', G. E. Moore, perhaps the most influential opponent of scepticism in this century, makes some assertions and, as he points out, does so in a very positive and definite way. In just this way, he says, for example, that he had clothes on and was not absolutely naked. Moore goes on to note that although he did not expressly *say* of the things which he asserted that he *knew* them to be true, he implied as much by asserting them in the way he did. His words are these:

... I *implied* ... that I myself knew for certain, in each case, that what I asserted to be the case was, at the time I asserted it, in fact the case. And I do not think that I can be justly accused of dogmatism or over-confidence for having asserted these things positively in the way that I did. In the case of some kinds of assertions, and under some circumstances, a man can be justly accused of dogmatism for asserting something positively. But in the case of assertions such as I made, made under the circumstances under which I made them, the charge would be absurd.[13]

I think that we may take it that, according to Moore, the reason he could not so be accused is that he was *not* dogmatic here.

[13] Moore, 'Certainty', p. 223.

And the reason for that is that he *knew* these things, e.g. that he was not naked, so that he was *justified* in being absolutely *certain* of them. And, so, in those innocuous circumstances of speech, he was justified in acting out of, or in accord with, his position or attitude of personal certainty. Moore was saying, in effect, that one could have this by now familiarly characterized attitude without any pain of being at all dogmatic in the matter: that no new experience or information will have any effect at all on one's thinking in the matter at hand, in this case, in the matter of whether at the then present or just past time, one is absolutely naked or not. Moore's position here is, then, quite of a piece with Malcolm's thought that it is not at all unreasonable of him to allow nothing to count as contrary evidence in the matter of whether an ink-bottle is before him. But Moore's point is more particular than Malcolm's, for he notes the *particular way* in which one who is certain might be thought to be unreasonable, or not justified, in his attitude: he might be thought to be such *in that* he is *dogmatic* in the matter. In situations where one knows, Moore implies, one is not at all dogmatic in having just such an absolutely negative position or attitude. It seems, then, that Moore was more sensitive than other authors to the possibility that *dogmatism* might at least almost always be charged of one who was absolutely certain, even when the person might rather plausibly claim to know. Now it strikes me as oddly unfortunate, in a way, that Malcolm, who actually spelled out, quite well I think, what was involved in being certain, was not so sensitive to this particular charge. For it is, I think, precisely the feature he spells out which makes the charge of dogmatism live and convincing. As Malcolm is anti-sceptical, this is to his credit. By the same token however, it is to Moore's credit that, even without articulating the key idea, he was able to sense the charge of dogmatism as a particular threat to his position, perhaps as the key one. Indeed, in the three full sentences I quoted, he refers to this charge as many times. We may put the substantial question, then in these words: was Moore referring to a charge of some real substance, or was he right in contending that (because he knew) there was really nothing to be feared?

Controversy being what it is, dogmatism is most often

associated with questions or matters where there does not seem to be a clear-cut answer either way. For example, someone might commonly be called dogmatic about whether some form of socialism is the most efficient form of government for the economic growth of a certain country now. Or someone might well be called dogmatic about whether the old-time baseball stars were better hitters than their modern counterparts. Perhaps, one might be recognizably dogmatic in the matter of whether Germany would have been defeated eventually had the United States not entered World War II. During a discussion of such matters as these, people commonly refuse to be moved *at all* by apparently forceful evidence for the other side; instead, they belittle that evidence as misleading or irrelevant. It is at these times that we say that people are just being dogmatic and that if they continue to have such an attitude, there can be little or no point in discussing the matter with them.

People may, of course, be more or less dogmatic in various matters. In my terminology, 'dogmatic' is a relative term. Linguistic tests serve to bear this out. At any rate, the more dogmatic someone is, the less the evidence he would admit as relevant and possibly damaging. Relative term though it is, when *nothing* is allowed to count, the person is *completely dogmatic* about the matter; this, even if the person is not so extreme along any other dimensions there may be in being dogmatic. Accordingly, it may be that some people who are dogmatic, even completely dogmatic, about a certain thing are not absolutely certain of that thing. Perhaps they would not risk so much on its truth; perhaps they would not be so ready to draw inferences from it, and so on. Thus, their exclusionary attitude towards new experience is not on a par with certain other things, as it might be in cases where matters seem clear-cut, e.g., where the matter is whether one is absolutely naked, or whether there is an ink-bottle before one. This may make people's dogmatism more obvious in controversial cases than in clear-cut ones. There are indeed a number of reasons for this discrepancy in obviousness, some themselves quite obvious and some not quite so obvious. In apparently clear-cut cases, there is, first of all, likely to be no disagreement on the matter itself, so no one is apt to question anyone else's view in the matter. But, more than that, each person is likely to be at least quite close to being perfectly certain of his (shared) position, at least if he has about as much experience or involvement in the matter as other parties present. So, no one is apt to question, either, the degree of strength of anyone's position, since anyone else's is quite close on that score to his own. You are about as certain of the thing as the next man; so his position seems fitting and perfectly all right to you. These are quite obvious reasons for there being no apparent dogmatism in matters where things appear to be certain, e.g. where people agree that it is quite plain that there is a rug on the floor where they are standing. But, here are some reasons which, though less obvious, may operate as well. In the first place, it may be that in many matters which seem certain, people are not really absolutely certain of things. This is what I suggested before, in Chapter II, section 4. If this is correct, then, as people will not be absolutely certain even, e.g. that there is a rug on the floor, any dogmatic feature of being certain will not be there to be noticed even in such cases, and so for this most elementary reason must of course not be noticed. All that will be noticed, then, might be everyone's agreement in the matter, and the apparent sameness in the strength of their positions. But if this is not so and people are certain, there will be further factors unobviously masking possible dogmatism anyway. And these may be at work as well when people are quite close to being absolutely certain of something. Whether people are perfectly certain or only nearly so, the sorts of experiences which might be pertinent to their becoming less certain, whether in actuality or only in description, are not likely to present themselves. They will likely range from extremely odd to utterly bizarre and fantastic. Thus, tests for spotting too great an adherence on someone's part, too exclusionary an attitude to contrary experience, are not likely to arise in such matters. Experiences to separate absolutely certain dogmatists from 'reasonably certain fellows' are not liable to turn up. With people being thus untested, any dogmatic feature on this score will go unnoticed in the normal course of life and conversation.

Still another reason for the masking of dogmatism might be the lack of a relevant inconsistency in such matters. This is suggested from our previous discussion, where we saw that personal certainty has several independent necessary conditions or, so to speak, essential dimensions. In a controversial case, the following sort of inconsistency often arises: a man who is very exclusionary in his attitude regarding a particular proposition may, at the same time, not be so willing to risk stakes or base inferences on it as on several other less controversial propositions. In other words, in such matters, people often are not even very close to being certain—mainly, at least, for failing to be close along dimensions other than the one of tenacity, or of exclusionary attitude. Thus, their tenacity in debate or discussion bespeaks an inconsistency on their part which is unreasonable and, in a way at least, dogmatic. This sort of dogmatism will not be present when people are even very nearly certain, or at least it will never be obviously present then. For, in such cases, the disparity involved will be, of analytic necessity, nothing or very small. Thus, in apparently clear-cut cases, it may be that the only way that you might be thought dogmatic is through the appreciation of an overly exclusionary attitude. No significant inconsistency, at any rate, is likely to bring such a charge.

There are quite enough reasons for our not noticing whatever dogmatism may be present in cases where matters are not controversial but apparently clear-cut. Accordingly, we may well suspect that in such apparently clear-cut cases, where you might well be at least very nearly certain of something, you might be dogmatic for having too exclusionary an attitude in the case. For your dogmatic feature is not likely to be brought to your attention. In consequence, we ought to be careful to guard against being prejudiced against the possibility that in apparently clear-cut cases people may often be dogmatic.

We may now, I think, more fairly assess the question of whether in cases where you are absolutely certain, supposing there actually are any such, your attitude is dogmatic or not. In such a case, there may be no relevant inconsistency, there then being no disparity between your tenacity and your willingness to risk and infer. And, it may well be that no one will ever disagree with you, or even be much less certain of the thing. For, when you are absolutely certain, as we are supposing, the matter is likely to be apparently clear-cut. But, even if nothing rubs the wrong way, from within yourself or without, your attitude in the matter is this: I will not allow *anything at all* to count as evidence against my present view in the matter. The case being apparently clear-cut, this attitude will, perhaps almost certainly, cause you no trouble nor bring any challenge. But, what are you to think of it anyway, even if no penalty or embarrassment is liable ever to occur. I think that any reflection at all makes it pretty plain that, no matter how certain things may seem, this attitude is always dogmatic, and that a man who has it will always be open to that charge even if circumstances mean that he will never be exposed to it. Indeed, as regards this matter, whatever else is true of him, we may say that he is completely dogmatic.

Now, in order to see more clearly why, even in the apparently most clear-cut and certain matters, there is something wrong with letting nothing count against your being right, it will *help* to describe some sequences of experience. I do *not* think that such an appreciation of detail is really necessary to gaining conviction that the attitude of certainty is always dogmatic and, providing there are no overriding considerations in its favour, to be forgone in favour of a more open-minded position. We must favour such an attitude in any case, no matter how certain something seems and no matter how little we may be able to imagine what experiences there might be which, should they ever occur, you had best consider seriously and not just disregard. This is the right view in the matter however poor our own imaginations might be. But, the strength of habits to the contrary being so great, it will be a big help if we can succeed in imagining sequences of experience which seem to cry out for serious thought. Even in the cases of things which at first seem quite certain, then, I will strive to be of service by imagining contrary experiences. These described experiences should help us grasp more clearly the idea that the attitude of certainty is always dogmatic and that, for this reason at least, being certain always means, in the matters at hand, complete dogmatism on anyone's part.

§7. *Helpful Experiences for Rejecting the Attitude of Certainty*

In quoting Malcolm's meditations on himself and his inkbottle, we looked at some sequences of experiences which, if they occurred, might rightly be considered to have some weight. Accordingly, they should result in the person's not being quite so certain as before that there is or was an ink-bottle before him. That would be the proper course for things to take. Malcolm says he wouldn't take those experiences as relevant here, that that is his attitude and that all of that is perfectly all right. I would disagree. But, in any event, it seems that we can easily imagine experiences which are more telling in this regard. And, also, with only more difficulty, we can imagine others which are easily more telling.

In respect of the matter of that ink-bottle, there are, it seems to me, all sorts of possible experiences which might cast some doubt. For example, you may be approached by government officials who seem to demonstrate that the object on your desk is a container of a material to poison the water supply, which somehow found its way out of government hands into your home. It was disguised to look like an ink-bottle, but it is seen to have many small structural features essential to such a container of poison but which no ink-bottles have. You might well think, then, that though this object holds ink it is *not* an ink-bottle but, rather, it is something else disguised as an ink-bottle. Perhaps, then, there never was an *ink-bottle* before you, but only some such other object. It seems, at any rate, that such an experience as this should not be disregarded out of hand, no matter what you eventually should come to think about whether an ink-bottle was before you. An attitude which would thus disregard it seems, then, to be a dogmatic one, on your part, on anyone's part, Malcolm's included.

The experience just described is, I suppose, less than completely convincing. And, even if it is admitted that the experience does have some weight, it seems easy enough to retreat to other statements which are not thus susceptible to experiential challenge. For example, you may be, instead, absolutely certain that there is before you something which looks like an ink-bottle, or that there is something with a circular top, or whatever the favoured things turn out to be. And, even sticking to our ordinary, 'unfavoured', 'material object' beliefs, though the sort of experience just imagined might go against one's being certain that an *ink-bottle* is or was before you, such a sequence of experience will not go against your certainty about many other things: that there are automobiles, that there have been automobiles for quite some time now, that you are not now absolutely naked, and so on. To get a more completely convincing case about the ink-bottle, and to begin to get a convincing case for these less susceptible things, your imagination must work more radically. Descartes was quite well aware of the problem when he imagined his evil demon. We may do well to follow suit, though in a more modern and scientific vein. But we will now use our 'contrast cases' in a way which is more direct than that of any of our classical arguments.

I begin to imagine a more radical sequence of experience by supposing myself to experience a voice, coming from no definite location, which tells me this, in no uncertain terms: All the experiences I am having, including that of the voice, are artificially induced. Indeed, this has been going on for all of my conscious life and it will continue to do so. The voice tells me of various experiences I have had, some of which I had myself forgotten almost entirely. It then says that scientists accomplish all of this with me; it seems to tell me what they are like, what I am really like, and, in great detail, how they manage to bring about these effects in me. To make its case most convincing, the voice says what experiences I will next have, and next after that, and, then, after that. First I will seem to fly off the face of the earth to a planet where the inhabitants worship me because I have only one mouth. After that, it will seem that I come back to earth and find that I have been elected Secretary-Treasurer of the International Brotherhood of Electricians. Finally, if that is not preposterous enough, I will seem to open up my body and find myself stuffed with fried shrimp, even unto the inner reaches of my thighs. Miraculously enough, I experience just this to happen. The experiences are not as in an ordinary dream, but are indistinguishable from what I call the most ordinary waking experiences—except, of course, for the apparently extraordinary content. Nor does this predicted sequence seem to take place in a flash, or in any very brief interval. To mirror what I take as reality, it seems to take a couple of months. After a convincing talk with the voice at the end of this experiential journey, I am left with a blue homogeneous field of visual experience, feeling little but wonder, to think over whether an ink-bottle was ever before me, whether there are now or ever were any automobiles, and so on. Of course the voice has told me that none of these things ever were, and told me why I thought otherwise. While engaged in the context of the less direct classical arguments, I thought of these things in way of rebutting a Moorean attempt at reversal (in Chapter I, section 8). What am I to think now; putting the matter directly, what *should my attitude be* towards such experiences?

My attitude towards these imagined experiences *is* that if they should occur I would be at least somewhat less certain than I now am about these matters. This is my present attitude. If things would not develop in accord with it, that would be something I can now only hope will not happen. Moreover, I think it pretty plain that this is the attitude which I *ought* to have and that anyone who held an opposite one would have a dogmatic attitude in these matters. That is, if your attitude is that these experiences will not be counted as having any weight at all, you would be dogmatic in these matters. Indeed, you would be completely dogmatic here, though I suspect that you are not.

Now, some people might have the attitude that if these experiences occurred one should think himself to be quite mad or, at least, to have had his capacity for judgement impaired in some damaging way.[14] My own attitude is more open than this. But it should be pointed out that even this attitude of prospective self-defeat is quite compatible with that of lessening one's confidence or certainty. Your total attitude, that is, might be that if the imagined experiences really came to pass you would both be less certain that there ever were automobiles *and also* be inclined to think that you must have become quite mad. All that I am claiming or need to claim is that you ought to have at least the first part of this total attitude or, more precisely, that you *ought not* to have the *opposite* attitude: that any such experiences will be completely disregarded.

It is easy to suppose that I am claiming quite a lot for these imagined experiences no matter how hard I try to make it clear that all I need to claim is rather little. One might suppose that,

14 Malcolm suggests this sort of view in his lecture 'Memory and the Past', *Knowledge and Certainty*, p. 201. He considers it in a somewhat different context, being most concerned there with the proposition that the earth has existed for no more than five minutes. I will treat such propositions as that in the section following this one. My thoughts on this view owe something to conversation with Michael Slote.

according to what I am saying, if the appropriate experiences turned up you ought to believe the opposite of what now seems to you to be absolutely certain—or that the proper attitude is one to this effect. But I am, in fact, saying no such thing. All I am saying is that your attitude should be that you will be less certain of those things than you formerly were. If you are now just as certain that there are automobiles as that ten and ten are twenty, then towards the possible experience of our voice denying the first while affirming the second your attitude ought to be that a difference will emerge: you will then be less certain that there are or were automobiles than that ten and ten are twenty. At least this much must be admitted, I think, *even if* you may properly have the attitude that you will never actually believe that there are no automobiles. Again, one might suppose that I have it that you must be prepared, in the face of such experiences, to abandon your position or view in, say, the matter of automobiles. But I am not saying even this. One might just as well, so far as what I say goes, continue to believe that there are automobiles. That one's attitude should be to this effect might be quite all right according to my argument here. What is not all right, I say, is to hold it *as certainly as ever* that there are automobiles. Now, *my own attitude* is that should such experiences as these actually occur and persist, I *would* consider my present experiences to be an induced illusion, just as the voice would say. And I would not only abandon my present belief about automobiles, I would believe the opposite of what now seems so certain to me. I think that there is nothing wrong with this attitude and I suspect that there is something wrong with any which is incompatible with it. These points may, however, strike some as being rather more controversial. It is for this reason that I have taken pains to put forward a much weaker and, I think, a quite uncontroversial claim about attitudes towards experiences. And, for just this reason, I have been careful to point out the difference between this safer claim and these others which I also believe to be true. Since only the safer claim is needed to establish that the attitude of certainty is, even in these simple matters, completely dogmatic, it is hard to deny that this attitude is indeed a dogmatic one.

While these remarks should have a good influence on our thoughts about certainty, a certain question may have occurred to one near the outset which may still receive some useful remarks. The question is this: Why should *my* future possible experiences be so important in any of this; why should *my* having some extraordinary new experience count any *more* against an apparently certain idea or proposition *than someone else's* having such an experience, even so far as my own view of the matter is concerned? The idea here is, of course, that if someone else claimed to you that he had crazy new experiences, like those just described, you would, if equally certain of there being automobiles, give no weight at all to his claims. You would give them no weight *even if you were absolutely certain that they were correct*, that they correctly reported experiences of his. You would think, perhaps, that something unfortunate must have happened to this claimant's brain, and that is why he had the strange experiences he reported. You would think nothing new about the matter of whether there are or ever were automobiles. And all of this seems perfectly all right on your part. So, if you may treat another's experiences in this way, if you may reject them quite out of hand, why not also with experiences of your own? What is so special about *me*, you might ask, and about *my*, experiences, that *anyone*, myself included, ought, even in such a certain matter as this, give them substantial consideration?[15]

This question presents some puzzling problems, but none, I think, which effect the case we are trying to make. First of all, even if we cannot *explain why*, in most circumstances, a given person ought to treat his own experiences more seriously than exactly similar experiences on the part of another person, we may have some confidence anyway *that* this is indeed so. Accordingly, I suggest that we may leave the puzzling problem of why all of this is so for some future occasion.

But, more than this, the assumptions that underlie this question may themselves be challenged. Is it really true that one *need not* give *another's* extraordinary experiences *any* regard in these matters, even if one accepts the idea that *one's own* experience should be given a *special* place? To me, the answer seems quite plainly negative. Suppose three or four persons, each believed quite trustworthy by you, as well as to be strangers to each other, each told you a similar story about his recent

15 This interesting question was put to me by John Taurek.

experiences. Each one told a story like our story about the voice, and each concluded by saying that, as a consequence, he was no longer so certain that there are or ever were any automobiles. Now, if only one of these people told you this, you might give little or no weight to his statements. But, with three or four apparently independent reports, then, I suggest, you would, at least you should, take them seriously. Your attitude should not be that even if they all closely concur, you would not be even a very little bit less certain about the automobiles. And, reflecting on this, it seems to me that a given person's report, while it ought to gain greatly in importance from the confirmation of two or three strangers, *should* be given *some* weight, however slight, even if it is the only one to occur. Otherwise we have the quite difficult task of supposing that from reports each of which need be given *no* weight, we may obtain a conjunction which must be seriously considered. This does not seem a good way to think about these matters.

§8. *Helpful Experiences for the Hardest Cases; Other Times*

In respect of almost any matter, the possibility of certain imagined sequences of experience makes quite a convincing case that one ought not, on pain of dogmatism, have the attitude of absolute certainty. There are, however, two sorts of matters where something more must be said to explain how such experience might help us to appreciate the wrongness of this severe attitude. I treat them in turn, proceeding from the less to the more difficult.

The first and lesser difficulty concerns certain sorts of matters about the past. The most famous of these, due to Russell,[16] is the matter of whether the world sprang into existence five minutes ago. But the matter of whether you have existed for more than a brief moment will pose the problem more clearly so far as sequences of convincing experiences are concerned. As you may remember, this is the context in which we discussed these matters in Chapter I, section 12. The problem may be put like this: If any sequence of experience is to be convincing, it must itself endure for much more than a brief moment. Even in advance of any experiences which might look to show that you have been in existence only for a brief moment, you can and

16 Bertrand Russell, *The Analysis of Mind* (New York, 1921), pp. 159–60.

ought to appreciate this fact about the conditions of convincing. Therefore, it is in any case quite all right to have the attitude that no possible experience will be counted as convincing evidence for the claim that you have existed only for a brief moment. Rather, you may disregard any new experience which purports to be to this effect. This is why, when we first discussed these matters, I said that the classical form of argument is not as effective in establishing universal scepticism concerning other times as it is in establishing the universal thesis for our alleged knowledge of the external world. But, though this reasoning appears to disarm our classical form of argument, perhaps we may now, in turn, use some more direct sceptical thoughts to disarm and even to upset this reasoning.

The difficulty with this reasoning is that it doesn't take into account how new experiences might make us view time differently. If our voice told us new things about time, we might not be able to disregard it without ourselves being dogmatic. Suppose that the voice says that you have been brought into existence only a brief moment ago complete with an accurate understanding of the length of temporal intervals. But you are also provided, the voice says, with an appealing consistent web of ostensible memories. To believe that you have experienced the things it seems to you that you have will be, then, only to believe what is false. Now, the recent experiences you indeed have had are, according to the voice, part of a sequence which has gone on only for a brief moment, a billionth of a second, to be quite precise. And, this includes these very messages that even now are coming to you. Though it seems to you that the experiences have been going on for some months, you have in fact been alive for only a brief moment and, indeed, the world of concrete things, including the source of the voice, has existed for less than a minute. In response to these vocal claims you might put forward some scientific, relativistic theory of time on which the claims would make no sense or, at any rate, on which they could not possibly be true. But, that would only be to adduce some theory. And, if there is anything scientific about science it is that one should never be too certain of any theory, no matter how beautiful, comprehensive, and powerful it may seem. So it seems that, no matter how you might wish to reply, you would do well to allow at least some influence for such a sequence of experience as the one just imagined. You should have the attitude, I suggest, that should it occur you will be not quite *so* certain as you otherwise might be that you have been alive for more than a brief moment.

§9. *Helpful Experiences for the Hardest Cases; Cartesian Propositions*

The greatest difficulty in finding possible experience a help in abandoning the attitude of certainty comes, I think, in matters where we are inclined to think that the only possible error must be a 'purely verbal' one. This occurs with matters of 'immediate experience', e.g. with whether one is now experiencing phenomenal blueness, or pain. And, it occurs with the 'simplest matters of logical and mathematical necessity', e.g. with whether two is the sum of one and one. Perhaps the most famous case, due to Descartes, is that concerning one's own present moment thinking and existence, e.g. whether one now exists. These are the cases of the 'Cartesian propositions' which we discussed in Chapter I, section 13. (Now, some philosophers have found it quite an article of faith to suppose that there might be anything to answer to the word 'I'. They would think, I suppose, that what one ought to be sure of is that *something* now exists, leaving it quite open, what that existent might be. For these philosophers, these more impersonal statements will count as Cartesian propositions, even if that is not much in the spirit of the historical Descartes.) When we first discussed such propositions or matters as these, we found our classical form of argument quite powerless and uncompelling. The indirectness of such arguments, the very feature which lets them initially work so well on us in other matters, fails to take hold with matters so apparently certain and simple as these. Can our more direct argument for ignorance be of more use to scepticism here?

Even if it is true that in such matters as these any error must be purely verbal, why shouldn't the possibility of just such an error make the attitude of absolute certainty dogmatic in these matters? I have never heard anything to convince me of the opposite. It is said that what one believes or is certain of are propositions or, at least, some things that are too abstract to have uncertainty over words interfere with their status (excepting the comparatively rare cases of those that are *about* words). Let us agree at the outset that we understand such attempts to downgrade the effect that words might have. But, nevertheless, ought not the following story about possible experience cause at least some very small doubts to enter our minds? Again, we have our voice. After going through the sequence of experiences I described before, the voice tells me that I become easily confused about the meanings of certain terms. It says that on many occasions, and now is one of them, I confuse the meaning of 'exist', a word which means, roughly, 'to continue on in the face of obstacles', with the meaning of 'persist', a word which, roughly, shares a meaning with the verb 'be', or 'am'. Consequently, in philosophical meditations, I often say to myself 'I exist' and 'It seems certain to me that I *exist* now.' And, I then seem to remember that I have never thought otherwise. But, in fact, of course, I am quite a change-able fellow and, so, I rarely if ever *exist*. It is true that I *persist*, as everyone does, and I *should* say *this* when I am engaged in such meditation. No doubt, I will soon change once again and say and think, rightly, that what I do is persist. This will then seem certain to me, which is better than its seeming certain to me that what I do is exist, since at least the former is something which is *true*. But, it would be far better still if *neither* ever even *seemed* to be absolutely *certain*. At the very least, the voice concludes, I ought never to *be* certain of these things, no matter how tempting that might be. This is especially true in my case because I am so changeable and, as a consequence, so often and so easily confused.

I have no doubt that many would want to protest against the idea that our voice should have any power here. That would only be confusion, they would say. Some might say that the matter of whether the words 'I exist now' express a truth and that of whether I exist now are two utterly different matters. Now, it is very true that these matters are very different. But, why should that lead anyone to protest against what I am saying? What I am saying is just that according to the appro-priate sort of attitude, under certain conditions of experience I will become less certain than before that I indeed *exist*, that one thing I do is exist. Indeed, I may be in just such an experiential situation even while believing that the words 'I exist now' do indeed express a truth. We may suppose, after all, another case, in which the voice tells me that I do continue on in the face of obstacles, and so that I ought to believe that I exist, as well as that I persist. Now, it *may* be that there is something deeply wrong with any of these vocal suggestions. But I can't see how anyone can be absolutely certain that *this* is so. As a consequence, I can't see either how anyone ought to be completely sure that any experiences such as these must be quite irrelevant to what he ought to think in these admittedly quite simple matters. And, as a consequence of that, so far as I can see, my attitude in any of these matters ought not to be that of absolute certainty. Perhaps I should develop these doubts a little further.

My own view is that what one believes, and especially what one is more or less certain of, is a function of what words one thinks in and, so, of the meaning of those words. And, I also think that, in most cases, the meaning of one's words cannot easily change fast. I think that one cannot quickly create new meanings at will for common words in which one thinks. I do not hold these to be necessary truths, but I do think these things to be true. If you have any inclination to share this view, you should be adequately affected, I suggest, by our recent discussion of 'exist' and 'persist'.

But, even if these beliefs of mine, despite their admitted vagueness, seem badly incorrect to you, how can you be absolutely *certain* that they are? After all, the main point here is not to be settled by how convincingly I might further speak on behalf of these ideas. Nor is it to be settled by how convincingly you can think to yourself in reply, on behalf of some opposite view. For there can always be more convincing spokesmen for either of these ideas than you or I. In particular, in circumstances such as those so recently described, our voice may establish its proper convincing power through success in other matters. If the voice then argues for the sort of position I am advocating, indeed, if he just assures you that that position is correct, you had better be at least a bit less certain, I suggest, of any contrary view you may hold.[17]

But doesn't this clinch the matter pretty conclusively, at least, for the view that doubts about verbal error can properly undermine certainty in even the simplest matters? For such voices advocating this view is enough, after all, to make it proper for you to be less certain of the opposite and, for that

[17] I owe this important point to Gilbert Harman.

reason, to be less certain that you now *exist*, which the voice
has so greatly denied. Thus, you ought not, really, to be
absolutely certain that you now exist, or that something exists,
or that you now feel pain, or whatever. Of course, the source
of uncertainty we have just uncovered is present in matters
which are not so apparently certain or simple. Thus, we may
now appreciate even more fully why it is at least a bit dogmatic
for you to be certain that there is an ink-bottle before you, that
there ever are any automobiles, or that you have existed for
more than a brief moment.

As I said earlier, these imagined sequences of experience are
only meant to be a help in coming to the idea that being certain involves being dogmatic. Their role is to exemplify some
situations where this feature of dogmatism might be rather
clearly brought out. I hope that the sequences I have described
have been thus revealing and, so, convincing. But that they be
so is hardly essential to making good our claim. For even if the
particular sequence of experience we are able to imagine does
not seem to jeopardize some statement which seems quite
certain, we shouldn't be *sure* that there isn't *any* such sequence—
possibly, even, one which a human imagination just can't
grasp in much detail. And, even if there is no sequence of
experience which ought to make us less certain, mightn't there be
some *other factor* information about which ought to give us a
pause? Perhaps, there are some currently obscure conceptual
truths about the nature of thought and reason, which show how
any thinking at all is parasitic on the possibility of error in the
case? No matter how comfortable we may feel in our philosophy
and our view of the world, I can't see how we might properly
be *certain* that there is *no way* that we could possibly be wrong.
We cannot properly be certain that we have given a complete
accounting of every sort of experience, evidence, and information which might possibly exist. For this reason, if for no other,
it will be dogmatic of us ever to have the attitude that we will
disregard *any* new experience, evidence, and information which
runs counter to what we hold.

What we have just been arguing for most directly is the
idea that the attitude of certainty, this attitude which is always
had in being certain, always means that one is (completely)
dogmatic in the matter at hand. And, for that reason, providing

there are no overriding considerations, this attitude is never all right for anyone ever to have. Now, mindful of examples like that of helping someone who is in trouble, one might object that the wrongness of this attitude, and the fact that it is entailed by being certain, do not themselves ensure that being certain is itself not perfectly all right. The idea would be that something's entailing something which is wrong is not enough to ensure that the entailing thing is itself wrong. This *general* idea is, we may grant, established well enough by the example of helping someone in trouble: again, as in section 2 of this chapter, helping someone in trouble entails someone's being in trouble, the latter being wrong or bad. But helping someone in trouble is itself right or good, and so, at least perfectly all right.

But the relation between being certain and having the dogmatic attitude of certainty is quite unlike that between helping someone in trouble and someone's being in trouble. In the latter case, there is something wrong and the attempt at least towards the righting of it. Or, there is a bad situation and the attempt at least towards the improvement of it. Nothing remotely like this goes on with someone's having the attitude of certainty and his being certain of something. On the contrary, as our arguments have already strongly suggested, the having of this attitude is something which *makes* being certain wrong, so long as no overriding considerations obtain. Indeed, even if there are other inherent properties of being certain which count in favour of it, they now seem heavily overriden by the dogmatism inherent in being certain. So, what we have been arguing for, though in a somewhat less direct way, is that the dogmatism of a certain attitude means that, in the absence of overriding considerations, being certain is not all right but always wrong. And, I suggest, even in this admittedly wider respect, our arguments have been rather compelling ones.

Our second, more substantive premiss is now supported at least quite as well as the first one. And, not only is the support of each derived from considerations quite independent of those supporting the other, but the support of each premiss is strong enough, I suggest, that we may accept them both together and draw rather obvious consequences from them for our further acceptance. One such consequence is our thesis of universal scepticism: Nobody ever knows anything about anything.

Excepting one important point, or set of points, still to come, this is our argument for ignorance, ignorance which is inevitable and universal. That point, or set of points, concerns an analysis of knowing. This analysis reveals knowing to be an absolute *justifying* state, condition, or position. As such, the analysis gives me much more confidence in my scepticism about knowing. For it shows 'know' to be an absolute term. It does this, not by giving a partial definition, but by completely defining the term. And this complete definition is as revealing as any sceptic might ever wish.

§10. *An Absolutely Clear Analysis of Knowing*

There is hardly a philosopher anywhere who has no desire at all to get some clearer idea of what it is for someone, himself for example, to know that something is so. Being sceptical about knowledge, I will try to give an analysis of knowing which favours the thesis of universal scepticism, which helps one towards accepting that thesis as true. Now, there is a certain trend in philosophy towards the idea that analyses of key terms and concepts should be neutral, in the sense, I suppose, of not helping to encourage belief in any position on any philosophical dispute involving the concept or the term. But to restrict analyses in this way seems quite plainly incorrect. For if one of the sides to such a dispute is the correct one, as one very well might be, then an analysis which is itself correct and also revealing, that is, a *good* analysis, should help us to see that that position is indeed correct. In particular, in so far as our arguments to date have force, we should suppose that a good analysis of knowing will be anything but neutral. On the contrary, it should help us to see why the concept of knowledge is an inapplicable one.

Happily, then, our analysis will not be neutral. It will also not be 'reductive', that is, it will not try to break knowledge down into several independent components. I think that this too is a good thing. For it seems quite implausible that sentences of the form 'S knows that *p*' should be abbreviations for conjunctions, for sentences of the form 'A and B'. The concept of knowledge seems more grand than that, to make its own special claim of importance. But while it will not be thus reductive, our account will be an analysis in the important sense that it will reveal the main logical features of our concept of knowledge. It will do this by relating sentences of the form 'S knows that p' to locutions in which absolute adjectives serve us in a systematic, and, so, instructive way.

We have already argued that 'know', in sentences of the form 'S knows that p', is a defined absolute term (as in Chapter II, sections 3 and 9). We have done this by arguing that the basic absolute term 'certain' provides a necessary condition of knowing and, thus, serves to define it partially. But, as one may be certain that p without knowing that p, we are not able to get from 'certain' a full definition of 'know' in these sentences. What I want to find is another basic absolute term, an adjective other than 'certain', to give just such a complete definition of 'know'.

My analysis will centre around the absolute adjective 'clear'. In the favoured schematism of the day, I put forth the analysis as a necessary truth of this form: S knows that p if and only if it is clear to S that p. Syntactically, the simplest way to write the right-hand side, or *the condition*, is this: that p is clear to S. In so far as this is an *analysis*, and not just a necessary bi-conditional, the that-clause in the condition should not be taken to purport to denote a fact, i.e. the fact that p. For even though S knows that p if and only if the fact that p is clear to S, S *might* not know the fact. The form *'S knows the fact that p' is a form only for marked deviance. A good deal later on, in Chapter VII, we will discuss these matters much further. For now, we just note that our analysis is *not* this: S knows that p if and only if the fact that p is clear to S. And we do not look to the 'that p' part of our condition for much instruction at this point.

The term 'clear' is a basic absolute term. It is also an adjective with a very great distribution in English discourse; a great variety of linguistic contexts can contain it. Yet there is no strong reason to believe that it means different things in different contexts. Accordingly, evidence of its absolute character in the simplest, 'physical' contexts may give strong evidence of its being absolute also as it occurs in the condition of our analysis. I take it that 'clear' means the same in each of these sentences:

The water was clear.
His meaning was clear (to her).

It was clear (to her) that he meant (that) there was clear water there.

In any event, in each of these sentences it is pretty clear that 'clear' is an absolute term.

If someone says that the water is pretty clear, he may be taken to have said that the water is pretty close to being absolutely clear; that is a good paraphrase of what he said. Similarly, if the water is not nearly as clear as the glass, the situation is this: either the glass is absolutely clear and the water is not, or else the water is not as close to being absolutely clear as is the glass. If his meaning was very clear (to her), that is not so much as if his meaning really was clear (to her). And, the reason for this is that in the first case his meaning was only very close to being absolutely clear (to her), while in the second it really was absolutely clear (to her). In connection with our third and last sentence, if it was fairly clear to her that he meant that there was clear water there, then it was fairly close to being absolutely, and perfectly, and completely clear to her that he meant that. Finally, if it was clearer to her that he meant that than that he was telling the truth—well, it's quite clear how we may best explicate what that situation is. In sum, it's quite (close to being absolutely) clear that 'clear' is, throughout an impressive variety of contexts, always a basic absolute term.

If our offered analysis is logically adequate, that is, if it gives a condition which is both logically necessary and also logically sufficient, it stands a good chance of instructively revealing knowing to be a demanding absolute limit. It will be that limit which is reached, if ever, when it is (absolutely) clear to someone that something is so. When we spell out what goes on with conditions or positions which progressively approach this limit, we will have spelled out much of what is involved in our concept of knowing. For 'S's knowing that p' will be just another form for marking this limit, a form for marking it with a verb. But first, we should assure ourselves that we have the makings of a correct analysis here, that is, that we have a condition which is logically necessary and logically sufficient.

The logical sufficiency of our condition is, I think, quite easy to perceive. Much argument is hardly needed on this count. If it is clear to me that philosophy is difficult, then I know that it is. And, if it has been clear to you that this was so ever since you read the *Meditations*, then you have known this ever since then. As I said, it doesn't take much to become convinced that this sort of clarity is enough for knowing.

More is needed to become convinced that someone can know something to be so *only if* it is (absolutely) clear to him (or her) that it is so. The trouble here, as it so often is with 'know', is that our tendency is to be much more liberal with this verb than with our locution with an adjective. We already encountered this disparity with 'certain', another absolute adjective whose proper application is necessary (in Chapter II, section 9). The case of the examined student comes to mind again. We would not normally say that it was clear to this student that the Battle of Hastings was fought in 1066, no more than we would say that he was certain of it. But, as we noted before, we would find it easy to say that the student knew that the battle was fought then. My position is, of course, that a discrepancy in our tendencies says no more about any *logical* relations of 'know' and 'clear' than one did before regarding 'know' and 'certain'. By properly applying our Method of Opposed Terms, and our Principle of Emphasis, the telling inconsistency quickly emerges: 'He really *knew* it, but it *wasn't* absolutely *clear* to him.' No matter what story we start to tell, if we finish with an assertion of knowing and a denial of this clarity, then so long as we properly attend to the key concepts, we can hardly fail to find that story to close with a contradiction. Accordingly, our condition is logically necessary as well as logically sufficient.

There remains to explain why our tendency is to be more liberal with 'know' than with equivalent locutions with 'clear'. Part of the reason is, I suggest, that the battery of modifiers with 'clear' gives us a ready retreat with that term, one which will systematically come to mind when something is thought to be not really clear to someone. For example, with 'clear' we may think: That was, if not really clear to him, at least clearer to him than it was to her. A similar consideration, it will be remembered, helped to explain why we are more liberal with 'know' than with 'certain'. The other suggestion we offered for explaining this last fact cannot apply to the present case however. That suggestion, as you may remember, was that knowing involves many things besides being certain, and so, that in denying knowing one may mislead others (or even oneself) into thinking that perhaps certain of these other things were absent as well. Accordingly, one may be liberal with 'know' in order to ensure that one avoids misleading in this way. But knowing involves nothing which is not equally involved in the thing's being clear to the person. Thus, we have no reason to think that withholding 'know' should mislead in any way that withholding 'clear' will not. And so, without any further points to chart a course here, the idea of misleading produces no explanation of our discrepancy with 'know' and 'clear'. All of this makes me wish that I had more to say towards explaining this discrepancy in our tendencies towards use. But I take this task to be a sign of my own inadequacy here, rather than a mark of any inadequacy in our analysis of knowing. So far as the logic of things goes, it does not seem to me that that analysis really can be faulted.

Granting that our analysis gives us everything we want in terms of logic, what does it give us in terms of insight? Logical equivalences are easy enough to come by; revealing ones are not. Only the latter can count as analyses. In what way is the equivalence we have provided in an *analysis* of knowing?

§11. *Some Implications of this Analysis*

Quite obvious entailments from this analytic condition are also entailments from knowing. This serves to confirm the logical adequacy of our analysis, and it also gives a small beginning towards revealing the explanatory value of the words of the condition. First, our condition 'implies truth'. If it is clear to Mary that they left, it follows that they left. It is inconsistent to say 'It was *clear* to her that they left, but they *didn't* leave.' Second, our condition implies that the subject is (absolutely) certain of the thing. If that thing is (absolutely) *clear* to Mary, then she is (absolutely) *certain* that they left. It is inconsistent to say 'It was *clear* to her that they left, but she *wasn't certain* of it.' Finally for now, our condition implies that it is (at least) all right for the subject to be absolutely certain; the condition is appropriately normative. If it really is perfectly clear to Mary that they left, then, providing there isn't any special reason against it, it's perfectly all right for her to be certain that they did. There can then be nothing at all wrong with her being absolutely certain of that thing.

The final implication gives us an insight into *why* the attitude of certainty might be at once so absolutely severe and at the same time justified by knowing, granting, of course, that there really is such a thing as knowing. The idea is this: When you *know* that something is so, the thing is absolutely *clear* to you. Thus, no further experience *could possibly clarify* the matter as far as you are concerned. Nothing which could turn up could make it even the least bit clearer to you that the thing is so. For as regards the matter of whether that thing is so or not, we have agreed, things are already for you as clear as they ever could be. What substantial effect or change would any new experience then have here? Any new experience which would serve to suggest anything one way or the other regarding this matter can, in so far as it has any effect at all, serve only to make things *less* clear, *never* any *more* so. Consequently no serious attention need or should be paid to any such suggestive experience. Most particularly, then, contrary experiences can surely be disregarded. The upshot is pretty clear: if we accept the idea that your knowing something is the same thing as that thing's being absolutely clear to you, we can uncover the implicit relationale behind the alleged extraordinary justifying power of your knowing the thing.[18] By means of the words of our analysis, we have revealed something about knowing; we have articulated an intuitive backing for an important entailment of knowing, the one expressed in our first premiss. So, our condition is beginning to look as though it really gives us an analysis. At the same time, of course, the analysis is serving to support our argument for ignorance.

The most revealing features of our condition, however, lie in how it helps linguistically to relate knowing to those states, conditions, or positions which, while lesser ones than knowing, are still more or less close to that absolute limit. One such position would be that where it is pretty (close to being absolutely) clear to Mary that they left. Another is where this thing is very clear to her. What is the relation of these two positions? And, what have they to do with 'attitude conditions',

---

[18] I owe these important points to Michael Slote.

like that of being certain, and with the justification of these 'attitudes'?

We may understand these relations in terms of these two parallel scales:

Clarity		*Certainty*	
L_1	S's knowing that p = Its being (absolutely) clear to S that p	L_2	S's being (absolutely) certain that p
E_1	Its being (E_1) clear to T that q	E_2	T's being (E_2) certain that q
D_1	Its being very clear to S that r	D_2	S's being very certain that r
C_1	Its being (C_1) clear to S that s	C_2	S's being (C_2) certain that s
B_1	Its being pretty clear to T that t	B_2	T's being pretty certain that t
X_1	Its being (X_1) clear to N that n	X_2	N's being (X_2) certain that n

The mutual relations of the items on the scale at the right, the Scale of Certainty, is already familiar. Each item further towards the top of the scale, and listed further towards the top of the page, is closer and closer to being one where a subject is certain, except of course in the case of the topmost position, where a subject is certain of a thing. Thus, at E_2 the subject T is to a certain very, very high degree, (E_2), close to being absolutely certain that q. At D_2 on this scale, the subject S is only very close to being certain that r. Accordingly T is closer to being certain that q than S is that r. Since he is at E_2 there may be no neat words to say non-comparativly how (close to being) certain T is that q. But, if so, that just means that there are more points or places on this scale than available words for conveniently talking of them.

The mutual relations of the items in the scale on the left, the Scale of Clarity, are exactly similar. At E_1 it is to a certain very, very high degree, (E_1), close to being absolutely clear to the subject T that q. At D_1 on this scale, it is only very close to being clear to the subject S that r. Accordingly, it is closer to being clear to T that q than it is to S that r. Remembering what we just said before about the possible paucity of convenient expressions for talking of scale positions, we notice now that there are just as many places on this scale which are not spoken of neatly in non-comparative terms. Whatever our linguistic resources, though, it seems quite clear that these scales provide orderlings which are, in certain respects at least, quite parallel. What can we make of these parallel series?

We can make a good deal, I suggest, of the relation of items on one scale to items on the other, of the relation between the scales. Most obviously, the items on the Scale of Clarity entail truth, while those on the Scale of Certainty appear not to. Thus items on the right *will not* entail or include parallel items on the left; but items on the left *might* entail the parallel items on the right. Do they? Suppose that we are at B_1 on the Scale of Clarity; does it follow that, with the same subject and the same matter, we are also at B_2 on the Scale of Certainty? In other words, if it is *pretty* clear to T that *t*, does it follow that, at that time, T is *pretty* certain that *t*? I think not. For, T might be *more* certain than that that *t*, for example, T may be *very*, *very* certain that *t*. What does seem to follow is this: T is *at least pretty* certain that *t*. Thus, what *is inconsistent* to say here is this: 'It is *pretty clear* to Mary that they left, but she *isn't even pretty certain* of it.' The 'even' is needed here for the inconsistency. Otherwise, we might add on 'she's *more* than that; she's *very* certain of it.' In that way, we could bring out clearly the *consistency* of 'It is *pretty* clear to Mary that they left, but she *isn't pretty* certain of it; (she's *more* than that; she's very certain of it).' We may, then, begin to understand the relation between the scales by saying this: When someone is at a certain point on the Scale of Clarity, it follows that he is on at least as high a point on the Scale of Certainty; but he may be on a higher point. For example, we must allow that even if it was clearer to Mary that they left than that the party was boring, Mary may be more certain that the party was boring.

While these comparisons are possible, it is quite clear that all is not well in the compared situations. For even if Mary *is* more certain that the party was boring, it appears that she *shouldn't* be. If it is clearer to her that they left, then, in the absence of any overriding considerations to the contrary, Mary *should be* more certain that they left than that the party was boring. What is wrong here is that Mary is more certain than she is justified in being about the party's being boring. The fault does not lie, it is plain, in her not being sufficiently certain that they left. So the relation between the scales in normative terms is this: If a subject is at a certain point, with respect to a certain matter, on the Scale of Clarity, he is *justified in being* at the parallel point on the Scale of Certainty (unless there are overriding considerations). He *cannot be* at a lower point with respect to that matter on the Scale of Certainty. He *may be* at a higher point, but, again, *if* he is, and if there are no special considerations to make that all right for him, then he *should not be*. He should be only at a lower point than that. In particular, he should be at the point made all right by his position on the Scale of Clarity, i.e. by how close the thing is to being absolutely clear to him. For example, if it is pretty clear to Mary that the party was boring, and no special considerations obtain, then she should be pretty certain of that and no more.

These remarks apply to any places along the scales, as well as to any beings and matters. In particular they apply to remarks about the limits, to the places or points which are the limits of the scales. Thus, someone *may be* (absolutely) certain of something even though that thing is not (absolutely) clear to him. But, if he is, and if there are no special considerations present, then he shouldn't be. Apart from such overriding considerations, the only time that that may be all right is when the thing is (absolutely) clear to the subject. And then, if our language is to be believed, it is perfectly all right. So knowing is the limit of a scale of *justifying* states, positions, or conditions. In relevant sentences we use 'know' to purport to refer to this limit, however obliquely, and whether or not that limit is ever actually reached. That same limit, we have been at pains to see, may be equally referred to by means of a suitable adjective, by means of the basic absolute term 'clear'.

For understanding this limit, the verb 'know' is less perspicuous than the adjective. Its grammatical relations do not so directly mirror or reveal its logical ones. Consequently, we look to adjectival terms to give us an *analysis*, to help to reveal the logical features of 'know'. Now, if 'know' is thus less perspicuous than expressions with 'clear', why do we have this verb *also* to refer to this limit? What need have we of a less perspicuous redundancy in our language? Perhaps part of the reason we have these sentences with 'know' is that they are shorter, more convenient locutions. Perhaps part of the reason is that 'know', because of its grammatical category, helped give rise to some other verbs, or to certain important uses of them. These uses syntactically parallel the relevant locutions with 'know': 'He not only saw the frog; *he saw that it was a frog.*' Where these syntactic parallels obtain, there is a *perspicuous entailment to knowing*. And, then, this can in turn bring to mind the entailment from 'He saw that it was a frog' to 'It was clear to him that it was a frog.' Perhaps 'know' and 'clear' may be mutually helpful in getting us to appreciate their shared logical place in our language.

The term 'clear' is reminiscent of Descartes, whose lead I often follow. (At least it reminds me of standard English translations of his work.) Our reliance on the term is of course quite different from his. He looks to clear and distinct *ideas* as the mark of true knowledge. We look to *things* which are clear *to the subject*. These latter are, at least generally, *not* ideas; they are parts of the truth (as will be argued in Chapter VII). Still, despite this very substantial difference between us, the connection of 'clear' with Descartes encourages me to favour this absolute adjective for expressing my analysis. A more important reason for this favouring is the great distribution of 'clear' in our discourse, including the physical or visual occurrences which give us a helpful slant on its absolute character. But, of course, what I have just been saying implies that there are other absolute adjectives which could also be used, which in the same linguistic frames give logically equivalent conditions. These will not have such physical or visual uses, nor will they be so closely connected with Descartes: 'obvious', 'evident', 'plain', and 'apparent'. That these other words also work well to explicate 'know' is important for us. It gives us a reason, I suggest, for thinking that our analysis represents much more than any precious connection of 'know' with any other word. Rather, the analysis tells us some important things about knowing.

Our analysis naturally extends to other relevant sorts of sentences about knowing. In all of them, it shows 'know' to be an absolute term, indeed one which is supposed to justify our absolute certainty about things. This is true, not only of sentences of our standard form 'S knows that p', but also of those which are suitably related: If Mary knows where the box is, then it is absolutely clear to her where it is. If she knows how much the box will hold, it is clear to her how much it will hold. If she knows where to place the box, then it is clear to her where to place it. And, if she knows how to open the box, it is clear to her how to open it. In each case she is, according to our thought and language, justified in being certain about where the box is, about how much it will hold, about where to place the box, and about how to open it.

In each case, when these things are clear to her, she is, according to our language and our common thought, justified in having the attitude of certainty. If it is (absolutely) clear to her how to open the box, then it is (perfectly) all right for her to have this attitude: in so far as I care about being right in the matter, no new experience whatsoever will make me any less certain about how to open the box. But, this attitude is actually completely dogmatic. And so, without overriding considerations, it is not really all right for her to have the attitude. Hence, Mary does not really *know* how to open the box, where to place it, how much it will hold, and so on. Thus, we must be sceptics about even more alleged knowing than *may* be implied in our offered thesis of universal scepticism about knowledge, the thesis that nobody knows anything to be so.

Philosophers have taken an interest, largely due to Gilbert Ryle, in the question of whether sentences of our form 'S knows that *p*' can *give an analysis* to sentences of the form 'S knows how to x'.[19] This question is not an entirely clear one, I think, but it is quite interesting what can be done with it anyway.[20] But while this work may be of philosophical importance elsewhere (and in Chapter VII we will see some of its metaphysical implications), it is quite irrelevant to treating the main problems of epistemology, that is, to dealing with the (insuperable) challenges of scepticism. For whether or not we can analyse knowing how to in terms of knowing that, we have just seen that we can directly give an absolutist analysis of knowing how to. Directly for sentences with 'know how to', this analysis shows 'know' to be an allegedly justifying state for being absolutely certain of something. This gives us enough confidence to generate a parallel argument for ignorance concerning these cases, an argument which we have just seen to be quite convincing. Accordingly, scepticism about knowing how to is, in any case, quite as inevitable as the scepticism for which we have argued at such length.

[19] Ryle, *The Concept of Mind* (London, 1949), Ch. 11, 'Knowing How and Knowing That'.
[20] See Zeno Vendler's *Res Cogitans* (Ithaca, N.Y., 1972), especially pp. 103-5.

As can happen so often in epistemology, once we think of the fundamental issues as all involving absolute terms, and once we see what the basic ones involve, we can see the minor issues as just that. Fundamentally, the absolute clarity required by knowledge can never be attained. For it is to perform the impossibly magical task of justifying an attitude which is in fact wrongly dogmatic. Knowledge seems to give every bit of the essence of certainty a good name. But no matter what name it may masquerade under, dogmatism must remain the same thing.

§12. *Taking Stock of our Scepticism*

By this point, we have done quite a bit, I think, to support our thesis of universal scepticism about knowledge or, perhaps artfully, our thesis of universal ignorance. Most recently, we have brought our comprehensive analysis of knowing to the support of this thesis. The analysis, as noted, does this largely by giving support to our direct normative argument, mainly by supporting the argument's first premiss. It supports the second premiss too, though, in that it helps articulate an alleged rationale for rejecting an absolutely severe attitude: If I *know*, then no new experience can possibly do anything to *clarify* any further for me whether the thing is so; the only significant effect it might have is to make it somewhat *less clear* to me. In supporting these premisses, our analysis, along with other supporting data put forth in this chapter, gives support to our explanatory hypotheses of Chapter I. The reason we accept the analysis, and also accept the analytically connected parts of those hypotheses, is that we are speakers of English, who have incorporated semantic relations which are embodied in this language. Accordingly, our analysis and our classical arguments support one another: The analysis helps explain further why those arguments should be sound. And, for their part, of course, the powerful intuitions aroused by the classical arguments then greatly enlarge our intuitive basis for thinking the analysis correct. Further, by supporting our analysis in this way, our classical arguments have a powerful new way of giving support to our new, more direct argument for ignorance. For its greater directness in utilizing the dogmatic flaw in knowledge, this new argument can effectively undermine certain statements about knowledge against which the less direct classical arguments are quite powerless (as in Chapter I, section 13). Along these structural lines, we have made, I think, quite a convincing case for the idea that ignorance is absolutely universal. And because we have grounded our case in the absolute justifying power which our language requires of knowing, we have been able to extend our treatment of absolute terms to give an analytic basis for our argument. The argument, then, is seen to turn on connections which are both normative and analytic. And this explains why our ignorance is, not only universal or complete, but, in the strictest sense, absolutely inevitable and necessary.

Now, while I am thus ready to repose some fair confidence in our thesis of universal, necessary ignorance, I should not close this chapter without saying a few words directed towards certain ideas which others might naturally have now.

The first set of remarks is aimed at one who, convinced of most of what I have said, remains less than convinced by my ideas in section 9 of this chapter. We may call him a *conservative sceptic about knowledge*. He cannot accept our second premiss, given the absolute universality of that crucial proposition. Now, as regards this premiss, one may be in sympathy with its spirit, but may think it takes things too far. Philosophy has traditionally distinguished between statements about one's own present moment existence and experience, on the one hand, and on the other, statements about things further removed from one's momentary consciousness. It has also separated the simplest or most intuitive logical truths from those which might better be called derivative. Despite everything I have said, one might still adhere to this tradition, feeling that as regards statements of these first two classes there is no real possibility of error, and that only some confused argumentation might look to show otherwise. But little scepticism is then lost for our conservative sceptic. For if he takes this position, which is not an entirely implausible one, he may restrict our argument and, accordingly, accept the sceptical theses in an only slightly restricted form. First, he may accept our first premiss:

(1*q*) If someone *knows* something to be so, then it is all right for the person to be absolutely certain that it is so providing only

that no overriding (consideration or) considerations make(s)
it not all right,

for he has voiced no cause for denying it. And, then, he may
restrict the matters on which the second will be taken to hold
true. Let us call the statements which he favours, 'statements
of type x', and the correlative matters, 'matters of type x'. Thus,
the statement that something now looks blue to one might be
allowed as a statement of type x, and the matter of whether
something now looks blue to one would then be a matter of
type x. Our conservative sceptic may then say that he thinks it
quite all right for one to be certain that something is so,
provided that it is in a matter of type x. But then also, he may
accept this restriction of our second premiss:

(2qR) In respect of any matter which is not of type x, it is
never the case that it is all right for someone to be absolutely
certain that something is so if no overriding (consideration
or) considerations make(s) it all right.

From these two premisses, he will obtain the correlatively
restricted form of scepticism:

(3R) In respect of any matter which is not of type x, nobody
ever *knows* that anything is so.

Thus, we have a quite obvious refuge for one who thinks that
some confusion must have come upon me when I claimed the
attitude of certainty to be *everywhere* dogmatic. He need not
abandon scepticism about knowledge entirely. All he need
refuse is a small part of what the universal thesis claims. He
will accept the idea that, while a few simple sorts of things
might be known, almost all the sorts of things which people
claim to know to be so are never really known by anyone at all.

The second sort of thinker I will here address may be called
a *normative nihilist*. In his view, no normative statements are
ever true. Even if it is not without a truth-value at all, he
thinks, any statement to the effect that anything is right or
wrong, or, for that matter, that it is all right, is a statement
which is false at best, perhaps necessarily false. There is no place
in this present work to canvass the arguments which may
underlie this position. But, while I cannot fully accept them, I

think that some are sufficiently powerful for me to have *some* inclination, at least, towards holding this extreme position. Now, a normative nihilist may be put off by our own argument for ignorance, as presented in this chapter. For the way we *supported our premisses*, especially in the case of the more sub-stantive second premiss, did involve our making certain normative judgements. For example, I said that one *should* have a more open-minded attitude in various matters, that the attitude of certainty was *wrong* for one to have and so on. But the normative nihilist would be unfortunate if he lost out on scepticism for concentrating too greatly on these merely supporting remarks. They are for the benefit of those, usually myself included (!), who are not so extreme as he. They show this great majority that, even if *some* things may be all right, even without special considerations in their favour, someone's being absolutely certain of something *never* is one of these things. Now, the first premiss of our argument is a purely conditional analytic statement about knowing; it shows 'know' to be implicitly a normative term. And the arguments for that premiss are not restricted to those which make normative assumptions. At the same time, the crucial second premiss is an entirely *negative* proposition which, while containing a norma-tive element, can hardly offend a normative nihilist. For he thinks that it is *never all right* for anybody to do or to be *anything*; just as it is never *right*, or *wrong*, for them to be it, or to do it. Thus, it *follows* from his view that, in particular, our premiss is correct: that (granting certain considerations are not present) it is *never all right* for anyone to be absolutely certain. Conse-sequently, if he can effectively argue for his position, the normative nihilist will not have undermined our own argument for ignorance. Rather, he will provide the means for a more sweeping argument for ignorance, one which will make our present argument an argument *a fortiori*. We may, then, say 'More power to him!' For it will mean more power to us.

My final passage must emphasize again that I have nowhere in this essay used any key terms, neither 'certain' nor 'know', in any special or technical or philosophical sense. I have used them in an ordinary sense and, so far as I can discern, their *only* ordinary sense in the relevant sentences of philosophic interest. It is in virtue of certain shared aspects of their sense or meaning that these words do not allow for simple positive sentences which express anything true. Now, a fairly standard attitude for a philosopher to take at this last juncture is the one of being gracious in defeat towards the sceptic's allegedly empty victory. This attitude comes easily to a third sort of person to whom I shall say something, a *sceptical isolationist*. These following are some words which such an isolationist might use to express his position: 'I will give you the words "know" and "certain", and never use them in the sorts of sentences and claims to which you have objected. Nor will I ever believe any such to be true. And, for good measure, I will be prepared to accept your use of "ignorant", and to believe accordingly. But, this still allows me to say and think almost everything I formerly did, for rather few of our statements or beliefs are about whether people know or are properly certain of things, or, correlatively, about whether or not they are ignorant. So, though scepticism may be right, it need not have much consequence even so far as the truth or falsity of things goes, much less regarding practical problems. The victory of scepticism about knowledge is as unimportant as it is isolated.' What are we to say to this response? We must agree with at least the last remark, that in so far as it is isolated scepticism's victory is bound to lack much significance. But our objector has produced no evidence that any such isolation must be accepted as a consequence of victory. Surely, nothing which we have said in sceptical argument entails as much and, indeed, some things, like our experience with 'regret' and 'sad', come upon as early as in section 2, point quite the opposite way. We need not, then, acquiesce to this hopefully disarming agreement from any former dogmatist. On the contrary, we may look forward, undogmatically of course, towards examining the question of what consequences our newly won scepticism might have. Perhaps, practical matters will not be much effected. But for those of us for whom truth matters, we may wonder at least that the consequences of scepticism might be quite material.

IV

Some Wages of Ignorance

In comparison with what has gone before, from here on out, I will offer little further in the way of new arguments for scepticism about knowledge. One thing I will do is adduce considerations which, I think, reinforce the arguments already offered, often in suggestively systematic ways. But these considerations will emerge from inquiries whose main intended bearing is on the question of what might follow from our ignorance. For, I hope and will trust that what I have already said makes total, inevitable ignorance rather hard to deny, and that it at least makes the acceptance of a very great amount of ignorance all but impossible to refuse. Accordingly, my main objective in the present chapter, as well as in much of the rest of this work, is to examine what will follow in so far as ignorance does indeed prevail.

These examinations have occupied me for some years now. Under another description, they began even before I took scepticism with sufficient seriousness. For, what follows from ignorance is just the negative of the entailments to knowledge, and an interest in the latter might come upon any philosopher, no matter what his inclinations regarding the thorny issues of knowledge and scepticism. Having been involved in these studies with both main sorts of inclination on those thorny issues, at different times of course, I feel that these examinations may be conducted quite impartially, and that they may be of intellectual profit to philosophers of quite various epistemological persuasions. Indeed, the results which seem to emerge should be of interest as much to those who concentrate on the philosophy of mind and on the philosophy of language as to any who think mainly about the more traditional questions of epistemology itself.

But of course these results will be much more exciting if

scepticism is indeed correct. For then, our sceptical isolationist will be refuted precisely in the isolationist part of his position. With the falsity of our claims to know, we will have also the falsity of many, perhaps most, of our statements about our 'mental relations to things'. Great stretches of our ordinary thought will be undermined or, perhaps better, exposed as incorrect. Accordingly, in so far as anything like truth is a goal, we will have to revise a good deal of our language and, so, of our present way of thinking. Trying to be impartial, or at least judicious, but filled with this exciting idea, I will now try to lay bare some entailments to knowledge or, from our sceptical point of view, some consequences or wages of ignorance.

§1. *The Patterns our Language Reserves for the Central Concepts of our Thought*

It is intuitively quite clear that the concept of knowledge is a central one in our actual thinking. No matter how impossibly absolute a conception it may be, the concept of knowledge does seem to have this place. A philosopher who wanted to say something about each of our main ideas would naturally include a chapter on knowledge in his ambitious but selective work. Perhaps for reasons like those we have already presented, the concept of knowledge should be abandoned in favour of more lenient, workable concepts. Perhaps certain concepts dealing with the idea of belief could do all of the worthwhile epistemological work ever wanted from the idea of knowledge. But right now, these suggestions are beside the point.

It is my belief that there are only a few concepts which have a central place in our thought; all of our ideas are not on a par. This is no doubt a rather common thought for a philosopher to have. It is also my belief that the way that our syntax works is to provide an extremely economical way for these more central concepts to exert their dominance, their importance, their centrality in our way of thought. In this way, our English syntax is in the service of our natural semantics. If this is right, then we should expect to find some very simple syntactico-semantic patterns to hold between much of what we can most economically say about people, on the one hand, and, on the other, sentences about what these people do or do not know. That this is indeed the case is the thought which guides the remainder of this chapter, as well as a fair amount of our work which follows it.

To get down to details, I will present my argument for this guiding thought by presenting several intimately related hypotheses: a couple about the semantics of verbs, a couple about adjectives, and, in the chapter to follow, a couple about nouns. I will first present some of these hypotheses in a very simple formulation. The hypotheses will then be revised in order to accommodate a few counter-examples. But the very paucity of these counter-examples is itself instructive evidence, as are the semantic explanations of them. Finally, while I will try to end with some hypotheses which are absolutely without exception, I realize that I may very well fail in such an ambitious task. As orderly as I believe English to be, even I can appreciate the complexity to be expected of a natural language at a stage where substantial development has taken place. But, even if there are exceptions to my final formulations, my hypotheses will hold, I think, for the great bulk of our linguistic phenomena. While I will not always be careful to write in an appropriately muted way, it is this slightly more modest idea for which I will argue.

§2. *Constructing some simple Sentences and Talking about some Entailments*

One very simple sort of English sentence is that of the form 'S verbs'. We interpret our form by insisting that the letter 'S' be replaced only by the name of some being, or by a pronoun suited to a being, that the word 'verbs' be replaced only by a single word which would intuitively be classed as a verb in an appropriate tense, and that our second replacement follow directly upon our first in our generated sentence. Thus, 'John slept' and 'Mary believes' will be of our simple form, allowing that the latter sentence may be incomplete in the sense that it may be equivalent to some longer, more complex sentence with the same beginning (here, perhaps, to 'Mary believes something or someone'), which gives the verb an object. But both the sentence 'The boy laughed' and also 'John laughed heartily' will not be of our simple form, but only of a somewhat more complex one.

One way of obtaining more complex sentences is by starting

with the words of such simple sentences, and then following them immediately by a propositional clause. (This, even though we will often, by following this simple procedure, generate no proper sentence but only some non-sentential string of words.) A propositional clause is just a string of words which if it retained their same meaning and stood alone, with only the minimal changes necessary for such standing (such as whatever capitalization or punctuation might be needed), would serve as a propositional sentence, that is, a sentence which standardly expresses what is true or what is false. Thus, we may take 'Mary knows' and directly follow it by 'there are tables' to get the more complex sentence 'Mary knows there are tables.' We do *not* do this, however, when we take 'Mary wishes' and directly follow it with 'she was in the land of cotton' to get the sentence 'Mary wishes she was in the land of cotton.' For as they occur in the longer sentence, these words mean something different from what they mean in the sentence 'She was in the land of cotton,' the main factor being the different mood of 'was'. Accordingly, 'Mary wished she was in the land of cotton' is not a sentence of our simple form. (This will be of importance to us in section 5, where we claim that while a sentence like 'Mary incorrectly believes she was in the land of cotton' entails 'She was not in the land of cotton,' a sentence of our simple form never has the verb yield such a negative entailment.)

In each case where we do obtain a sentence, and not something like *'Mary hits there are tables', we may obtain a slightly longer sentence which means the same by placing the word 'that' right after our starting words, and only then tacking on our propositional clause right after the previous words. Thus, 'Mary knows that there are tables' means the same as 'Mary knows there are tables.' If we represent our propositional clauses by the letter 'p', we may say that these last sentences are of the form 'S verbs that p'. As sentences of this form always mean the same as sentences of the simpler form 'S verbs p', where there *is* a sentence of this last sort, we may say that in the former sentences the word 'that' has only minimal meaning. It is a sub-hypothesis of mine that sentences of the form 'S verbs word p' will mean the same as sentences of the simpler form just in case we replace 'word' by a word which there has the same minimal meaning which 'that' has in such a replacement. And, so, perhaps 'that' itself is the only word suitable for such replacement. We get obviously bad results when we try to put in something for 'word' which obviously must mean something different from our minimal 'that'. This happens with: 'Mary knows or snow is white,' 'Mary knows why snow is white,' and so on. Perhaps a good way to keep these facts before us is to represent the sentences we have been generating as all being of the form 'S verbs (that) p'. This seems an appropriate thing to do, given that my sub-hypothesis is right, even in cases where the 'that' cannot be optionally deleted: 'She asserted that he did it,' as against ?'She asserted he did it.'

There is an important semantic difference between the two sentences, 'Mary noticed it was raining' and 'Mary believed it was raining,' both of which are of our simple form, 'S verbs (that) p.' This difference may be expressed, at least in part, by saying that while the first sentence will express a truth only if it was raining, the second sentence may express a truth whether it was raining or not. And, this may allow us to say that the first sentence *entails* the sentence 'It was raining' while the second one does not. In making such an allowance we must suppose that the two sentences function in a relevantly parallel manner. Thus, for example, where we allow that the sentences 'John was a bachelor' entails 'John was unmarried,' we suppose that in the first sentence 'bachelor' means nothing like 'holder of the first or lowest academic degree', that in each sentence the name 'John' has the same referent, and whatever else may be needed for a relevant parallel to be established. Where such a parallel is not operating, there can be no question of whether a given *sentence* (as opposed to what it expresses) entails another *sentence*.

Quite obviously, the differentially entailed sentence 'It was raining' is that sentence which most closely corresponds to the propositional clause, 'it was raining'. As an understood convenience, then, we may say that our first sentence, 'Mary noticed it was raining,' *entails its completing (propositional) clause* while our second sentence fails to do so, meaning that the first sentence entails the sentence corresponding to 'it was raining' while the second one does not. While many sentences fail to entail their completing clauses, many others do yield such an entailment. As with 'Mary noticed it was raining,' the sentences

'Lionel knows four is the sum of three and one' and 'He regrets that he left the party early' entail their completing clauses.

If easy, intuitive argument isn't enough, recent work on proper names indicates them to have so little relevant meaning, if any at all, that these entailments can scarcely be attributed to the names which occur in these sentences.[1] And, the personal pronouns which might occur instead are no better bets for entailing here. Indeed, should we replace any of these with the innocuous word 'someone', our entailments will go through quite well. Thus, as a general rule, our entailments cannot be attributed to our replacement for 'S'. As a second point, we may notice that just as 'Mary noticed it was raining' entails 'It was raining,' 'Mary noticed four is the sum of three and one' entails 'Four is the sum of three and one,' and 'Mary noticed that snow is white' entails 'Snow is white.' Indeed, no matter which propositional clause we place right after our verb (at least so long as a consistent sentence is the result), we obtain a sentence which entails its completing clause. Thus, as a general rule, our entailments cannot be attributed to our replacement for '*p*'. By elimination, we are thus in a rather reasonable position to say that, in each case, our entailments are attributable to our replacement for 'verbs'. Whatever the meaning of this word allows or requires it to do in other linguistic contexts, it requires that it entails its completing clause in the simple contexts we are examining. Thus, when they occur in these contexts, such diverse verbs as 'notices' and 'regrets' yield us our entailments. The fact that they always do this says something about these verbs. We may focus on this fact by saying that, in certain sentences of the form 'S verbs (that) *p*' which entail their completing clauses, the *verb* entails the completing clause, and even that this word entails *its* completing clause. Of course, even with a verb like 'believes', we may pick *certain* clauses where an entailment is yielded. Thus, 'She believes that she has at least one belief' entails 'She has at least one belief.' But we don't get an entailment with *each and every* clause which can follow 'believes' here. Thus, in contrast, we do *not* say that 'believes' is a verb which, in sentences of our form, entails its completing clause.

[1] See Saul Kripke's 'Naming and Necessity' in *Semantics of Natural Language,* ed. G. Harman and D. Davidson (Dordrecht, 1972), pp. 253–308.

§3. *How Verbs Yield Entailments to Knowledge*

Of all the sentences of the form 'S verbs (that) *p*', those which will most commonly occur to philosophers as cases where the verb entails its completing clause will be sentences where the replacement for 'verbs' is an appropriate form of the verb 'knows', or 'to know'. Among such sentences will be 'John knew Mary went home' and 'Mary knows that there are tables.' Regardless of variations in tense, we may represent such sentences as all being of the form 'S knows (that) *p*' and call them *(simple) knowledge sentences*. Further, taking, for example, the sentence 'Mary noticed there are tables,' we may call the related sentence 'Mary knew there are tables,' the *corresponding* (simple) knowledge sentence; for the latter differs from the former only in that the verb is changed to a correspondingly tensed variant of the verb 'knows'. For generality of statement, we may say also that any simple knowledge sentence is its own corresponding simple knowledge sentence. Noticing that the sentence 'Mary noticed there are tables' entails, not only its completing clause, but also the sentence 'Mary knew there are tables,' we may fix this fact in our minds by saying that the verb, 'noticed', as it occurs in our original sentence, entails both its completing clause *and also the corresponding simple knowledge sentence*. Yet more vividly, we might say that here our verb entails *its* corresponding knowledge sentence. For, owing to the meaning of 'noticed', if Mary noticed there are tables, it follows that Mary knew there are tables.

In thinking along these lines, it is natural to put forth boldly, at least to examine, the entirely general hypothesis:

Whenever a sentence of the form 'S verbs (that) *p*' has the verb entail its completing clause, the verb entails its corresponding simple knowledge sentence.

Verbs which are positive instances of this hypothesis are many and varied: 'admits', 'ascertained', 'conceded', 'discerned', 'disclosed', 'discovered', 'foresaw', 'found', 'knows' (itself), 'learned' (at least in one sense), 'noted', 'noticed', 'perceives', 'realizes', 'recalls', 'recognized', 'regrets', 'remembers', 'revealed', 'sees', 'understands' (in at least one sense and also possibly, 'explained'), and so on.[2]

Thus, for example, 'Mary discovered that snow is white' entails 'Mary knew that snow is white.' We may evidence this by noting the contradictory feeling we get from 'Mary *discovered* that snow is white, but she did *not know* that snow is white.' It is especially important to notice the contradiction with our verb used in the present tense. 'Mary *discovers* that snow is white, but she does *not know* that it is.' For when one thinks of what must be true, in the past, for one to discover something, one is struck that, *before* the discovery, one *must not know* the thing in question. One might then think that 'Mary discovered that snow is white' will entail both 'Mary knew that snow is white' and also 'Mary did not know that snow is white.' Does this apparently innocent sentence get us into such *obvious* trouble? But, there is no trouble here because, while the first two sentences talk of the *same* past time, the last one talks of a time which is *further in the past*, i.e. an *earlier* time. We must understand these sentences in this way if we may understand them to function in such a relevantly parallel manner as will allow any entailments to obtain among them. This is nothing peculiar; this is generally what happens with our use of tenses. Thus, 'He was fat, but he was thin' is, as taken most naturally, expressive of a contradiction. To get even the feeling that no contradiction is expressed, we need to insert words as in 'He was fat, but before that he was thin,' or at least to use some distorting unbalanced emphasis as in 'He was fat, but *was* thin' (though, in this last case, a contradiction actually is expressed). Just so, we naturally understand a contradiction to be expressed only with 'Mary discovered that snow is white, and she did not know that it is,' and not with 'Mary discovered that snow is white, and she knew that it is.' Indeed, with the latter sentence, we might just as well have used a 'so' instead of the 'and'; indeed, perhaps we would have done better to do so. To sum up: when we understand our simple sentences (as well as others) to function in a relevantly parallel manner, there need be no problem of understanding which entailments hold amongst them.

[2] Many, perhaps most, of these verbs were first brought to my attention by Mr. Terry L. Smith.

To say that sentences of our simple form are *really* of the more complex form 'S verbs the fact that *p*' is both incorrect and irrelevant. It is incorrect because there are some sentences of the form 'S verbs (that) *p*' for which there is no sentence of this longer form with 'fact'. Thus, while 'Mary saw that they left' is a perfectly proper sentence, and of our simple form, we have only marked deviance with *'Mary saw the fact that they left.' We do have as a sentence, of course, 'Mary saw that it was a fact that they left,' but that is another matter altogether. (Compare 'Mary saw that it was a lie that they left.') So, if our simple sentences are each equivalent to some longer sentences where the verb has an explicitly nominalized object, and perhaps from which they derive, those objects will vary from case to case, or at least they won't always be the corresponding fact, the fact that *p*. But, more importantly, this sort of remark is quite irrelevant. Our hypothesis fully allows that our simple sentences each have some such more complex source as their derivation. It only implies that if they are thus derived, perhaps from different complex sources in different cases, the resulting simple sentences, of our form, will adhere to a certain semantic constraint. We might say, then, that this hypothesis articulates a principle to which all such simplifying transformations must adhere. This must be understood with all our hypotheses, the ones for adjectives and nouns as well.

The first word of our formulation, the word 'whenever', is a word of generality, borrowed from our talk of time. Here, in the jargon of the logician, the word indicates a 'qualification over' readings, or over sentences of our form with a particular meaning assumed or assigned. Thus, the sentence 'She learned that Columbus sailed the ocean blue in 1492' may have at least two readings. On at least one reading it entails 'Columbus sailed the ocean blue in 1492.' On at least one other it does not entail this. Our hypothesis, with its generalizing 'whenever', predicts that on any reading where this is entailed, there is also entailed the sentence 'She knew that Columbus sailed the ocean blue in 1492.' And, this does appear correct. So, our hypothesis gives a semantic principle to which ambiguities adhere. This principle is a very general 'filtering device' for the transformations that language allows for its verbs. Our hypothesis for adjectives, and still later for nouns, will articulate parallel 'filters' concerning those other main parts of speech. These filters must be passed through for any sentences where any agent or being is most closely tied, as close as our syntax will allow, to a fact, a 'propositional content', or whatever else is indicated by our replacement for '*p*'.

Some purported counter-examples to our offered hypothesis are obviously beside the point. But others are not so obviously so. Of course, it is obvious that 'Mary correctly believes it is raining' entails 'It is raining' but does not entail 'Mary knows it is raining.' Someone might, I suppose, put this forward as a counter-example. But it is just as obvious that this sentence is not of our simple form. For the occurrence of the adverbial word, 'correctly', prevents the verb from following right upon its proper predecessor, 'Mary'. What is a bit less obvious is that with such a sentence as 'Mary caused the window to shatter,' while it may be that the sentence entails 'The window shattered' but does not entail 'Mary knew the window shattered,' there really is no propositional clause in the original sentence. For, 'the window to shatter' is different from 'the window shattered', or 'the window shatters', or any other propositional clause. To get something like the original, but something which does have a propositional clause, we must trot out a sentence like 'Mary caused *it to be* (*the case*) *that* the window shattered.' And, now we have as complicating, intervening material, at least the words 'it to be'. There are many examples which, like the present one, turn out to be quite beside the point—if not in one way, then in another.

There are, however, a few genuine counter-examples to our offered hypothesis, at least the verbs 'guessed' and 'forgets'. For if someone forgets that Mary went home, it is entailed that Mary went home; and in at least one sense of the verb, if someone guessed that there are four hundred and eighteen beans in the jar, it follows that there are that many in there. But so far from it being entailed that these things are known, these verbs here entail quite the opposite, namely, that the subject does *not* know the thing in question. Noting that the negation of (what is expressed by) a simple knowledge sentence may always be expressed by a sentence of the form 'It is not the case that S knows (that) *p*,' with the replacement rules parallel to those already adopted, we may conveniently talk of the *negation* of any such knowledge sentence. Thus, the negation of the sentence 'Mary knew Jim came' will be the sentence 'It is not the case that Mary knew Jim came.'[3] In these terms, we may replace our original hypothesis by the following somewhat more complicated one, so as to accommodate our previously troubling verbs:

> Whenever a sentence of the form 'S verbs (that) *p*' has the verb entail its completing clause, then either the verb entails its corresponding simple knowledge sentence, or else the verb entails the negation of that knowledge sentence.

With this hypothesis, there are, I think, no clear, damaging counter-examples. But the disjunctive character of this hypothesis would seem to render it somewhat uninteresting unless we can give some idea, in some intuitive terms, of what the hypothesis says. I will try to put an adequate idea in this way: In our simple sentences, whenever a verb yields us truth, it yields us a *decision* as to the presence or absence of knowledge. Or, to put the idea a bit more grandly: Where our verbs are talking about and yielding us truth, they are doing so only in so far as and because they are talking about and yielding us a decision as to knowledge or else ignorance. With this being the import of our most recent hypothesis, that hypothesis does not seem *ad hoc* for all its disjunctive character. And the tremendously disproportionate number of decisions in the positive direction may then be understood as just a bit more evidence for thinking that each verb which intuitively *seems* to entail so much as its knowledge sentence is a verb which actually does do so.

§4. *How an Hypothesis may be Taken as a Governing Paradigm*
It will occur to the careful reader, no doubt, that such words as 'proved', 'demonstrated', and 'showed' *appear* to be pretty

---

[3] Throughout most of what follows, I will write negations of sentences in the shorter, more convenient, and less stultified form which is provided by internalizing' the words which carry the negation. Thus, for 'It is not the case that Mary knew Jim came,' I will write conveniently, 'Mary did not know Jim came.' I think that, in the simple sentences we are considering, the two forms are quite equivalent, as is suggested by the apparent consistency of 'Of course, Mary did not know Jim came, as there wasn't any such thing for Mary to know about.' But, whether equivalent or not, my claims all concern the longer form, the form of 'external negation'. So, where the reader has any doubts concerning the validity of my claims, and these doubts are based on suspicions about my using the shorter 'internal' form, he is quite free to rewrite my passage in the longer way and test the claims accordingly.

clear counter-examples to our disjunctive hypothesis. But this appearance may be regarded as deceptive, I think, if we regard our hypothesis as only applying to words when understood in their central, unextended meaning. When regarded in this way, our hypothesis may be understood as presenting us with an important paradigm which governs the use of our verbs. For, when we understand, say, 'proved', in its unextended sense, it is *required* that the verb take as its subject an agent, or being. I think that this is rather intuitive. Thus, while we might utter such things as 'Without his ever knowing that there is no largest prime number, John proved there is no largest prime number,' we will not be using our verb, 'proved', in its central, unextended sense. And, our utterance may be paraphrased as 'Without his ever knowing that there is no largest prime number, *John's doing* certain things proved there is no largest prime number.' This last sentence is quite on a par with 'Without his ever knowing that a boy can grow a foot in a year, John's growing a foot in a year proved a boy can grow a foot in a year.' And, similarly, our original sentence is quite on a par with 'Without his ever knowing that a boy can grow a foot in a year, John proved a boy can grow a foot in a year.' Thus, in so far as we allow 'proved' to yield us truth without any decision on knowledge, we allow it to take strange subjects and allow ourselves to use it well without its unextended meaning.

But, if our original is a genuine English sentence which might express a truth, then so is the sentence 'John proved there is no largest prime number' as well as 'John proved a boy can grow a foot in a year.' This is true even though both of these sentences has a verb which entails its completing clause without entailing either its knowledge sentence or the negation of it. And, the most reasonable conclusion from our recently employed test of paraphrase for unextended meaning seems to be, not that our hypothesis holds in any case, but that it holds just in case our verbs are used with their central, unextended meaning. It is in this sense, then, that we may understand our hypothesis as an important paradigm for governing English sentences.

By taking our hypothesis as helping us to find the central sense of our verbs, we may notice a subtle but important difference between the verb 'ensured', which has a connection with causality, and other causal verbs, like 'caused' itself. Thus, in its central meaning 'John ensured that Betty will leave' entails both that Betty will leave and, moreover, that John knew she will. Only by going without that meaning, and so by allowing our verb to take a subject that is not a being, may we get the first entailment without the second. Thus, in 'John's vomiting on the floor ensured Betty will leave,' we do get rid of the entailment to John's knowledge. But we do this, I think, only by allowing ourselves to use our verb in a sense which we intuitively feel to be at least a bit removed from the central meaning we take it to have. In contrast, no such removal is felt, I think, when we say 'John's vomiting on the floor caused it to be the case that Betty will leave.' Rather 'caused' seems to mean the same thing here that it does in the somewhat simpler sentence 'John caused it to be the case that Betty will leave.' Thus, in helping to reveal this difference in (central) meaning between 'ensured', which requires no extra words, and 'caused', for example, which does require some, our hypothesis receives a certain sort of support. But while we should grant that *some* verbs, like 'proved' and 'ensured', allow for an extended meaning and so for use without our paradigm, and, while we may suggest that these extensions even serve to support our hypothesis as a governing paradigm; we may also notice the many verbs which do not admit of any extended meaning or correlative non-paradigmatic use. Among such undeviating verbs are (most of) those exhibited in section 3, as well as other verbs. And finally, for this round at least, we may take as still further support for our hypothesis the fact that the verbs which allow for no deviation so greatly outnumber the verbs like 'ensured', which have an element of charity.

§5. *Why some Entailments from Verbs are not to be Found*

Just as we may easily develop the notion of a sentence which is the negation of another one, we may also develop the convenient idea of a propositional clause which is the negation of another one, that of a propositional clause being the negation of a sentence, and so on. Thus, much as before, we may say plainly enough that, for example; the sentence 'Mary falsely believes horses are fish' entails the negation of the propositional clause 'horses are fish', for it entails 'It is not the case that horses are fish.' Or, in other words, this sentence entails the negation of its own completing propositional clause. Here, it is pretty plain also that this entailment can be attributed to the occurrence of the adverbial word 'falsely'. By the same token, in order to get this particular entailment of the negation of a completing clause, we exhibited a sentence of a more complex form than those we have been considering. It is, then, natural to ask whether such an entailment is ever available with our simple sentences, or, more specifically, whether, in our simple sentences, a *verb* ever entails the negation of its completing propositional clause. My answer is in the negative, and we may put it in the form of an hypothesis:

> There is no sentence of the form 'S verbs (that) p' where the verb ever entails the negation of its completing clause.

As our previous hypothesis has many positive instances, should this second one hold, we would be able to say this about our language: In our simple sentences, while many verbs yield us truth, none yields us falsity. This would fit in well with what we said before: that those (many) verbs which yield us truth do so only in so far as and because they yield us a decision as to the presence or absence of knowledge. So, in so far as it can be counted on to hold, this second hypothesis is, in an illuminating way, quite closely connected with our first one. But, let us examine this hypothesis to see how far it holds.

The first thing to notice in connection with this hypothesis is, I think, this: those verbs which *most clearly* yield us falsity require the insertion of extra words into what would only otherwise be allowed as sentences of our simple standard form. Thus, 'John prevented *it from being the case* that Mary will get rich' clearly yields us 'It is not the case that Mary will get rich,' but we are equally clear about needing the words 'it from being the case' to get the verb to do the job. Interestingly, I think, this is but the other side of the coin of what would, if it could, most clearly count against our first hypothesis: such sentences as 'John caused *it to be the case* that Mary will get rich' and 'John brought *it about* that Mary will get rich.' For, these sentences, while they most clearly yield us truth without yielding any decision about knowledge, do so only with their extra words, their breaking of our simple form, their greater linguistic complication. Thus, by spotting the extra words in an array of such examples, we may serve to build confidence in our second hypothesis, and also in the closeness of its connection with our first one.

Proceeding along these lines, we may notice how such verbs as 'disproves' and 'refutes' strikingly contrast with their opposites, i.e. such verbs as 'proves', 'shows', and 'demonstrates'. Thus, the closest we can come to our standard form with the first group is to produce such sentences as 'John disproved *the claim* that Mary will get rich' and 'John refuted *the statement* that all cows chew their cud.' The string *'John refuted that all cows chew their cud' is far from being a sentence of English, while the string 'John proved that all cows chew their cud' is so clear a case of being one. Of course, John may refute Bill's conjecture. But even if Bill's conjecture *is* that there is a largest prime, John will never *refute *that there is a largest prime.* This is so even though John may, in the course of his reasonings, *prove that* there is no largest prime. And, in the central, unextended sense of 'prove', he will do so only in case, in the course of those reasonings, John will come to know, if he doesn't already, that there is no largest prime number. So, our 'contrast with extra words' test, which we have just gone through in several ways, provides a complimentary argument to our test of 'paraphrase for unextended meaning' that we offered previously. Thus, while getting some evidence for our second hypothesis, and for the closeness of its connection with our first one, we are also confirming the idea that our first hypothesis exhibits an important paradigm for the verbs of our language.

To be sure, there are some verbs that *at least appear* to yield us falsity while requiring no extra words to get us to the negation of their completing clauses. One thinks of such verbs as 'imagine', 'pretends', 'fancies', and so on. But, is it really true that 'John imagines that he is a prince' *entails* 'John is not a prince'? Or, might it be that, on many occasions, (the utterance of) the first sentence only *suggests* the truth of what the latter expresses? I want to argue that only something like the latter may best be construed to be really what is going on here. *So long as* John does *not know* that he is a prince, and *especially* if John is quite sure that he is no prince, it seems quite possible for John to imagine that he is a prince. Especially on this last condition, John may pretend or fancy or imagine that he is a prince even while he is in fact just that. So, when I try to view the matter most sensitively, I find no clear counter-examples with any of these initially promising verbs. On reflection, I suggest, they do *not entail* the negation of their completing clauses but only do so much as *suggest* that these negations hold. What it is about these verbs which allows them often to promote such suggestions is a problem which needs more thought than I can now provide. But it is likely, I think, that an adequate account here will be but part of a more general explanation of how it is that our language allows us to suggest things which are neither said by us nor entailed by what we say.

Now, some persons have told me that there are certain verbs, in fact belonging to a very special class, which fit our form but still give negative entailments.[4] One of these would be the verb 'misbelieves', another 'misremembered'. I have no clear intuitions to the effect that there really are such sentences as 'She misbelieved that they left' and 'He misremembered that her name was "Marie".' To me, these strings seem deviant. But this may be due only to a lack of experience on my part. Suppose, then, that these are genuine sentences, and that they entail, respectively, 'They did not leave' and 'Her name was not "Marie".' What follows from this? Our second hypothesis will then be wrong; it does not work for *every* verb. But it does work for almost all. And, more than that, these counter-examples can be explained in terms of the hypothesis. The very existence of verbs like these, made up out of a special prefix, 'mis-', followed by a simpler, more central verb, 'believes' or 'remembered', wants some explanation. Why don't we have negative verbs occurring just as simply and centrally as others: like *'nelieves' and *'nemembered'? Because generally and centrally, verbs conform to our semantic principle, to our hypothesis. Thus, special resources are required to give a simple expression to ideas, which, according to the main drift and theme of our language, find no ready expression.

In any event, we could place an obvious restriction on our hypothesis to exclude these special examples. But, what would

---

[4] These examples were given me by John Kearns, John O'Connor, and Myrna Breskin.

be the point? So long as the exceptions to our hypothesis are so few, and so long as we can so comfortably understand what is exceptional about them, our hypothesis is without damaging counter-instances. In that case, we can treat our hypothesis as giving an important semantic principle. We might even be excused from speaking of it in wholly general terms. Indeed, for simplicity's sake, I will often take this liberty.

It is my suggestion, then, that our second general hypothesis is immune from any damaging counter-examples. What might be the full import of this second paradigm? To uncover its import, let us suppose for the moment that it does *not* hold. What would we have then? The answer is quite easy, of course: we would have, in our simple sentences, verbs that yield us falsity, i.e. the negations of their completing clauses. But, then, what would these verbs also yield? They would yield, and for the most *trivial* of reasons, the absence of knowledge, i.e. the negations of their knowledge sentences. For, the verbs would yield us in the case at hand, that there is nothing to be known in the first place. Knowing that *p*, if it requires anything, requires that it be, *not false*, but true that *p*. So, it is quite obvious that if this second, complementary hypothesis did not hold, we would have verbs which entailed an absence of knowledge for an entirely trivial reason. But then, by parity of reasoning, if the hypothesis *does* hold, as it appears to do, any verb which, in our simple sentences, yields us an absence of knowledge will do so for a reason which is not entirely trivial. Thus, in so far as we may spot verbs which, in this relatively non-trivial way, yield us an absence of knowledge, this complementary hypothesis takes on considerable interest. So, we now ask: Are there, in our simple sentences, verbs which, while they do not yield us falsity, nevertheless do yield us the absence of knowledge?

Remembering that in formulating our first hypothesis we had to be disjunctive, we realize that our answer must be affirmative. For there we noted that, in our simple sentences, 'forgets' and 'guesses', while they yielded *truth*, i.e. entailed their completing clauses, yielded as well the absence of knowledge, i.e. entailed the negation of their knowledge sentences. For example, at least in one sense of the verb, if John *guessed* that Harry did it, then, while it is entailed that Harry did it, it is also entailed

that John *did not know* that Harry did it. But is it only those
few verbs which, while yielding truth (and not yielding knowledge), yield ignorance as well? Or, are there *also* verbs which,
while they do *not* yield truth nor, of course, falsity *do* yield an
absence of knowledge? A consideration of such verbs as 'sus-
pects', 'hopes', 'fears', 'expects', 'conjectures', 'feels', and
'decided' makes it pretty clear that the answer here must also
be affirmative. Thus, if John really fears that the horse he bet
on lost, it is entailed that John does *not know* that the horse he
bet on lost. And, if John *expects* that the horse won, it is entailed
that John does *not know* the horse won.

We should notice, further, that in all cases where our verbs
entail that something is not known by someone, they also entail
that its negation is not known. Or, in other symbols, if our
verb yields us the negation of its knowledge sentence, it yields
as well so much as the most closely corresponding sentence of
the form: 'It is not the case that S knows *whether* (or not) *p*.'

To sum up: there are a few verbs which entail their completing clauses, as well as several which do not, all of which
entail not only the negation of their simple knowledge sentences, but so much as the most closely corresponding sentence
of the form 'S does not know whether (or not) *p*.'[5] This result,
along with the many positive instances of our first hypothesis,
lends further interest to both of our general hypotheses, just as
it evidences the closeness of the connection between them. But,
more than this, the composite picture we have developed indicates, about as strongly as one might like, what I have been
suggesting all along: that in our simple sentences, our verbs are
never importantly concerned simply with truth (and falsity).
In so far as they have any concern with that, it is only through
their being importantly concerned with knowledge and ignorance, that is, with the presence and absence of knowledge.

§6. *Sentences with Adjectives and some Hypotheses about them*

Which sentences with adjectives give the closest parallel to our
simple sentences with verbs? If we stick to the simple sort of
instructions which we used for our form for verbs, which we

---

[5] Correlative with my remarks in footnote 3, this 'internalized' form may be
looked at simply as a shorter way of writing sentences of the longer form, where
the negation is brought out to the front.

certainly want to do, we will not get any proper sentences from the form 'S adjective(s) (that) p'. We do not have quite such simple sentences for adjectives in English, but only non-sentential strings like *'Mary happy it is raining.' Concerning adjectives, the simplest sentences for connecting our 'S' and 'p' require us to place, between our replacement for 'S' and any word which would be functioning as an adjective, like 'happy', a single word variant of the verb 'to be'. That is, the best we can do is to insert an 'is' or 'was' between our personal subject and its adjective. Thus, we must focus on sentences of the form 'S is adjective (that) p', like, 'Mary is happy it is raining.' This is the closest parallel to the form 'S verbs (that) p' which English has to offer. It is the simplest way in English for an adjective to join an agent or being and a fact, or 'propositional content', or whatever else our 'p' indicates.

The parallel is not peculiar to sentences with a propositional clause following behind. Thus, we have in addition to the form 'S verbs (that) p', the even simpler one 'S verbs'. But we have no sentences of the form 'S adjective'. Adjectives, in any case, need a form of 'to be' to separate them from their subjects. Thus, we get 'Mary swims' and 'Mary is hot,' but not *'Mary hot.' So, where we follow parallel instructions, we may have some confidence that, between the forms 'S is adjective (that) p' and 'S verbs (that) p', we have a parallel which runs both close and deep. The one form is to adjectives as the other is to verbs.

Just as we may spot a difference between 'John noticed Mary was home' and 'John believed Mary was home,' we may spot one between 'John is happy Mary was home' and 'John is convinced Mary was home.' In each case, only the first of the pair entails that Mary was home. Just as we may reasonably say that the verb 'noticed' entails its completing clause, we may say that the adjective 'happy' entails *its* completing clause. The reasoning follows that in section 2, now in connection with adjectives instead of verbs.

Indeed, all of the terminology used in stating our two hypotheses for verbs may be carried over in the most obvious way for talking about adjectives. What we want to say about adjectives, then, will be conveyed in parallel hypotheses for them. We have this primary hypothesis for adjectives:

Whenever a sentence of the form 'S is adjective (that) *p*' has the adjective entail its completing clause, then either the adjective entails its corresponding simple knowledge sentence, or else the adjective entails the negation of that knowledge sentence.

And, we have this as our second, complementary hypothesis:

There is no sentence of the form 'S is adjective (that) *p*' where the adjective ever entails the negation of its completing clause.

It is quite clear, I trust, that what these hypotheses say about adjectives is what the previous two said about verbs. So, in these new hypotheses, we have parallel hypotheses for adjectives. That we easily see. What we still must look to see is how well our newer hypotheses fare. In their domain, do they hold as well, or about as well, as our hypotheses for verbs did in theirs? We had better get an affirmative answer here for any further questions relating them to be of much interest.

§7. *Adjectives which Confirm our First Hypothesis*

Our new first hypothesis says that where our adjectives are yielding us truth, they are yielding us a decision as to the presence or absence of knowledge on the part of our subject. In so far as this is right it gives a sense to saying that, in such simple sentences, the concept of knowledge plays an essential role in governing the semantics of these adjectives. Still more sense may be given this claim if we find that the great majority of adjectives which make such a decision on knowledge decide in the positive direction. For, if it is the concept of knowledge that is primary here, and that of ignorance only secondary, the preponderance of adjectives (which entail truth) should yield us knowledge. Thus, we should expect many more adjectives to fall under the first disjunct of our consequent, that is, to entail their knowledge sentences, than to fall under the second, that is, to entail the negations of those knowledge sentences. This turns out to be the case.

Among the many adjectives which have this positively decisive character are: 'amazed', 'amused', 'angry', 'annoyed', 'ashamed', 'astonished', 'astounded', 'aware', 'delighted', 'depressed', 'disappointed', 'elated', 'embarrassed', 'excited', 'furious', 'glad', 'grateful', 'happy', 'horrified', 'irritated', 'over-joyed', 'pleased', 'proud', 'sorry', 'surprised', 'thankful', 'tickled', 'unhappy', 'upset', and, to put a stop to this impressive parade, 'impressed'.[6]

Many of these adjectives, including the last; in some sense derive from clearly related verbs. But that does not disqualify them, along with many others, from being adjectives of state, and thus, from being adjectives. For in the most ordinary sense of 'state', these adjectives generally help us to say what state someone is in. Thus, if you embarrassed me, then I am or was embarrassed. But then, also, I am or was in a state of embarrassment, or, more or less equivalently, in a state of being embarrassed. Perhaps you pointed out that my bicycle was a 'girl's bicycle'; in that way you might have embarrassed me by making me embarrassed that my bike was of a certain sort. But, then, whatever else you did, you caused me to be in a certain state, whether that state be in any important sense 'relational' or not. And, you may say that I am or was in this state by saying, simply, that I am or was embarrassed.

To convince ourselves that, whether derived from a verb, whether importantly relational, or whatever, each of our adjectives does entail its knowledge sentence and not just its completing clause, we may best begin by trying the test we tried before with verbs. Thus, we start by saying 'John is surprised that his mother is working in a garage, but he does not know his mother is working in a garage,' which we hear to be a contradiction. And, this feeling of contradiction can only be enhanced, I think, by tampering with the sentence so that we get something which, while it expresses the same idea, highlights just those terms our hypothesis picks as responsible for any contradiction that really might be there. Such an increase in feeling may be obtained, I suggest, by our emphasizing the key words in the sentence: 'John is really *surprised* his mother is working in a garage, but he does *not* actually *know* that she is doing so.' Or, one might say 'Though John was *happy* that Mary went away, he did *not* really *know* she did that,' but with no more consistent a

---

[6] Almost all of the words in this list were brought to my attention by Robert M. Gordon in a number of discussions. See his paper, 'Emotions and Knowledge', *Journal of Philosophy*, vol. lxvi, No. 13 (1969).

result. No matter what sentence we generate here, the more we emphasize what we would expect to be the responsible terms, the more we get the feeling that, while what is expressed must be true or false, it cannot possibly be true.

A further way to test these adjectives is to cook up an example where our subject satisfies many conditions apparently essential to his having knowledge, but where he falls short of knowing the thing. We then ask: Although he doesn't really *know* the thing, is his satisfaction of all those other conditions perhaps enough to entail that the subject, say, is happy that the thing is so? Let's take a case where our subject is justified at least in believing the thing, the thing is true, his grounds are quite good, but the subject fails to know. One case is where a reliable source tells the subject something which, while it happens to be true, is not known to be so by the source. Perhaps on this one occasion the source just wanted to fool the subject into believing the thing, and succeeded in doing so. The source, say, tells the subject that he, the subject, has just won a new bike in a raffle, getting the subject to believe just this because the subject knows the source to be, in general, very reliable on such matters as this, as well as on other matters. Unbeknownst to the source, the subject *has* won a bike, so our subject's belief that he has won one is, not only justified, but correct. But, is our subject, who *doesn't know* he has won a bike, *happy that he has won a bike*? Or, is it only something like this: our subject is happy because he thinks he has won a bike, and, as it happens, he has? It's pretty clear, I think, that only something like the latter even approximates what ought to be said about the situation; it is not true that our subject is happy that he has won a bike. No matter how we pile up the conditions our subject meets for knowledge, so long as he falls short of actually knowing the thing to be so, he can't possibly be happy, or angry, or impressed that it is so. This test works just as well with verbs. And, so, it helps us further confirm our first hypothesis for them.

Still another way to test these adjectives is to take what seems plausible as being a very severe necessary condition for knowing and, then, to try to see whether we can consistently say that the adjectival sentence holds even though the subject fails to meet this stringent condition. One such condition, which in Chapter II I advocated as indeed necessary for knowledge, is that the subject be *completely sure,* or *absolutely certain* of the thing. Like the other two tests, this one will work with any relevant verb: 'John *regrets* that he quit school, but he is *not* absolutely *certain* he did' surely looks to be something true or false but nothing which could possibly be true. The same goes with 'John really *remembers* that he quit school, but he *isn't* completely *sure* he did that,' and so on. And, like the other tests, it is not hard to tell that this one works as well with adjectives. When I say, for example, 'John is really *angry* that his mother has quit her job, but John really is *not* completely *sure* that she has done that very thing,' I find myself unable to pass over the matter and allow that I might have said something which could possibly be true. As I have not here been just playing about with so many words, I have, willy nilly, expressed a contradiction. A contradiction is also expressed with 'John is *elated* that he won the prize, but he is *not* absolutely *certain* he won it,' and also with 'John is *surprised* that the girls ran away, but he *isn't* perfectly *certain* that they did,' and so on. Even if we didn't suspect knowledge, we should now conclude that our listed adjectives require absolute certainty. If they require knowledge too, as they by now surely seem to do, it will not be any easy 'knowledge' but the real thing: knowing with absolute certainty.

An extension of this third test, or, if one likes, a fourth test, is to try the same thing with severe necessary conditions which also are logically sufficient ones. This works well both for our verbs and our adjectives. Thus, the condition we just mentioned, knowing with absolute certainty gives us these contradictions, which confirm our hypotheses: 'Mary *admitted* that the party was boring, but she *didn't know for certain* that it was,' 'John is *surprised* that she behaved so badly, but he *doesn't know with absolute certainty* that she did behave that way,' and so on. In particular, the severe condition of our analysis gives us contradictions, and so it too appears entailed by our simple sentences: 'John was really *delighted* that they returned his wallet, but it *wasn't* absolutely *clear* to him that they did' and 'Mary *regretted* that she behaved badly, even though it *wasn't* perfectly *obvious* to her that she did.' This is pretty impressive confirmation, I submit, for our primary hypotheses about verbs and adjectives. At the same time, we are forced to the idea that, whether or not knowledge is required, these adjectives and verbs here require things to be absolutely clear to their subjects. All of these points will be highlighted when, in section 11, we draw out the consequences of our linguistic study for both epistemology and the philosophy of mind. For now, we may stick to this study and note that this last is at least the third intuitive test which converges on our hypothesized result: In our simple sentences, our many listed adjectives all do indeed require so much as knowledge on the part of the being or subject.

In looking for adjectives which entail ignorance, or a lack of knowledge for our subject, we should not expect much if our experience with verbs is much of a guide. For the only spotted verbs which yielded ignorance, and so satisfied the first verbal hypothesis through its second clause, were 'forgets' and, at least in one sense, 'guessed'. I should think that there must be several more verbs which entail both truth and igmorance, but, still, my experience indicates that there probably aren't very many in all. With adjectives, I find the field here still more barren. The only adjective which, so far as I can see, clearly fits our form and yields both truth and ignorance is 'unaware'. Thus, 'John is unaware that Mary was home' entails, with tolerable clarity, both 'Mary was home' and 'John does not know that Mary was home.'

Matters are worse with other adjectives which one might suspect of doing the same thing. They generally fail to give us examples that are even tolerably clear. Thus, our favoured word, 'ignorant', and 'oblivious', for example, cannot fit in the simple sentences we require. The string *'John is ignorant that Mary came' is not an English sentence. To get one from it, we must interpose some extra words between our adjective and its completing clause: for example, 'John is ignorant *of the fact* that Mary came.' Or else, we must do something else which complicates: 'Mary is ignorant *as to whether* the party was boring.' Thus, our hypothesis about adjectives seems often confirmed through words that yield a positive decision on knowledge while hardly ever confirmed by words which yield a negative decision. So far, at least, this hypothesis seems quite on a par with its parallel for verbs.

§8. *How some Adjectives Disconfirm this First Hypothesis*

From my trials at disconfirmation, I can spot only two adjectives which are clear counter-instances to our first hypothesis. Fortunately, I think, they fall into a natural group, both syntactically and semantically. They are 'lucky' and 'fortunate'; 'unlucky' and 'unfortunate' do not so clearly fit our form. Though 'John is lucky Mary was home' entails 'Mary was home', it entails neither that John knows this to be so nor that he does not. The truth of our original is compatible both with John's knowing the relevant thing and also with his being ignorant of it. It is hard not to notice that these violating adjectives are semantically quite close together while being rather far removed from any on the list that confirm the hypothesis. The syntactic difference of the groups is only a little harder to appreciate. Syntactically, 'John is lucky that Mary was home' is closely related to the (virtually) equivalent sentence 'The fact that Mary was home is lucky for John.' Indeed, there might well be a good point to saying that, in some sense, the former is derived from the latter. But, when we try to take our being's name out of subject position with any word from our confirming group, and try to do this in a parallel way, we get strikingly bad results. Thus, 'John is angry Mary was home' goes into nothing like *'The fact that Mary was home is angry for (of, with) John.' So, only with our disconfirming adjectives do we have a case where they do not require, in their central sense, a being as their subject. Indeed, their primary subject, so to speak, seems to be some fact, or factive expression. Still, sticking to our quite precisely defined forms, we must allow that they are counter-examples to our hypothesis. What we can say, though, is that, as their deviation gets an explanation which relates well to the hypothesis, they are not *damaging* counter-instances. Just as our first hypothesis for verbs served as a governing paradigm for that part of speech, so our first adjectival hypothesis gives a paradigm for adjectives.

Accordingly, even where disconfirmation strikes, we have a parallel with our verbs. For, the counter-instances to our first verbal hypothesis came with this semantically and syntactically related group of verbs: 'proves', 'demonstrates', 'shows', and 'establishes'. Here, we had to allow that these words had a sense where they did not require a being as their subject, but allowed for facts or events (etc.) to start them off. We remember that, in one sense, 'John proved that an infant can grow a foot in a year,' while it entails 'An infant can grow a foot in a year,' entails no relevant knowledge or ignorance on the part of John. But, in precisely such a sense, where it breaks our paradigmatic hypothesis for verbs, 'proves' may take as well a fact or event-like subject. Thus, in this sense, our original goes into or comes from the (virtually) equivalent 'The fact that John grew a foot in a year proved that an infant can grow a foot in a year,' or, equally, 'John's growing a foot in a year proved that an infant can grow a foot in a year.' So, in very much the same way that 'proved' and its fellows violate but provide no damaging counter-instances for our first verbal hypothesis, 'lucky' and its company do so for our first adjectival one. Even where they depart from reality, our hypotheses for verbs and adjectives do so hand in hand, on parallel courses.

Still, these reflections leave us with a definite problem. That problem is of course that of formulating hypotheses which, while much the same in conception as these hypotheses about verbs and adjectives, really do fit the facts, and not just in the way a paradigm 'fits' them. With these original, disconfirmed formulations as our base or springboard, we must try to formulate, both for adjectives and verbs, parallel hypotheses which have no exceptions at all. But, I will postpone this project for just a while, so that we may look at our second hypothesis for adjectives. We want to see its relation to our other hypotheses, and also to the facts in its domain.

§9. *The Absence of Adjectives which Entail Falsity*

We experienced little trouble with our second hypothesis about verbs:

There is no sentence of the form 'S verbs (that) *p*' where the verb ever entails the negation of its completing clause.

So far as our experience with it went, there were no very intuitive, clear counter-instances to it. Any verb which clearly seemed to yield us falsity, seemed just as clearly to require extra words, and so not to be of our simple form. Thus, *'John refuted that all cows chew their cud' and *'John prevented that Mary will get rich,' while comprehensible if uttered, are no sentences of our language. To get sentences, which will indeed entail the negations of these clauses, we need more words than our simple form allows. As we may remember, we will need such more complex sentences as 'John refuted *the statement* that all cows chew their cud' and 'John prevented *it from being the case* that Mary will get rich,' which break our form for containing the words emphasized. To get the entailment to the negation, to falsity, we need extra words to help.

Our parallel hypothesis for adjectives is of course:

There is no sentence of the form 'S is adjective (that)-*p*' where the adjective ever entails the negation of its completing clause.

In so far as this hypothesis holds, we shall be able to say that, in our simple sentences, while many adjectives yield us truth, none of these words yields us falsity. I think that this hypothesis, quite like its parallel for verbs, holds up extremely well.

If any adjectives might be expected to disconfirm our hypothesis, we should expect trouble from such apparently tailor-made words as 'wrong', 'incorrect', and 'mistaken'. But, ?'John is wrong that Mary is coming' is deviant. To return to standard English, we must interpose some extra words, as with 'John is wrong *in thinking* that Mary is coming' or with 'John is wrong *about the fact* that Mary is coming.' The fact that these adjectives demand such extra words may best be viewed as but the other side of a coin whose face is the fact that such adjectives as 'right' and 'correct' also require extra words. Thus, ?'John is correct that Betty went away' is deviant as well. To construct things properly with these adjectives we must interpose the same sort of words that we did on the other side. We then get sentences like 'John is correct *in saying* that Betty went away,' 'John is right *about its being the case* that Betty went away,' and so on. Thus, for the same reasons that 'correct' and company fail to yield truth without deciding knowledge, 'incorrect' and its fellows fail to yield falsity in any case. This evidences both of our hypotheses about adjectives, as well as the closeness of a connection between them.

There are other adjectives which serve to indicate falsity, while saying something more than 'incorrect' and 'wrong'.

Here, we have such verb-derived words as 'deceived', 'confused', 'misinformed', and so on. But with these, as with the words just examined, to get a sentence we need some extra words. Thus, instead of the mere string ?'John was deceived that it was raining,' we must have the sentences 'John was deceived *into thinking* that it was raining,' 'John was deceived *about the fact* that it was raining,' and so on. Indeed, in so far as I can make out, there is no word that provides any clear disconfirmation of our second hypothesis about adjectives. Perhaps some adjectives with a special prefix, like 'mis-', yield counter-instances. This parallels what I allowed might go on with verbs. But, while I am so unfamiliar with 'misbelieves,' that I would not want to judge strings with it to be deviant, at least the candidate adjective 'misinformed' is more familiar to me. And, according to my intuitions, there is deviance in, say, ?'John was misinformed that it was raining.' I judge to be better such longer strings as 'John was misinformed *about whether* it was raining,' and perhaps 'John was misinformed *to the effect* that it was raining.' But even if we allowed some such adjectives as counter-instances, we could say the same about the resulting situation here as we did before with verbs. First, the only candidates that even seem at all promising are special 'manufactured' or compound words. Their variation from the norm is itself (partially) explained in terms of our hypothesis's holding generally, its holding for more 'natural' adjectives. And, second, any counter-instances there may be will be very few as compared with all of the adjectives that fit our simple form. So the hypothesis holds at least very generally. Accordingly, we may be excused, again, I think, if we proceed to reason and write as if, or on the assumption that, our second hypothesis holds without any exceptions at all.

In our previous reasoning, after confirming the two hypotheses for verbs, we argued for the closeness and importance of their connection by noting that any verbs which would still yield the absence of knowledge must then do so for a nontrivial reason. We may make the same argument with respect to our hypotheses about adjectives. First, we have form-fitting adjectives which are enormously close to certain form-fitting verbs: 'fearful' to 'fears', 'hopeful' to 'hoped', 'worried' to 'worries'. Next, we have form-fitting adjectives which relate to other sorts of verbs: 'frightened' to 'frighten', 'terrified' to 'terrify'. Finally, we have at least one that goes closely with no particular verb of any sort: 'afraid'.[7] And, then, unlike all of the foregoing, which do not entail their completing clauses, there is at least 'unaware', which does. Each of these adjectives entails, not only the negation of its knowledge sentence, but also that its subject does not know the opposite either. Thus, if John is really afraid that Betty was there, John does not know *whether* (*or not*) Betty was there. If Betty is hopeful that Paul will come, then it follows that Betty does not know *whether* (*or not*) Paul will come. This is exactly what held for verbs like 'hopes' and 'fears'. In short and in sum: whatever held for verbs, holds as well for adjectives. Our simple sentences show no favourites with any part of speech. Both verbs and adjectives are importantly concerned with knowledge, its presence and its absence.

§10. *Reformulating our First Hypotheses for Verbs and Adjectives*

We may be quite well satisfied with the at least virtually exceptionless character of our second hypotheses for verbs and adjectives, and also with the evidence for their closeness with our first, primary hypotheses. Thus, except for the exceptions to our first hypotheses, like 'proved' and 'lucky', we may be quite well satisfied that we have hit on some generalizations which say a great deal about our language. What we want to do now, then, is to get parallel primary hypotheses for verbs and adjectives which, while having the same basic import as our original formulations, and while connecting just as closely with our second hypotheses, differ from our original formulations by having no exceptions whatsoever, or at least by having such special exceptions, and so few of them, that they can be regarded as being virtually exceptionless. These new formulations, or new hypotheses, for their being without substantial exceptions, will not be instructive in ways that our originals have already been seen to be. For, the ways in which and reasons why 'proved' and 'lucky' deviated from our paradigms taught us something, I think, both about words quite like them as well as about words quite unlike. Perhaps those lessons,

---

[7] Regarding these 'ignorance-entailing' adjectives, I am indebted to discussion with Robert Gordon.

which are of some interest to us in any case, can be applied to help us reformulate and get exceptionless hypotheses.

In every case which went against either of our primary hypotheses, the situation allowed, though of course it did not require, that our subject *not even believe that p*. Regarding such contrary words, it is this important semantic lack which let them take factive subjects. While facts and events cannot so much as believe things, they may be our subjects if not even belief is required. Thus, if John proved that an infant can grow a foot in a year, while it *may* be that John knew this to be so, it *may also* be that John didn't even believe that an infant can do this. Thus also, if John is lucky that Mary was home, while it may be that John knows this, it may also be that he doesn't even believe that she was home. For, no such belief is required for a fact involving John to prove that an infant can do that, or for the fact that Mary was home to be lucky for John. By taking only sentences which entail that their subjects at least believe that *p*, we rule out, quite naturally, any such problem sentences as these. At the same time, requiring this of our subjects will not rule out any of the verbs or adjectives which gave us such satisfaction before, like 'regrets', 'angry', and so on. For if John regrets that he did the deed, as it follows that he knows that he did it, it also follows that he at least believes that he did. And, if John is angry he did it, it similarly follows that John at least believes that he did. Thus, we may first reformulate, as follows, simply adding this extra entailment requirement on our original sentences:

> Whenever a sentence of the form 'S verbs (that) *p*' has the verb entail its completing clause and has it also entail the corresponding sentence of the form 'S at least believes (that) *p*', then either the verb entails its corresponding simple knowledge sentence or else the verb entails the negation of that knowledge sentence.

And, we formulate similarly for sentences with adjectives. These formulations rather strikingly complicate our hypotheses. But, it may be quickly recognized that this second condition in our antecedent rules out the verbs, and any adjective, which made us originally place a second clause in our consequent: If someone really forgot that Mary was home, then it does *not follow* that (at that time) the person at least believed that she was. And, similarly, this does not follow from someone's being unaware that Mary was home. In both cases, the person might not even have any belief in the matter. Thus, for both verbs and adjectives, by adding a new (conjunctive) condition to our antecedent, we may remove a (disjunctive) condition from our consequent. In formal terms at least, *if* we are now formulating hypotheses which are *any* more complex than our original ones, they are not more than a bit more complex. With at least this formal point to content us, we may then state, and try to argue for, our new, at least virtually exceptionless, primary hypotheses for verbs and adjectives:

> Whenever a sentence of the form 'S verbs (that) *p*' has the verb entail its completing clause and has it also entail the corresponding sentence of the form 'S at least believes (that) *p*' then the verb entails its corresponding simple knowledge sentence;

> Whenever a sentence of the form 'S is adjective (that) *p*' has the adjective entail its completing clause and has it also entail the corresponding sentence of the form 'S at least believes (that) *p*', then the adjective entails its corrsponding simple knowledge sentence.

As we remarked in Chapter I, section 5, our added condition is compatible with our subject's actually *knowing* that *p*, which it of course must be if it is to be at all serviceable here. That is why I include the words 'at least' in this formulation; they give us good insurance to that effect. (Philosophers with certain 'reckless' inclinations will drop these words). These newly formulated hypotheses are of course confirmed by a great many verbs and adjectives; all those we listed positively before, in sections 3 and 7. Is there a rationale at work behind these hypotheses, or has our alteration been *ad hoc* despite no loss in (formal) simplicity? There is a rationale: In simple sentences, when our language has a verb, or an adjective, entail both 'truth' and also 'belief', these are *not* two unconnected entailments. What *explains* why the two are so often found together is that, in each of these many cases, there is an entailment to knowledge, to that central, dominant conception.

Our condition picks out an essential feature of the verbs and adjectives which confirmed our originals. This semantic feature is, roughly, that these words talk about a relevant intellectual aspect of the subject. Conversely, verbs and adjectives, like 'proved' and 'lucky', which violate our original formulations can now be seen to have a semantic feature which serves to explain their violation. Whenever they violate, they do *not* talk about any relevant intellectual aspect of the subject. And we remarked, this feature fits well with the way these words allow factive subjects. This feature also fits with the fact that, while, as our second hypotheses state, there are no verbs or adjectives which yield falsity, there are various words of both sorts which yield ignorance, like 'forgets', 'hopes', and 'fearful'. For, about as completely as any sceptical isolationist might ever fear, this feature and this fact conspire to indicate that the concept of knowledge does govern, for verbs and adjectives alike, the syntax and semantics of our simple sentences. Any account of our language which gives no place to the dominance of this concept must be, then, at least rather badly incomplete.

§11. *Some Wages of Ignorance; Their Scope and Substance*

We have conducted a systematic study of one way that the syntax of our verbs and adjectives relates to their semantics. I hope that this is some contribution to the philosophy of language, and even to linguistic study more generally conceived. But the most substantive import of our study is for those common beliefs of ours whose content is supposed to be a primary concern of the philosophy of mind. By connecting our thoughts about knowledge to sentences with so many verbs and adjectives, our study helps to undermine a great deal of our ordinary language and thought. As a small by-product, it helps undermine a great part of two areas of philosophy as they are presently conducted. It helps undermine epistemology, which, as currently conducted, starts with our ordinary thinking to the effect that we know this and that. And, it does much the same for the philosophy of mind, which starts with our ordinary beliefs about our mental and emotional lives, states, and relations. If there is to be much left of either of these fields, it appears that they must begin anew; they must be conducted in quite a different way. Conceptual innovation is what they should provide, not just a charting, however intricate, of our actual, ordinary, but erroneous beliefs.

Our semantic results connect the philosophy of mind with epistemology in two main ways. Both of them concern scepticism about knowledge. Along the lines of the first way, the fact that verbs and adjectives appear to give so many entailments both to one's knowing and also to one's being absolutely certain provides further evidence for the already plausible idea that the former entails the latter. It fits with the more direct evidence of apparent contradictions from sentences like: 'John *knew* that he quit school, but he was *not* completely *certain* that he did.' And, it confirms the results we got before with only a few words, 'regrets' and 'happy' (as in Chapter III, section 2). There are now many more appearances which can most simply be explained by supposing the entailment from knowing to being absolutely certain. This one supposition unifies the phenomena and accounts for it all. Our basis of linguistic evidence is now not only much wider; it is systematically connected. And, so, it is far more difficult to suspect, much less to deny. By evidencing in this way the connection between knowing and being absolutely certain, our semantic results at least strengthen our case, presented in Chapter II, for the proposition that people know at most hardly anything to be so. In that it thus helps further scepticism about knowledge, our study uses materials of the philosophy of mind to help bear on a main epistemological question. The same points apply in like manner to the results we obtain in testing the condition of our analysis. All of our entailing words, verbs and adjectives, give sentences which entail that p is (absolutely) *clear* to S. As we have already agreed, they also entail knowing. Again the simplest explanation is that there are not unrelated entailments here. And, given the data we displayed in Chapter III, sections 10 and 11, the simplest explanation of these many entailments is this: knowing something and the thing's being clear entail each other. Hence, these results give a broad systematically connected base of confirmation for our analysis of knowing. As this analysis indicates knowing to be impossibly demanding, and serves to support our argument for ignorance, our semantic study thus gives a broad, connected basis for thinking that ignorance is universal, and that it is inevitable or necessary. Accordingly, we may repeat a point just recently made, but now with greater force: By way of our examined semantic relations, a greal deal of material standardly reserved for the philosophy of mind may be seen to point towards a very striking and sweeping epistemological thesis. This is one main way, in the direction of epistemology, that our semantic results connect these two philosophical areas. But perhaps the more striking connection goes in the other direction.

To get the full force of our study for the philosophy of mind, it's best to start with a familiar thought one has from within epistemology. This is the thought of the sceptical isolationist: 'If knowing is so demanding, and thus impossible, what's so important about *knowing* anyway? Even without actually knowing that something is so, I might very firmly and quite reasonably believe that it is. If the thing actually is so, as often happens, then what I believe will be true whether I know the thing or not. And, even without knowing the thing, my belief may be based on very good grounds, the sort for which I would be praised rather than ridiculed. So, even without *knowing* anything, it seems that a man might get on quite well in the world, indeed, at least as well as if he really knew. It should be easy for us, then, to forget about problems with *knowing*.' The obvious force of these reflections makes scepticism about knowledge seem a view without much consequence. Even if scepticism about knowledge is right, the whole issue of knowledge and scepticism appears quite isolated and unimportant. Indeed, the very things which made scepticism seem right, e.g. the requiring of justified absolute certainty, are precisely the things which make it seem so irrelevant to anything else.

If our semantic results about verbs are right, these initially quite plausible reflections must be discarded. Not only will scepticism entail that nobody ever sees or remembers that anything is so, our universal ignorance will also entail that nobody ever admits anything about anything, nor ever regrets anything at all. To get these results mapped out completely, we would have to relate sentences where our studied verbs take other grammatical objects, e.g. gerundial phrases and prepositional phrases, to those where they take a propositional clause. The details look to be intricate and interesting, and difficult problems forestall a comprehensive articulation. But it is quite safe to say, I suggest, that not much truth will be expressed by any sentences with complex objects if none is expressed by those which end in a propositional clause. Thus, if John doesn't really know *that he quit school*, it won't be true that John regrets *having quit school*; if Mary doesn't really know *that John quit school*, it won't be true that Mary remembers *John to have quit school*. Now, it may be that even if one doesn't know anything, one can still notice certain rocks, but one will not notice *anything about* those rocks, e.g. that they are quartz, or that they are chipped. Though certain verbs, like 'notice', 'see', and 'remember', *might* still be correctly applied with relatively simple objects, like 'the rocks', others like 'admit' and 'regret' will never correctly apply in the absence of knowledge, at least not in any relevant sense of these terms. (The relevant sense of 'admit' here is opposite to 'conceal' not to 'turn away'.) If John admits his guilt, then he must admit that he is or was guilty; if he regrets his behaviour, he must regret that. . . he behaved—. And, whenever it might be true that John admits the rocks, it must be true that John admits that . . . the rocks—; if John regrets the rocks, John must regret that . . . the rocks—. If these last are true, it will follow that John knows that . . . he behaved—, or that . . . the rocks—. So, just as universal ignorance will entail that nobody ever sees, or remembers, or notices anything *about anything*, it will entail that nobody ever admits or regrets anything *at all*.

If our results concerning propositional adjectives are right, the wages of ignorance are even more striking. For, if nobody ever really knows anything, then nobody will ever be angry, or happy, or surprised about anything. Though the details are again hard to articulate comprehensively, we may put the point generally for adjectives by saying that if no sentences of the form 'S is adjective (that) *p*' are true, then at most very few of the form 'S is adjective PP' will be true either (where the letters 'PP' stand for any prepositional phrase which will be the complement of the adjective). Thus, not only will nobody ever be angry *about* anything, nobody will ever be angry *at* anybody, or angry *with* anybody, and so on, unless scepticism is wrong. Not only will nobody ever be amazed *about* anything, nobody will ever be amazed *by* anything, *at* anything, and so on.

Now, with some of these adjectives, it is pretty plausible to suppose that they may be applied correctly, even if they never get a completing prepositional phrase. Thus, it's pretty plausible to think that one might be happy, and perhaps even angry, even if one is never happy or angry about anything, or with anybody, and so on. It isn't completely clear that this is possible, but it's pretty plausible to think it might be. But with other adjectives it's not so plausible. Thus, if nobody is ever amazed about anything, or by anything, and so on, it's hard to see how anybody could ever be amazed *at all*. If this strong conclusion holds, and if there is universal ignorance, then nobody *is* ever amazed. At least in their central senses, such conclusions seem to hold for a substantial group of adjectives which are verb-derived, ending in '-ed', not only 'amazed', but 'astonished', 'impressed', 'embarrassed', 'disappointed', and so on. With other adjectives of this type, results are less clear: 'depressed', 'elated', etc. Passing to the more 'independent' adjectives, we may still surmise, I suggest, that, just maybe, nobody is ever actually happy or unhappy either.

In connection with our distinction between absolute and relative terms, these remarks relate back to some we made in Chapter II, section 2. We said there that certain adjectives which looked to be relative terms turned out, on examination, to be *defined* absolute terms, either in certain linguistic contexts or, perhaps, even in all. If they work that way in all contexts, then of course they will be defined absolutes pure and simple. We may now appreciate more clearly how great is the scope of these remarks. Most, if not all, of our adjectives which entail knowing look to be relative terms: If Mary is very disappointed, she is just that; she is not very nearly disappointed; if she is rather happy with her work, it hardly follows that she is rather close to being happy with it. And, if she is not as pleased by their gift as by the fact that they thought of her, it is not even allowed that she might be closer to being pleased by that fact. So, if we judge by our first intuitions, as well as by our syntactico-semantic tests, these words are as clearly relative, in any context one chooses, as any words one ever might examine. Once we see, however, that, in these contexts at least, these terms all require the application of 'know', as well as that of the more perspicuously absolute terms 'certain' and 'clear', the thought of their being relative, in these contexts at least, quite shortly is undermined. And, in so far as we may surmise that the same holds for other contexts, these adjectives, despite their initial appearances to the contrary, must be accepted as defined absolutes pure and simple. (This is not to say that a word like 'disappointed' has no relative criteria. Along some dimension of its application, it does. But, if knowing is always required for it, facts about any such other dimension will never have a chance to bear on reality.) Accordingly, the idea of absolute terms permeates our language and thought at least very extensively; how extensively, is a matter for much further analysis and exploration. Moving back to the material mode, even in advance of this exploration, we may be rather confident about at least this much: if nobody knows anything to be so, nobody can ever be happy or unhappy about anything, or proud of anything, disappointed with it, pleased by it, and so on. For more conservative sceptics, other, more particular consequences lie in store: if nobody ever knows anything about anyone else, then nobody can ever be sad or glad about anyone else's successes or failures, and so on, and so on.

These claims are quite enormous. At least two sorts of negative reactions to them are likely. First, one might just turn around and say, 'Well, if scepticism requires this much, it can't *possibly* be right. In effect, you've just given a convincing argument against scepticism.' While this response would have some plausibility in most conversational contexts, at this point in the present work it begins to smack of dogmatism. It is hard to think that the sorts of considerations we have just drawn out really make the case against scepticism. Further, *even if knowledge doesn't* require absolute certainty or any absolute, and *even if* we do *know* a fair amount, *these propositional verbs and adjectives do seem to require absolute certainty anyway.* And, even if knowing isn't so hard to come by, being absolutely certain seems to be rather rare indeed. If this last is right, then, as all sorts of evidence conspires to suggest, we won't be happy, or angry, or embarrassed about very much even if we were to know. And, scepticism about our allegedly widespread absolute certainty is not easy to debunk. It's not easy, that is, to take seriously the response, 'Well, you've just given a convincing argument to show that we must be absolutely certain about all sorts of things!'

This rejoinder of ours takes on even more bite when we remember that the same points apply to the condition of our analysis. Even if they know, our results indicate, people won't be *happy* their friends are succeeding *unless* it is absolutely *clear* to them that their friends are. It is, we recall, inconsistent to say, 'He really was *happy* that Charles was succeeding, but it *wasn't* absolutely *clear* to him that Charles was.' But how much is really absolutely clear to anyone? Given what we have uncovered about this absolute justifying term, it seems that nothing is. Hence, even if knowing were not an absolute, and people knew a lot about their friends, no one could ever be happy or sad about them, or about anything for that matter. The enormity of these wages won't shrink one bit, it appears, even if we (wrongly) give back the idea that people have knowledge. There seems, then, especially little to favour anyone's claim to know, to favour our first sort of negative reaction.

The other reaction is to deny that any of our claimed entailments hold, except perhaps the relatively unobjectionable ones claimed in our antecedents. It was largely to forestall such a reaction that we sought exceptionless, integrated hypotheses about our language. A few stray intuitions might be brushed aside; perhaps they could be easily ignored by a sceptic who wished to think his commitments slight. But when integrated hypotheses bring together, and account for, a great many linguistic intuitions, each particular intuition cannot be so easily dismissed. At such a point, it is better to suppose, I think, that our concepts of knowledge and certainty are not isolated freaks. Considering the scope of our semantic results, it is now best to suppose this *whether or not* knowledge and certainty turn out to be impossibly demanding conceptions. This means that we are not well advised to suppose any more that they must be either isolated or else easily satisfied. So, neither sort of likely reaction to our sceptical conclusions will get us any way out. These wages of ignorance look to be what must be had. They are a legacy of our having the concept of knowledge, and of having a language in which that concept is so central.

§12. *A Problem of what to Say and Think*

Once we give up the possibility of correctly applying our simple entailing sentences, as we have argued we must do, we are left with depleted resources for talking and thinking about people, many of their emotional relations, and many of their other 'mental' relations as well. An example can start to make this acute problem tolerably clear. Suppose that Mary was fearful that they would not arrive, having heard that a storm was brewing. However, they did arrive. There was a smile on Mary's face, and good feeling ran through her. We might naturally say right after this that Mary was happy that they arrived. In this way, if all went well, we would purport to express Mary's 'emotional relation' towards the relevant thing here. We would say not only what made Mary happy here but what she was happy *about*. We now realize, however, that we can't truly say that Mary was happy that they arrived. For the truth of such a statement requires that Mary knows them to have arrived, and our ignorance means that this is impossible. What we would like to do now is roughly this: To say consistently all of what is expressed by 'Mary was happy that they arrived' without expressing, or minus, what is expressed by 'Mary knew that they arrived.' But, how do we eliminate the culprit without losing a lot more as well? There is a problem here (which we already indicated in section 7). This problem may appear trivial or at least easily solvable. But given our present linguistic resources, it is, I suggest, actually insuperable. We will now try to solve this problem if only to appreciate its difficulty, its seriousness, and its scope.

In trying to express as much content as we feel we want, one thing we might say is this: 'Mary was happy because she correctly believed that they arrived.' Granting (the at least somewhat doubtful idea) that Mary's being happy need not entail her knowing anything to be so, this might very well express a proposition about Mary at that time which was true. In that case, this sentence is, in some sense, along the right track, or a right track. But though we now have one thing which is true, and which would be true if, *per impossibile*, Mary was happy that they arrived, it is a thing which gives us at best a small part of the picture. Suppose that Mary was happy on all those occasions when she had correct beliefs to the effect that certain people arrived, but was only occasionally happy when such beliefs were not correct. Bizarrely, we may suppose this to come about by the works of an eccentric deity who can tell what her beliefs are and when they are correct. When Mary has a correct belief of the appropriate content, the deity causes certain brain-activity in her which naturally results in feelings of happiness on her part. Otherwise, he doesn't bother to intervene, and these feelings do not so regularly occur. It seems to me that this is a fairly clear case of Mary's being happy because she correctly believed that they arrived. Yet, it doesn't display very much of what goes on in situations where we would say 'Mary was happy that they arrived,' taking ourselves, erroneously, to speak the truth. It is compatible with this case that Mary not even approximate well a person who would be, *per impossibile*, happy *about* their having arrived. Indeed, in this presented case, it is far from clear that, though happy, Mary is happy about anything at all.

If we could use an appropriately placed 'about', as in 'Mary was happy about their having arrived', we could take a long step towards having solved our problem. Even so, we might still want to speak more specifically. For perhaps Mary could be happy about their having arrived in being happy that their having arrived was so well publicized by her broadcasting company. And, thus, it might be that Mary was happy about this event without being at all happy that they arrived. But, in any case, we have already seen that Mary can't be happy about anything (X), without her being happy that something is so (that . . . X—). So, as welcome as it might possibly be, no available locution with an appropriate 'about' seems likely ever to be of any assistance.

While it doesn't do enough for us, it is obvious that the 'because' in 'She was happy because she correctly believed that they arrived' can't just be taking the place of a complementary 'that'. But we don't get what we want by substituting the latter for the former: 'She was happy that she correctly believed that they arrived.' In the first place, this sentence, to be true, requires Mary to know at least as much as our original, 'She was happy that they arrived.' For she must now know that she *correctly* believes *that they arrived*. So, this sentence can't be true, as even a conservative sceptic would agree. Secondly, even if true, this sentence does not express the appropriate content. What it tells us about is not a Mary who is happy about something concerning others, but a Mary who is happy about her own 'state of mind', and her achievement thereof, in particular, about the correctness of a certain belief of hers. The positive part of this description may be a bit crude, but the point is clear enough. If we drop the 'correctly' from our sentence with 'that', then, for a conservative sceptic at least, we solve the first problem: 'She was happy that she believed that they arrived.' Such a sceptic will allow that Mary may know about her own beliefs, anyway, though our argument for universal ignorance renders even this hard to accept. Much as before, however, even if this sentence is true, its content is far from what we want. It talks of a Mary whose primary feeling here does not importantly concern others. She is now not involved with her belief's correctness, but she is too much involved with its mere existence. If this content is all that holds of Mary, we have no Mary whose feelings are related to others in anything like the ways we commonly suppose our own feelings to be.

Having looked at some of the more straightforward sorts of locutions available, we may also look at some of those which are, if not more idiomatic, at least more roundabout or in-direct. For example, we may consider the parenthetical sentence: 'She was happy, as she correctly believed (or thought), that they arrived.' But this sentence entails: 'As she correctly believed (or thought), she was happy that they arrived.' And this entails: 'She correctly believed (or thought) that she was happy that they arrived.' But, this entails 'She was happy that they arrived,' and that is our problem in the first place. Now, this fatal entailment can be avoided if the adverb 'correctly' is left out at the start: 'She was happy, as she believed (or thought), that they arrived.' This sentence has, it appears, two interpretations. On one, it means the same as 'Just as she believed (or thought), she was happy that they arrived.' This is of course no good, since it gets us our problem entailment all over again. On the other, the sentence means, near enough, 'According to what she believed (or thought), she was happy that they arrived.' But this means little different from 'She believed (or thought) that she was happy that they arrived.' While this last avoids our problem entailment, it does so at the cost of having no content even remotely like what we want. She might have believed this without being happy at all, or while being happy about something else entirely, and so on.

Accordingly, with this parenthetical device, either we get our problems back or else we get very little.[8]

We need not, of course, resort to any parenthetical devices to get belief or thought in the picture. But, how much can we make of thought or belief in any case, given the limits of our available English locutions? We may consider the sentence 'She was happy in the belief (or at the thought) that they arrived,' but this holds true even if they never arrived. And, we want her happiness to be suitably connected with the arriving of those others. If we put 'correct' in, we get the entailment to their having arrived: 'She was happy in the correct belief (or at the correct thought) that they arrived.' But, so far as this sentence goes, her happiness may have no actual connection with their having arrived. The entailment to the fact of their arriving from 'She was happy that they arrived' may be viewed as a consequence of the sentence expressing a relation or connection between her happiness and their arriving, which connection is essential to saying what Mary is happy about. In the present case, in contrast, the addition of 'correct' secures the entailment to that fact, but the fact is left unconnected. What we want is to talk about people's feelings being related to various things, often things 'going on outside of them'.

A dramatic way of seeing the inadequacy of this sentence comes from our musings about electrodes. Suppose, again, that all of your experience is the result of electrical patterns impinging on your brain in certain ways through implanted electrodes, those electrodes being hooked up to a computer which may (or may not) in turn be operated by an evil scientist. We may suppose that the experience it or he induces naturally leads you to the belief or to the thought that there are many kind and generous people in the world and that, believing or thinking this, you become 'appropriately' happy. You are happy in the belief, or at the thought, that there are many kind and generous people in the world. But you are nowhere near being happy that there are such people. Even if there are many such people,

[8] This parenthetical sentence was suggested to me by Gerald A. Cohen. Something which is suggested by this parenthetical sentence, but which doesn't look to be an interpretation of it is this: 'She was happy. As she believed, she was happy that they arrived.' As the latter part is (virtually) equivalent to one or another of our previously exhibited interpretations, this suggested discourse means hardly any advance.

and so, even if you may be happy in a correct belief, or at a correct thought, you will have no appropriate contact with them. So your happiness here is unconnected with the world. Now, even if such unconnected happiness is better than any misery, it does not seem a fully satisfactory happiness. Rightly or not, you want more than this. At least some of your happiness, you feel, should be related to things 'outside of yourself' in ways in which this happiness so definitely and dramatically is not. But how are we to describe in any detail the situation which you would prefer to obtain, the one which seems so much more satisfactory than this artificial one? Dramatically put, this is our problem all over again. While I have not canvassed all of the resources of our language, the data point to a tentative conclusion: English, perhaps like other languages, provides no consistent way for us to describe the emotional situations we feel to be most satisfactory.

Now, part of our problem occurs even if we ignore scepticism and even if we avoid any fine questions about knowledge. In everyday life, we often make mistakes about the facts. Thus, if on hearing that they arrived, Mary is happy, we may say, shortly thereafter, 'She was happy that they arrived.' We say this on the assumption that we all know that they arrived, Mary included. But it may well develop later that Mary only heard a *false* report to the effect that they arrived, and that they never did arrive. What do we say, now, about Mary's emotional situation at that past time? We can no longer allow that she was happy they arrived, since they never arrived. We might try some of the locutions previously canvassed. But, even though certain problems are absent in this case—there is no problem of being appropriately connected to a certain fact, for there is no such fact—an intuitively adequate description is hard to come by. A remaining problem goes like this: If she was just happy in the belief that they arrived, she might well be a person whose happiness was based on delusionary thinking, and who had no real concern for others and their safety. We want to characterize an emotional situation quite different from this, and to do so clearly and adequately. But, just as happened so dramatically in the cases endangered by scepticism, we don't seem to have the resources available. Our lack of linguistic resources means an everyday problem for us, *whether or not*

scepticism is any problem. This everyday problem is little recognized by us, even in philosophy and certainly in everyday
affairs and conversations. Why is it so little recognized? The
answer is, I think, this: Our way of thinking about our feelings
discounts those that are not appropriately connected with, or
based in, reality, at least if they are of the sort, like happiness
but perhaps not hopefulness, which are 'supposed to be based
in reality'. I think that this way of thinking, which makes the
artificially induced emotions of the electrode patient seem so
glaringly unsatisfactory, is culturally inherited. If these thoughts
are on the right track, then we may perhaps accept a conjecture
which would explain, though not answer, all of these problems
and questions.

The conjecture goes like this. Those who developed our language, or who developed its main ancestor(s), may well have
thought as follows. Feelings which are not based in reality are
not worthy of our aspirations, they can contribute little or
nothing towards a good life. Feelings which are based in
reality are what we should seek to arouse and maintain, in
others as well as in ourselves. And our 'negative' feelings will be
talked of in ways following the worthwhile 'positive' ones. Such
a great premium might thus be placed on thinking about positive feelings which are based in reality that other emotional
and mental situations might be thought not very important to
describe adequately. Thus, no adequate resources were developed for that purpose. That is why we have the everyday
problem; the problem of the thing's turning out to be false.
The sceptical problem, as a wholesale difficulty, comes with the
absence of knowledge, the absence of the presumed basis for
those feelings which would be part of a satisfactory life. We may
rehearse this in terms of our semantic study. Entailing sentences
of our simple forms were designed to express just these feelings,
and just such mental states or relations of other sorts as were
similarly well based. Other adequate locutions were systematically connected to these through a network of entailment relations. There being nothing else developed here for us to do
anything much like the same, we now have nothing adequate
to say or think on these matters.

If this is right, or even very nearly so, we might suspect that
it is a very difficult task to replace these stretches of language,

which now must go by the board. When trying to do it, we should take care to create connected ways of avoiding our everyday problem. This might be a bonus for completing a task which, so far as our interest in truth goes, the truth of scepticism places before us. How are we *consistently* to express what we might try to express with the inconsistent 'She was happy that they arrived, but she didn't know they arrived'? The work which would answer this question requires insightful innovation. The new locutions, systematically connected in appropriate ways, will be the product of psychological insight, as well as of linguistic dexterity and expertise. Unfortunately for me here, my own talents and inclinations, such as they are, run in other, more negative directions. Accordingly, I leave others with this difficult job, with this perhaps most troubling of these exhibited wages of ignorance. Doing little positive about these problems, I will now try to uncover some other consequences of our ignorance, indeed, some which look to mean at least as much trouble.

V

From Ignorance to Irrationality

SCEPTICISM about knowledge is a thesis which, even in a very strong form, whether or not a totally universal one, many people have found forceful and appealing. We have argued, indeed, at a considerable length, for the universal form of this thesis, for the view that nobody ever knows anything to be so. Prior to our results of the fourth chapter, at least, I suspect that quite a few people would have found our arguments quite convincing. Indeed, even now, after encountering the substantial consequences that our fourth chapter brings to light, I have some expectation that quite a few of these still agree with me that scepticism about knowledge is to be accepted. A main thought behind my expectation is this: Just as I once did, others may have the idea that people may be *reasonable* and *justified* in various things; in particular, in believing various things to be so. One of these believed things might even be the universal thesis of scepticism about knowledge or, what amounts to the same, the proposition that we are inevitably and universally ignorant.

If your thoughts run along these lines, as mine at one time did, then you are involved in a natural retreat from the battleground of argument concerning scepticism about knowledge. One who takes this course of retreat will distinguish between two types of scepticism. Scepticism about knowledge, whether in a universal form or in some weaker one, is only a first type of scepticism. A second type of scepticism, which may also be advanced universally or in a weaker form, is scepticism about being reasonable and justified. The latter view may be conveniently distinguished by the expression 'scepticism about rationality'. At least on the face of it, scepticism about rationality seems logically independent of scepticism about knowledge. It seems that universal scepticism about knowledge will not entail any significant scepticism about rationality.

ICS—H

As I have so recently said or implied, on my becoming more convinced of the truth of scepticism about knowledge, I tried the retreat to the position that at least people are reasonable and justified in all sorts of things. But in this chapter, I will argue that this retreat is impossible. I will argue that universal scepticism of the first type logically entails universal scepticism of the second: If it is true that nobody ever knows anything to be so, then it follows that it is also true that nobody is ever (even the least bit) reasonable or justified in anything, in particular, in believing anything to be so.[1] I shall also argue, later on, in section 7 and following, that a partial but strong form of scepticism about knowledge entails a form of scepticism about rationality which is almost as strong. Somewhat roughly put, this latter is the idea that if in the case of every person there is at most hardly anything that he knows to be so, then in every case there is not much more than hardly anything in which the person is (even the least bit) reasonable or justified. This is done mainly for the benefit of any conservative sceptics about knowledge.

As I have previously argued that there is so little, if anything, which anybody knows, I must end by taking any present argument as motivating more than just the conditional proposition

---

[1] I think that this agrees with one of Descartes' leading ideas. But many contemporary philosophers take a line which is against this one. In contemporary writings, philosophers usually talk about things being certain or only being probable rather than of people knowing those things or only being reasonable in believing them. If the issue fundamentally concerns people, as I think it does, then such statements as these directly conflict with our Cartesian line: 'Thus, if my reasoning is sound, it is at least misleading to say that unless something is certain nothing can even be probable'—A. J. Ayer, 'Basic Propositions', in Max Black, ed., *Philosophical Analysis* (Englewood Cliffs, N.J., 1963), p. 70. 'Whether any degree of doubtfulness attaches to the least dubitable of our beliefs is a question with which we need not at present concern ourselves; it is enough that any proposition concerning which we have rational grounds for some degree of belief or disbelief can, in theory, be placed in a scale between certain truth and certain falsehood. Whether these limits are themselves to be included we may leave an open question'—Bertrand Russell, *Human Knowledge* (New York, 1964), p. 381. On the Cartesian side, we find few contemporary figures, but here is a statement which does favour our position: 'It is true that in order that the difficulties posed by scepticism be met, it is essential that there be *some* knowledge which is more than probable, and that such knowledge be pertinent to nature and experience'— C. I. Lewis, *Mind and the World Order* (New York, 1956), p. 311. (The italics here are Lewis's.) While the wording differs from case to case, it seems that, in epistemology, almost every philosopher of any ambition has expressed an opinion on this important issue.

which links the two types of scepticism. I might respond, of course, by giving up scepticism about knowledge. But I do not think that this is the only possible response, nor even the one which all the arguments of our essay, taken together, most strongly motivate. Of course, there seems to be a paradox in accepting all these arguments. For, even from our conservative sceptic's point of view, they have it that there is at most very little in which one will be justified or reasonable, and they strongly suggest that, in particular, one will never be justified or reasonable in accepting those arguments themselves. This is quite disconcerting. But, on reflection, I think that there really is no paradox here. The arguments may be sound and effectively forceful—one who considers them may be brought to believe what is *true*. If he cannot be *reasonable* or *justified* in believing what is true, that may be only because the ideas of *being reasonable* and *being justified* are so impossibly demanding. This need not reflect badly on my arguments; rather, that will be their whole point. To stress what's relevant, we may say that it's misleading to remark, 'One will not be reasonable or justified in accepting *those arguments*.' One puts the pressure where the culprits lie by remarking, 'One will not be *reasonable* or *justified* in accepting those arguments.'

§1. *The Basis in Knowledge Argument; Being Reasonable*

In the case of at least almost any argument, however it is presented, you can then go on to argue for or against its premises. I will begin to link our scepticisms by putting forth the premisses of what I call the Basis in Knowledge Argument (for Scepticism About Rationality) or, for short, the Basis Argument. I do this so that I may validly deduce my linking conclusion from these premisses. Actually, I will present two parallel arguments of the same form, calling each of them the Basis Argument. This is just for convenience. I will first present the argument for the linking conclusion that if nobody ever knows anything to be so, then nobody is ever *reasonable* in anything. Later on, I will consider a parallel argument for the parallel conclusion about the necessity of knowing for anyone to be *justified* in anything. First, concerning being reasonable, there are three premisses of my Basis Argument.

The first premiss of this argument is the proposition:

(1) If someone S is (even the least bit) *reasonable* in something X, then there is something which is *S's reason* for X or there are some things which are *S's reasons* for X.

For example, if Ralph is reasonable in thinking that it was raining, then there is something which is Ralph's reason for thinking that it was or else there are some things which are his reasons for thinking it was raining. If he is reasonable in running to the store, then something must be his reason for that or else some things must be Ralph's reasons for running there. If nothing is his reason for it and no things are his reasons, then Ralph is not reasonable in running to the store.

My second premiss is the proposition:

(2) If there is something which is *S's reason* for something X, then there is some propositional value of '*p*' such that S's reason *is that p* and if there are some things which are *S's reasons* for X, then there are some propositional values of '*p*' and '*q*' and so on such that S's reasons *are that p and that q* and so on.

For example, if there is something which is Ralph's reason for thinking it was raining, then there is some propositional value of '*p*' such that Ralph's reason is that *p*, e.g. that *Fred's hat was wet*. And, if there are some things which are Ralph's reasons for running to the store, then they must be that *p* and that *q* and so on, e.g. that *he needs milk* and that *the store will close at six* and so on.

The third and final premiss of this argument is the proposition:

(3) If S's reason (for something X) *is that p*, then S *knows* that *p*; and if S's reasons (for X) *are that p and that q* and so on, then S *knows* that *p* and S *knows* that *q* and so on.

For example, if Ralph's reason (for running to the store) is that the store will close in twenty minutes, then Ralph *knows* that it will close in twenty minutes. If, on the other hand, his reasons are this first and also that he needs milk, then he knows that the store will close then and he *also knows* that he needs milk. And, if Ralph's reason (for thinking that it was raining) is that Fred's hat was wet, then Ralph *knows* that Fred's hat was wet.

These three premisses let us deduce the conclusion:

(4) If someone S is (even the least bit) *reasonable* in something X, then there is some propositional value of '*p*' such that S *knows* that *p*.

For, if someone knows that *p* and knows that *q* and so on, then it follows that, in particular, he knows that *p*. Even if not most explicitly, and even if in schematic form, this conclusion serves to express our idea of sceptical linking. And, the completely explicit and universal statement we want is scarcely far to seek.

It is quite clear that our argument will not depend on which people or things (or propositions) we choose and that, in any case, it proceeds in a way which may be generalized. This allows us to frame in English the universal conditional: If anybody is (even the least bit) *reasonable* in anything, then he or she *knows* something to be so. So far as being reasonable goes, this is the conditional which, when contraposed, states most explicitly the connection between the universal forms of our two types of scepticism: If nobody knows anything to be so, then nobody is (even the least bit) reasonable in anything. And, of course, from this the more particular connection, aimed epistemologically, trivially follows: If nobody knows anything to be so, then nobody is (even the least bit) reasonable in believing anything to be so. This is my Basis Argument. In effect, what this argument says is that someone's being reasonable (in something) must find a basis in some knowledge which that person has, in something which he knows to be so. If there is no such basis to be had, as we have argued at length in Chapter III, then the person can't possibly be reasonable in anything. That is why I call this argument my Basis in Knowledge Argument (for Scepticism About Rationality). The philosophical interest in this argument lies, of course, in its three premisses, for the argument is deductively valid. I shall try to defend these premisses, each in turn, so that the import of each is not misunderstood.

§2. *The First Premiss: The Step from one's Being Reasonable to one's Reason or Reasons*

To begin my argument, I claim that (1) if someone S is (even the least bit) reasonable in something X, then there must be

something which is S's reason for X or else there must be some
things which are S's reasons for X. The consequent of this
conditional is a disjunction between S's reason and S's reasons.
One might think this a needless complication, but I think that
we must make room for both the singular and the plural alternatives. The possessive form indicates uniqueness, at least relative to the context at hand and perhaps even universally. Thus,
if S has more than one house, there is nothing which is S's
house. Rather, there are things which are S's houses, and each
of them is *one of S's* houses. Neutrally, whether S has only one
house or more, any will be *a house of S's.* The point is of course
quite general. In the present case, we must consider the fact
that we often say that a number of things are someone's
reasons for something. If what we say is correct, then there
is nothing which is the person's reason for the thing; each
of the things is but one of his reasons for it. One might think
that his reasons might be viewed as conjoining to form one
big reason. But, this can't be. For if there is *one* big reason
here, then *it is his reason*, and then those others can't be the
person's *reasons*. Thus, wanting to focus on the singular construction, but needing to allow truth in our talk of people's
reasons, we must advance the disjunction of both the singular and the plural alternatives. A small fact of our language
requires a small complication in stating our first premiss. But,
what of the substance of this premiss?

Our premiss asserts only that whenever one is reasonable (in
something) there is *something* which is one's reason, or *some* things
which are one's reasons. It does not say anything about what
these might be. And, of course, it allows that this or these might
be different for different people and different situations. Now,
someone's reason for something might be quite different from
what anyone might suppose, including the subject himself; or
at least this premiss allows for this to be so. Suppose that a
foreigner wanted to know what word we use for referring to
toothbrushes. He holds up one and asks 'What is this?' You
say, 'It is a toothbrush.' What is your reason for saying this,
or your reasons for it? Perhaps you thought that he wanted to
know what toothbrushes were called, and you wanted to be
helpful to the foreigner. Now, if you were right about what he
wanted, that is, if he did want to know what they were called,

then your reasons might be these: that he wanted to know what we call toothbrushes, and that you wanted to be helpful. If you were wrong, however, about what he wanted, and all he wanted was for you to explain why your dirty toothbrush was on his new dresser, it is not so clear what your reason was, or reasons were. Perhaps, a reason of yours was, still, that you wanted to be helpful. This is somewhat plausible. Perhaps, a reason of yours was that *you thought* that he wanted to know what they were called. This is a bit less plausible. Why does the fact that *you thought* something to be so mean any reason here for *anyone*, let alone for you, to say anything to this foreigner, much less to say 'It is a toothbrush?' Of course so far as our premiss goes, your reason for saying the thing *might* be that you like tuna fish, or it even *might* be that China is the most populous country. Still, the *plausibility* of the premiss depends on our being able to pick out plausible reasons for any cases where, going by appearances anyway, someone is reasonable in something. In the present case, if you were wrong about what the foreigner wanted, the most plausible alternative seems this: There *was no reason* for you to say 'It is a toothbrush'; hence, you *had no reason* to say it; hence, *nothing* here was *a reason of yours* for that; and hence, finally, you were not (even the least bit) *reasonable* in saying that thing at that time. In any case, our intuitions about people's being reasonable and there being people's reasons emerge and disappear together. Taking any case, and viewing it in any way, we find them joined.

These intuitions and the truth of our premiss may both be lost if one wavers from the locution with 'reasonable' that our premiss in fact employs. It is crucial to our premiss that it gives a condition for *someone's* being reasonable in something. It is the person himself that the premiss focuses on. Thus the premiss allows that *what someone says* may be reasonable even if nothing is his reason for saying the thing, and no things are his reasons for it. And, the premiss also allows that it may be that *what someone does* in saying a certain thing may be reasonable even if the person has no reason at all for saying the thing. All sorts of *things* might be reasonable; but *the person himself* will not be reasonable *in anything* unless there is something which is his reason or some things which are his reasons for whatever is at hand. This is the reason that the sentence, '*What he believes* is *reasonable*, but *he* has *no reason at all* for believing it,' sounds and actually is quite *consistent*. It is also why it sounds and actually is *inconsistent* to say, '*He* is *reasonable* in believing that, but *he* has *no reason at all* for believing it.'

Finally, though it is a rather simple and obvious matter, one should not confuse being reasonable with *not* being *unreasonable*. The former quite clearly implies the latter, but the converse may well not hold. Thus, if *it is perfectly* all right for someone to run to the store, that may imply that it *is not unreasonable for* him to run there and that, if he does run there, *he is not unreasonable* in running to the store. All of this might be if, say, the matter is so indifferent or unproblematic that no reason is needed on the person's part for it to be perfectly all right for him to run to the store. In such a case, though, supposing that the person has no reason here, he will not be *reasonable* in running to the store. There are many locutions which do *not* imply that there is anything that is the subject's reason or any things that are his reasons. But, then, none of them imply that the subject is (even the least bit) *reasonable* in anything. Because one may be confused by or about these locutions, one may object to our first premiss. But it seems that there is no valid objection to it. If the Basis Argument is to be stopped, it must be further along the line.

§3. *The Second Premiss: The Step from one's Reason or Reasons to the Propositional Specificity of these things*

I want to end this argument in the idea that if someone is reasonable in anything, he must know *that something is so*. To this end, we employ the premiss: (2) If something is S's reason for something X, then there is some propositional value of 'p' such that S's reason is that p, and if some things are S's reasons for X, then there are propositional values of 'p' and 'q' and so on such that S's reasons are that p and that q and so on. What this premiss does is to line up one's reason or reasons in a way where they are propositionally specific. In this way, they can line up with what is known when one knows that something is so. Now, so far as this premiss goes, one's reasons may or may not actually be the same things as certain things which one knows to be so. For example, what are known might be true *propositions* and one's reasons might be parallel *facts*, even if such facts and propositions are distinct. But, that they be the same things is not the point. The point is this: as long as at least a parallel may be established between any of one's reasons and things which one might know to be so, that will be enough to set the stage for the next step of this Basis Argument.[2]

In saying that reasons are propositionally specific, we are recognizing them to be on a par with beliefs at least in this one respect. But they are equally on a par with less familiar items for philosophical contemplation in this regard: arguments, excuses, objections, discoveries, and so on. In parallel with what we said about reasons, we may say about arguments: If there is something which is S's argument (for something X), then there is some propositional value of 'p' such that S's argument is that p. For example, if something is Arthur's argument (for not building the Dinobomber), then his argument is that p, say, that the Dinobomber will soon be obsolete. Similarly, if there is something which is Oscar's objection (to Arthur's argument), then Oscar's objection is that q, say, that that argument does not consider the jobs of the bomber builders.

In certain cases, language may not be rich enough to specify reasons—or for that matter anything else—in any interesting way. But, we can generally indicate the way in which things are propositionally specific anyhow. Thus, there may be little to be said about this, that, and the other which we can rightly say. We may then, in order to indicate how they are propositionally specific, only be able to say such things as this about someone's

---

[2] In Chapter VII, I argue that the *thing* known, when someone knows *that something is so*, is something which is part of the (whole) truth (about the world), and not, e.g. a fact. This is indicated by the following sentences and deviant string:

Ben knows that it was raining.
Ben knows the truth about whether it was raining, namely, that it was raining.
*Ben knows the fact that it was raining.

A person's reason seems to be neither of these things, nor a proposition, as appears indicated by the following sentence and deviant strings:

Ben's reason is that it was raining.
*Ben's reason is the truth about whether it was raining, namely, that it was raining.
*Ben's reason is the fact that it was raining.
*Ben's reason is the (true) proposition that it was raining.

People's reasons not being parts of the truth, I conclude that they are not things known, but are only in parallel with things people know. They seem to be in a category all their own.

beliefs: His belief is that this is more like that than the other is. Similarly, if something is the person's reason for preferring this to the other it will also be propositionally specific even if we can only indicate that in such bare terms as before: His reason is that this is more like that than the other is. The extreme case in regard to our inability to indicate things with words might be the one where all we can say is that someone's reason is that things are the way they are, where these words are used not as a banal tautology but as the poor expression of the all but wholly inexpressible idea that here things are a certain, particular way. If someone's reason is that things are the way they are, that will satisfy the demands of this premiss as well as anything. Accordingly, I can't see how any significant controversy could arise over this second premiss. Indeed, this seems to be, if anything, the least promising place to try to stop the Basis Argument.

§4. *The Third Premiss: The Step from one's Propositionally Specific Reason or Reasons to one's Knowing*

The most distinctively epistemic step of this argument is the one expressed in the third and final premiss. In this premiss, it is claimed that (3) If S's reason (for something X) is that p, then S *knows* that p, and if S's reasons (for X) are that p and that q and so on, then S *knows* that p and S *knows* that q and so on. In standard English, the premiss says that if someone's reason (for something) is that something is so, then he or she *knows* that it is so, and if his or her reasons (for the thing) are that this is so and that that is so and so on, then he or she *knows* that this is so and *knows* that that is so and so on. Even if you do not at all misunderstand this premiss, it may take some doing to convince you of its truth. But if you do misunderstand it, then you will never be convinced. I begin to advance this premiss, then, by trying to avoid any misunderstanding.

Perhaps the most common source of misunderstanding is the idea that this premiss makes it out that you are always aware of your reasons, that you always know what they are. If you think that this is what the premiss says, then you might reject the premiss quite out of hand. But this way of thinking confuses our premiss with the following quite different proposition: If someone's reason (for something) is that thus-and-so, then the person must know what his or her reason is, i.e. he or she must know *that his or her reason (for it) is that thus-and-so*. But this is clearly not what our premiss is saying. This proposition entails what the premiss says, but it says much more. The premiss says only that if someone's reason is that thus-and-so, the person must know *that thus-and-so*; it does *not* say that he or she must know *that his or her reason is* that thus-and-so. This misinterpretation has the premiss saying that a lot more must be known by the subject.

A second source of misunderstanding is the idea that this premiss will have it that there are many more unconscious reasons than common sense dictates is really the case. This may occur as a reaction away from the first misunderstanding. But this premiss says nothing at all to this effect either. It only articulates a logical requirement for what may be your reasons: If something is your reason, then there must be something which you know to be so, which known thing, if it is not your reason, at least parallels your reason in the indicated way. The premiss allows that you may know all sorts of things to be so. It also allows that none, few, many, most, or all of these things may lie dormant, as it were, so far as providing the material for your reasons. In our convenient terms, the premiss just says that your reasons must always find a *basis* in your knowledge, or in what you know to be so.

A third source of misunderstanding is the conflation of *S's* reason *for* X with *the* reason *that* S X-es. S's reason for something will be the reason, or at least one of the reasons, that he does, prefers, believes, etc., as he does. But the converse generally does not hold. *The* reason *that* someone eats many sweets may well be that he needs an especially large amount of sugar for his health; but if he is ignorant of his biological condition, then that will not be *his* reason *for* eating many sweets. In such a case, it may be that nothing is his reason for eating many sweets even though something is the reason that he does precisely that. Somewhat similarly, it might be that *the* reason *that* someone washes his hands a great deal is that he is afraid of being impure. We may consistently suppose, however, that he does not know that he is afraid of this. But, then, that will *not* be *his* reason *for* washing his hands all the time. I think that people's conflating this distinction makes them think people have reasons much more often than they do. For example, if you are wrong about our foreigner, then it may well be that the reason, or one of the reasons, you said 'It is a toothbrush' was that you thought he wanted to know what toothbrushes are called. But that does not mean, as many people may be likely to suppose, that your reason, or one of your reasons, for saying it was that you thought that. Rather, as we remarked before, it seems that you had no reason to say it and, so, that *nothing* was *your* reason, or one of *your* reasons, *for* saying 'It is a toothbrush.'

In clearing up these misunderstandings, we have, I think, cleared the way for accepting our third premiss. Now I must argue for the premiss itself. In giving the argument, we are off to a good start in noticing that if someone's reason for something is that p, then it follows that it is true that p. In this respect, our locution, 'S's reason is that p', is like other important locutions with 'reason'. If *the* reason someone does something is that p, it also follows that p. Going directly to our point, it is inconsistent to say 'His *reason* was that the store was going to close, but it *wasn't* going to close' just as it's inconsistent to say 'The *reason* is that it was going to close, but it *wasn't*.' If the store wasn't going to close, then *that* can't possibly be Ralph's reason for running there. If anything is his reason here, it will have to be something else, perhaps, though probably not, that *he thought it was going to close*. But, then, if *that* is his reason, then *it* must be so. It is inconsistent to say, 'His *reason* was that he thought the store was going to close, but he *didn't* think that.' The same points apply to things which are Ralph's reasons.

Another necessary condition of knowing which is entailed by our key locution is that the subject *at least believe* that the thing is so. If Ralph *doesn't even* believe that the store is going to close, then that can't be his reason for running there. And, concerning his belief that it was raining, it is inconsistent to say, 'His *reason* was that Fred's hat was wet, but he *didn't even believe* that it was.' One might consistently say, for example, that Ralph's *fear* was that Fred's hat was wet though he didn't even believe that it was wet. But that is another matter. Again, the same points apply to Ralph's reasons.

We have noticed two quite independent necessary conditions of knowing to be entailed by someone's reason. This is grounds at least for suspicion. But neither of these conditions is either a very severe or very unusual one. Each is entailed by things which do not entail knowing, e.g. by someone's *correctly believing* something. But a very demanding condition of knowing is also entailed by someone's reason. If someone's reason is that *p*, then he must be absolutely *certain* that *p*. That someone be absolutely certain is something which is entailed by little which does not also entail knowing. But it is entailed by someone's reason. It is inconsistent to say 'Ralph's *reason* was that Fred's hat was wet, but he *wasn't* absolutely *certain* that it was.' Also inconsistent is: 'Ralph's *reason* was that Fred's hat was wet, but he was *more certain* that there was water on the ground.' If Ralph is not absolutely and perfectly certain and sure that the hat was wet, then that can't be his reason for anything. Perhaps something else is; perhaps, though probably not, that he thought it was wet. But, then, *that* must be something of which Ralph is absolutely certain. Once again, Ralph's reasons follow suit.

By now, we have got pretty fair evidence for our premiss by checking out necessary conditions of knowing. Let's approach the problem from the other side to see how some more of the evidence looks. Accordingly, I will now look to describe a situation where many necessary conditions of knowledge *are* satisfied, but where the person still does *not* know that *p*. Suppose, then, that Mary believes that the crops will grow now and she says that her reason for believing it is that it was raining. But Mary does *not know* that it was raining, even though she meets many necessary conditions of knowing it. The following situation makes this quite clear. Does it also make it clear that it is *false* that Mary's reason is *that it was raining*, despite what she may say? We must expect that it does.

In this situation, it is true that it was raining. And, Mary is perfectly certain that it was. Moreover, Mary's certainty is based on grounds which are quite good. But here is how all of this happened. Mary was indoors but then she came outside and looked around. The ground and objects outside were all wet just as if wetted recently by falling rain. And, other indications all pointed to its having rained. Indeed, this is why Mary is certain that it was raining. But, unbeknownst to Mary, while it did in fact rain, the rain was rapidly evaporated due to some extraordinary events: For one, the temperature outside went up to 130°F. for an hour. Right after the evaporation, some huge spray-and-sprinkle trucks swept by and covered the area with water again, and they did it in just the way that rain does. So, it all looked just as if nothing had evaporated. Because she sees the water, Mary is certain that it was raining. And, because she is certain of this, Mary thinks that the crops will grow now. Now, it is of course true that it was raining. But is it true that Mary's *reason* for thinking this about the crops is *that it was raining*? She says that it is. But it seems to me quite clear that that can't be her reason. Perhaps, though probably not, her reason is that she thinks it rained; perhaps, it's that there's water on the ground, and perhaps, even, there is nothing here which is her reason. It may not be completely clear what, if anything, it is best to say about such a case in a more positive direction. It is quite clear, though, that it must be false that Mary's reason is that it was raining. And, the reason for this seems also quite clear: It must be false because Mary doesn't *know* that it was raining. It is equally clear, I take it, that, for her lack of this knowledge, that it was raining couldn't be one of her reasons either.

Our tests converge to suggest strongly that if someone's reason is that *p*, then that person must know that *p*. Any necessary condition of knowing must be satisfied for something to be someone's reason and, on the other side, no matter how many conditions are satisfied the thing will not be the person's reason unless the person knows. All of this must remind us of our experiences in testing our entailing verbs and adjectives, in Chapter IV, section 7. We are also reminded, then, to try here, finally for now at least, a condition which is at once logically necessary and logically sufficient for knowing. I mean of course our perspicuously absolute condition that *p* be (absolutely) clear to S. Is it consistent to say, 'Ralph's real *reason* is *that it was raining*, but it *isn't* absolutely *clear* to him that it was?' I think it pretty clear that it is not. Moreover, it is inconsistent also to say, 'His reason is that it was raining, but it is clearer to him that the ground was wet.' These experiences should encourage us to look for some syntactico-semantic connections between our crucial occurrences of 'reason' and our key occurrences of our entailing verbs and adjectives. In section 6, we shall do just this, in order to give a broad base of linguistic support for our crucial third premiss and, so, for our Basis Argument. But, even now, we can say that the more closely we examine this argument, the more acceptable we find it. The only way to reject this Basis Argument appears to be to misunderstand what it says.

§5. *The Basis Argument again; Being Justified*

In the presentation just considered, the Basis Argument concerned the idea of someone's being reasonable in something. It showed that a logical part of his idea is that the subject knows something to be so. To put this linguistically, it follows from the meaning of 'S is reasonable in X' that there must be a truth of the form 'S knows that *p*'. Now, in some different language, say, Martian or Indonesian, there may be a word which means something rather like our word 'reasonable'. But, this word may never require any knowledge on the part of the subject for the truth of its key personal sentences. What would this show? I think it shows that their word, say, 'queasonable', however like 'reasonable' in certain respects, must mean something crucially different from our word. Accordingly, it shows that being queasonable is something crucially different from being reasonable in it. If nobody knows anything to be so, then we all might still be queasonable in many things, but that doesn't mean that anyone will be reasonable in anything at all. So even if our argument may rest, in some sense, on points of our own language, that is nothing against either the soundness or the importance of this argument.

The Basis Argument does not rely on any small, isolated feature of our language and thought. We have other locutions which are allied in meaning to 'S is reasonable in X'. Though modifiable in different ways, they convey the same main idea as that conveyed by our examined locution. One notable locution with much the same meaning is, of course, of the form 'S is rational in X', and the idea of a man's being rational in something differs little from the idea of his being reasonable in it. In this connection, we might most directly talk, in parallel with one's reason, of one's (rational) basis. In parallel with one's reasons, we might talk of parts of one's basis for the thing (in which one would be rational). Closer to more standard discussion in epistemology, we have locutions of the form 'S is justified in X'. Having been brought up philosophically in such discussions, I will focus on these locutions now. Fortunately for our sceptical linking, but as might be expected, we can provide a parallel (presentation of our) Basis Argument in terms of this allied idea of being justified.

The three premises of this parallel argument are:

(1') If someone S is *justified* in something X, then there is something which is *S's justification* for X.

(2') If there is something which is *S's justification* for something X, then there is some propositional value of '*p*' such that S's justification *is that p*.

(3') If S's justification (for something X) *is that p*, then S *knows* that *p*.

These three premises jointly entail the parallel conclusion:

(4') If someone S is *justified* in something X, then there is some propositional value of '*p*' such that S *knows* that *p*.

Generalizing on (4'), we get the parallel result that if anybody is justified in anything, then he or she must know something to be so. And, we get the conditional to link most explicitly the universal forms of our two types of scepticism: If nobody knows anything to be so, then nobody is justified in anything.

The only difference in wording between the two arguments, other than the use of different key terms, is that now we don't make room for a plural alternative. So far as I can tell, when we take 'justification' seriously, so that it has something to do with someone's being justified, then *a* justification will always be what one appropriately has here. When someone is justified, we can't correctly say that his *justifications are* that *p* and that *q*. Rather, we say that his *justification is* that *p and q*. In addition, we may perhaps say that *part of his justification* is that *p*, and that part of it is that *q*. If I am wrong about this, the argument may of course easily be rewritten with room for the plural alternative.

The points now to be made on behalf of this Basis Argument are so similar to those for the argument with 'reasonable' that I won't bother to defend these premises independently. But, I should say something, I think, to make sure that the third premiss, (3'), is taken correctly. Some people seem to think that as long as someone *offers* something *as* a justification (for something X), then that can be counted properly as *his justification* (for it). They seem to think that 'justification' can be understood on a quite complete parallel with, say, 'excuse' and 'argument'. Now, we can speak of someone's excuse or argument (for something) even if the person *has* no (real) excuse or argument (for it), so long as he or she *offers* something *as* an excuse or argument. That is, there need be nothing which excuses him (or, e.g. his behaviour), and nothing which argues for him (or his position) in the matter. We need not raise our eyebrows, so to speak, when we hear these words used like this. There is a literal interpretation of the forms 'S's argument is that *p*' and 'S's excuse is that *p*' with such a more lenient meaning. But 'justification' works differently. If we say 'John's *justification* was that it was raining, but he *didn't* really *have* any justification,' we have to put at least implicit scare quotes on the first occurrence of 'justification' to get, or to imagine, anything consistent. If there is something which is someone's justification, he cannot just offer something as such, there must always be something which justifies him there (in his behaviour, his position, etc.). Contrary to lenient thoughts, there's always more to something's being one's justification than one's offering something as such. What more there is involves at least this: One must *know* something. In section 6, we shall further discuss these rather subtle linguistic distinctions. But even if I am wrong on these matters of meaning, and even if there is such a lenient sense of 'justification', it won't be any sense which figures in our argument. Our argument will go through as long as there is at least one sense of the term where 'S's justification is that *p*' entails 'S knows that *p*', and so long as it is in this sense in which the former sentences are required by S's being *justified* in something. There is just such a sense available. We *can* hear it as inconsistent to say 'His *justification* was that it was raining, but he *didn't know* that it was.'

For our argument, at least, one's justification must connect with one's being justified. And, we can specify quite clearly what the relation is: Whenever one is justified in something, something or some things *justify* one in it. These things are facts. Thus, if S is justified in X, the fact that *p* justifies S in X or else the facts that *p* and that *q* and so on justify him in it. If what justifies S is *the fact that p*, then S's justification, in the only relevant sense for us, is *that p* and S *knows* that *p*. If the things which justify S are the fact that *p* and the fact that *q* and so on, then S's justification is that *p* and *q* and so on. Here, part of S's justification is that *p*, part is that *q*, and so on. Finally, it then follows that S *knows* that *p* and also that *q* and so on. Our parallel argument, then, rests on no equivocation of 'justification'. If such an equivocation is possible at all, which we should doubt, that will only allow one to *seem* to avoid our conclusion; that is, it will only allow for an equivocation *away* from our argument. Any relevant sense of the term ties one's justification to facts which justify one, and the correct application of the term in that case clearly requires that the subject knows the relevant thing(s) to be so.

In that we have parallel arguments to conclusions which are essentially the same idea, we are not trading on any fine features of our language or thought in our linking of the two types of scepticism. We find no precious claim in our conclusion that universal scepticism about knowledge entails universal scepticism about rationality. This is why I have referred to the two as but two presentations of the Basis in Knowledge Argument (for Scepticism About Rationality), and it is why I think this argument so important to a serious sceptical philosophy.

§6. *Two Hypotheses about Nouns*

To give us further confidence in our Basis Argument, in both of its presentations, I will try to provide a broad linguistic basis for its final and most distinctively epistemic premiss, or premisses. I will try, that is, to find such a basis for the idea that sentences of the form 'S's reason is that *p*', and of the form 'S's justification is that *p*', all entail corresponding sentences of the form 'S knows that p'. I will try to fit these sentences into a large pattern of English which supports our intuitions, already aroused in sections 4 and 5, to the effect that these claimed entailments hold. Once this is achieved, we may have more confidence that entailments to knowledge also hold from more complex but obviously related sentences, e.g. from sentences of the forms 'One of S's reasons is that *p*' and 'Part of S's justification is that *p*'.

In these quite apparently entailing sentences, the key words are nouns, 'reason' and 'justification'. In parallel with our established talk of propositional verbs and, more lately, of propositional adjectives, we may say that, at least as they occur in these sentences, these words are *propositional nouns*. In any case, neither should be confused with any other word of any other part of speech, including the propositional verb 'reason'.

In Chapter IV, we saw how the concept of knowledge governs the semantics of verbs and adjectives in a parallel way. First, we defined a form of sentence for verbs and, then, we found the closest parallel form for adjectives. We were then able to formulate parallel hypotheses which held good for the parallel forms of sentence. As the hypotheses were parallels, they conformed to a pattern. What I want to do now is to find a parallel form of sentence for nouns.

The key idea is to get sentences where an agent or being is tied or related to a 'propositional content', or fact, or whatever, by a single word of the part of speech in question, and by as little in the way of additional words as our language allows. This is why the form of sentence which we picked out for verbs is the quite simple form 'S verbs (that) p'. The parallel form of sentence for adjectives is, then, the form 'S is adjective (that) p'. How we generate sentences from these forms, and so what the forms mean, is already clear from our introduction of them in Chapter IV, sections 2 and 6. It is also quite clear, from our discussion in those sections, that these forms do indeed give our simplest ways of tying an agent or being to what may be given in an appropriate propositional clause. But we have said nothing yet about nouns in this regard, about our third main part of speech.

For our sentences with nouns, we will need *some* linguistic material beyond the noun itself to separate the subject from the propositional clause: The form 'S noun (that) p' will get us at best such a non-sentential string as **'John belief that snow is white.' Staying with names, the way to keep the material to a minimum, as even a quick look at our deviant string suggests, is to put a possessive element on our starting name and, then, place a tensed copula after the noun and before the 'that'. In this way, we get sentences like 'John's belief was that snow is white.' Thus, our parallel form of sentence for nouns is the form 'S's noun is that p'. The instructions for our new form are parallel to those for the old ones. Thus, in painstaking detail:

If we start with a name, we now put the name in the possessive case, which here just means tacking an ''s' on the name. If we start with a pronoun, we now use the possessive case for it: 'His' instead of 'He', and so on. We next replace the dummy 'noun' by a single word which is here a noun; we replace the 'is' by a single word variant of itself, that is, by an 'is' or 'was'; we replace the 'that' by itself; and we replace the letter 'p' by a propositional clause. What is apparently the most notable difference between this new form and the ones for verbs and adjectives is that in the new form, the 'that' is generally not deletable; hence, we have not bracketed it here. In the old forms, we remember, that 'that' is generally (though not universally) deletable; hence, we bracketed it there. Thus, while, 'John believes it was raining' is grammatical, *'John's belief is it was raining' is not. But this difference is, I suggest, a relatively trivial one. It is trivial because the 'that' in our nominal sentence has minimal meaning, as against, e.g. the 'why' in 'John's belief is why it was raining.' (Perhaps, a deity was displeased that John had, or was going to have a certain belief, e.g. the belief that frogs are animals.) Accordingly, forgetting about deletability, and going by our other motivation for bracketing 'that' in our old forms, we might bracket it here as well: 'S's noun is (that) p.' Still, I will not bother to do this. Whatever our symbolism, though, the main point here should be quite clear: These sentences with nouns are the closest parallel our language has for our studied sentences with verbs and with adjectives.

Various sentences of our simple form for nouns may be regarded as being, in some important sense, incomplete. Thus, while 'John's belief is that it was raining' is no more incomplete than 'John believes it was raining,' the sentence 'John's reason is that it was raining' appears to be incomplete in comparison with both of the first two. We feel a need to have some sentence say what, in the case at hand, John's reason is a reason *for*. Thus, a sentence of the form 'S's reason is that p' will not only stand or fall with, but, in some important sense, be elliptical for, a longer correlative sentence of the form 'S's reason for X is that p'. For example, 'John's reason is that it was raining' will be thus elliptical for some such sentence as, say, 'John's reason for taking his umbrella is that it was raining.' But even where we have sentences which are importantly elliptical, we may take them to be of the same form as sentences which are not. Thus, we may take 'John's reason is that it was raining' to be of the same form as 'John's belief is that it was raining,' namely, of the form 'S's noun is that p'.

In the case of our sentences for verbs, we may easily spot a difference between 'Mary perceived that her horse won' and 'Mary believed that her horse won.' And, in the case of our sentences for adjectives, we spot the same sort of difference between 'Mary is happy her horse won' and 'Mary is hopeful her horse won.' In line with our remarks before, we express the differences by saying that, in each case, the first of our pair entails the sentence 'Her horse won' while the second one does not do that. And, in a clear enough sense, we may say that in the first case it is the verb 'perceived' which is (primarily) responsible for the entailment, and in the second it is the adjective 'happy' which is (primarily) responsible. With either of these words, but not the two others, no matter what propositional clause we tack on behind it, we will get the entailment. This motivated our terminology: in the sentence 'Mary perceived that her horse won,' the verb entails *its* completing clause; and in the correlative sentence 'Mary is happy her horse won,' the adjective entails *its* completing clause.

Can we spot the same sort of difference in the case of our sentences for nouns? If we can, then we may extend our motivated terminology to talk about this new range of sentences. Do certain nouns entail their completing clauses? From the sentences 'Mary's discovery was that it was raining' and 'Mary's belief was that it was raining,' we get our positive answer. The former, but not the latter, entails the sentence 'It was raining.' We may understand the difference to be due only to a difference in the semantic function of the nouns, 'discovery' and 'belief', for the sentences are otherwise identical. No matter how we change the other replacements, so long as consistent sentences are the result, the entailment will always go through with 'discovery' and usually (though not always) fail with 'belief'. (The sentence 'Mary's belief is that nineteen is the sum of nine and ten' may, I suppose, entail the completing clause. And, it's pretty clear that 'Mary's belief is that she has at least one belief' does entail its clause. But it's also clear that in both

cases, the noun 'belief' is not itself adequate to do the job.)
Thus, we may extend our motivated terminology and say: In
the sentence 'Mary's discovery was that it was raining,' the
noun entails *its* completing clause. In 'Mary's belief was that it
was raining,' the noun doesn't do that.

To what extent are these entailments from nouns just another
way of expressing entailments from verbs (or from adjectives)?
In these simple sentences with nouns, do we have a genuinely
new semantic domain, or is it, more or less anyway, the same
phenomenon all over again? A quick look reveals nothing, or
very little, new to concern us. For example, in the case of our
last two sample sentences, the semantic difference can be explained, quite well I think, in terms of the difference between
related sentences with verbs. There is little semantic difference
between 'Mary discovered that it was raining' and 'Mary's
discovery was that it was raining.' And, there is also little
between 'Mary believed that it was raining' and 'Mary's belief
was that it was raining.' The entailment from the noun, or the
lack of it, can here be explained in terms of the power, or the
powerlessness, of the 'root' verb.

But though we may understand certain nouns in terms of
certain verbs, this sort of understanding is not always available.
For example, the sentence 'Mary's problem was that it was
raining' does entail 'It was raining,' while 'John's idea was
that it was raining' does not. But there is no verb 'problem' to
help our understanding, nor any verbal associate of the noun
'idea'. With our key nouns, 'reason' and 'justification', there
are associate verbs, '(to) reason' and '(to) justify'. But, these
verbs give us little to explain why the nouns entail their completing clauses. For, 'Mary reasoned that it was raining' does
not entail 'It was raining.' And, *'Mary justified that it was
raining,' is no sentence at all. To get a sentence here, we must
insert extra words, e.g. 'the claim': 'Mary justified the claim
that it was raining.' But, then, this sentence does *not* entail the
wanted 'It was raining.' Of course, we should not expect it to.
What Mary justified is bound to be quite different from her
justification of it. Many entailments from nouns are not fruitfully reducible to, nor explicable in terms of, any entailments
from verbs. Nor do adjectives give us any sufficient help here.
So, while mindful that verbs often yield us semantic insight for

nouns, we will look to the semantics of verbs more for parallels than for foundations.

If a large pattern of English exists to make our domains parallel, then for our third main part of speech we should expect this primary hypothesis to hold:

> Whenever a sentence of the form 'S's noun is that p' has the noun entail its completing clause and has it also entail the corresponding sentence of the form 'S at least believes (that) p', then the noun entails its corresponding simple knowledge sentence.

It is no feat to see that this hypothesis makes a statement about nouns which exactly parallels the statements made about verbs and adjectives by our previous two primary hypotheses. Nor is it hard to see that the closest parallel in the way of a second, complementary hypothesis now is this:

> There is no sentence of the form 'S's noun is that p' where the noun ever entails the negation of its completing clause.

The question remains, of course, to what extent these new hypotheses, which round out our generalizing, actually do hold for our new domain. I proceed to examine them each in turn beginning with the first. As it is for our purposes by far the more important of the two, I will spend by far the greatest time and effort on its examination.

Before we can tell to what extent this primary hypothesis does hold, we have a bit to do about getting clearer exactly which sentences we take to *correspond* to the sentences of our form 'S's noun is that p'. Certain nouns, if not all, require us to be quite careful about the times to be associated with the properly corresponding sentences. The sentence 'Mary's belief is that it was raining,' it seems to me, entails the proposition that right now Mary believes that it was raining. If Mary did believe that it was raining, but now does not, then, I think, there is nothing which *is* Mary's belief on this score, and so our nominal sentence here expresses no truth. Accordingly, 'belief' requires no new thought about times, or so it seems to me. But, unlike 'belief' the noun 'discovery' does seem to require some new consideration. The sentence 'Mary's discovery is that it was raining', it seems to me, may hold true even if Mary now does not discover anything, and even if she now does not even believe that it was raining. For, so long as Mary did in the past discover that it was raining and, so, at that time did at least believe it was, there is something which then was *and which continues to remain* her discovery, here, that it was raining. With 'discovery', then, we cannot define a general relation to a unique corresponding sentence of the form 'S at least believes (that) *p*', much less to a unique simple knowledge sentence. What this means, of course, is that, if it is taken in the strictest parallel to our previous primary hypotheses, our new hypothesis simply has no implication concerning 'discovery'. However, we can relax our understanding of the hypothesis, in an obvious way, thus getting it to concern this noun. And, then, it seems clear, the behaviour of 'discovery' will serve to support the hypothesis.

On our relevantly liberal interpretation of it, it's quite clear, I think, that certain unproblematic nouns, like 'discovery', fall under our hypothesis as positive instances. Many other nouns do not. We have already seen that 'belief', while fitting in our sentence form, bypasses our hypothesis; it fails to satisfy the first conjunct of the antecedent. Nouns like 'statement', 'assertion', and 'theory' fail to satisfy each of the antecedent's two conjuncts. And many other nouns, while going smoothly into our form, fail to satisfy the antecedent of this hypothesis for failing, at the least, to satisfy the first conjunct of it. Here is a list of only some of them: 'assumption', 'conjecture', 'expectation', 'fear', 'feeling', 'guess', 'hope', 'hypothesis', 'hunch', 'idea', 'impression', 'judgement', 'opinion', 'prediction', 'story', 'suggestion', 'suspicion', 'supposition', 'thesis', 'thought', understanding', 'view', 'worry'. It is quite clear, then, that our first conjunct does a lot of work. But, how much work, then, does the second conjunct do; or is it just installed for parallel appearances, thus to make our Basis Argument look good?

To see the work of the second conjunct, we may compare 'discovery' with 'problem' and related nouns: If Ben's discovery is that girls don't like him, it follows that (at least at some time) Ben at least believes that they don't like him. If he never even has any belief here, then that can't be his discovery. But, it might be his problem, or his trouble, shortcoming, misfortune, of difficulty. This is worth observing because these latter nouns do entail their completing clauses: If Ben's problem is that girls don't like him, it does follow that they don't. Now the second clause comes in: Even if he never even has any belief as to whether they like him or not, that they don't may be Ben's problem. For example, we may suppose that if they did he would be president of the senior class. Just so, 'problem', 'trouble', 'misfortune', 'shortcoming', and 'difficulty' fail to fit the second clause of our antecedent. Thus they also clearly by-pass our hypothesis. Our second conjunct does real work for us; the parallel with our earlier primary hypotheses is no idle or empty one.

Many of the nouns which fit our simple sentences fall into three related classes. Our hypothesis treats nouns of the first two classes quite differently from those of the third. This is no accident. Rather, I suggest, it is the reflection of an epistemological, even a psychological, theory, which is embodied in our language. Our first class of nouns contains, not only 'discovery', but also 'insight', 'finding', in one sense, at least, 'proof', 'observation', and so on. They confirm our hypothesis positively. This is because these nouns all concern the acquisition of knowledge. The nouns we are most concerned with, 'reason' and 'justification', belong to a second class. The second class concerns knowledge in another way: at least roughly, these nouns have to do with the function or utilization of a being's knowledge as a basis for things. Other nouns in this class are 'basis', 'data', 'evidence', and 'ground' or, perhaps better, 'grounds'. We may notice, for example, the inconsistency of 'His evidence was that it was raining, but it was clearer to him that the ground was wet.' These nouns also confirm our hypothesis in a positive way, though perhaps not quite so obviously as do those of the first class. Their positive fit may be understood, I suggest, in terms of their function: to mediate, or to denote mediations, between a being's knowledge and various other things for which he may want or need a basis in knowledge. These other things are denoted, at least generally, by nouns which fall into a third class, by far the largest. As they denote things which may have a *basis in* knowledge, and for which such a basis is often *needed*, it is not surprising that these nouns do not themselves entail knowledge. It is nouns of this class which occur on our list beginning with 'assumption'. Including our familiar friends, 'belief', 'statement', and 'theory', it is only to be expected that they and they alone, amongst these three kinds, should bypass our hypothesis.

Here is how nouns of the three classes may provide an explanation of why a certain person believes a certain thing: Ben's discovery (first class) that gremlins cause chicken pox will provide Ben with the knowledge that they do. In the case at hand, this will, in turn, provide Ben with a reason (second class) for his belief (third class) that chicken pox is a cute disease, namely, that gremlins cause it. This little story shows the relation of these main groups of nouns which fit our simple sentence form. A main feature of our hypothesis, then, is to sort out nouns in these groups by means of their relation to the key concept of their theory, our dominant, central concept of knowledge. Other nouns which fit our sentences are, as it were, economically filtered by our language to follow suit. Not so central to this guiding embodied theory, their behaviour bears special watching. But while they reveal special features, they present none which contravene our hypothesis.

In Chapter IV, section 3, we discussed how our hypothesis for verbs might serve as a 'filtering device'. So far as I can tell, the ambiguities with verbal sentences are generally lexical; two (or more) meanings of 'learn' account for as many meanings of simple sentences. In the case of nouns, syntactical ambiguity appears to be the more predominant kind. There are at least two meanings for the sentence 'Arthur's argument (for not building the dinobomber) is that the plane will soon be obsolete.' But I do not think that this derives from two meanings of 'argument' which fit that linguistic frame. Rather, I would suppose that the sentence derives, in some sense, from two distinct sources, each having 'argument' with the same meaning. One source is something which entails this: 'There is at least one argument (for this thing), namely, that the plane will soon be obsolete, an argument which may exist even if no one should ever happen to offer or even think of it, and Arthur has or had one such argument.' This source entails that the plane will soon be obsolete, that Arthur at lease believes it will be and, finally, that he knows the plane won't be useful long. A distinct source is roughly this one: 'Arthur offers or offered something as an argument (for not building the dinobomber), namely, that it will soon be obsolete.' On a reading associated with this source none of the just noted things is entailed. Our hypothesis for nouns thus places constraints on which readings are allowed for simple sentences. This is what I call its 'filtering power'. The filtering power is at work, in a similar way, with a whole group of nouns, each more or less closely related to 'argument': 'answer', 'complaint', 'criticism', 'defence', 'objection', 'explanation', and so on. Accordingly, the filtering power of our hypothesis has quite enough work to occupy it.

I do not think that our simple sentences with 'reason' are ambiguous in any way. But, it is interesting to notice that they entail the same sorts of things that sentences with 'argument', etc. entail on their first reading. Thus, 'John's reason (for not building the dinobomber) is that it will soon be obsolete.' This entails that there is at least one reason (for not building it), namely, that it will be obsolete soon. It also entails the two conditions of our antecedent and, finally, that John knows this plane will soon be outmoded. Similar remarks hold good for 'grounds', 'evidence', 'basis', 'data', and, I think, for 'justification'. Now, in section 5, we allowed that simple sentences with 'justification' *might* be ambiguous, though this seemed doubtful. We may now more fully understand what is going on in case they are: There will be a source which entails that there is some justification for the subject, namely, that p. This source will entail that he has it, that our antecedent's conditions are satisfied, and, finally, that he knows that p. This is a source which must hold true if our subject is to be *justified* in the thing for which his justification is that p. If there is another meaning, where knowing is not required, it would seem to be one which entails none of these things. And, that, we may presume, is because it comes from a source like this: 'John offers or offered something as a justification (for X), namely, that p.' We remarked to this effect before, in section 5, but now we may understand these points more fully, against a wider background of linguistic phenomena.[3]

In examining our primary hypothesis I will conclude by returning to consider 'problem' and related nouns. There is, I

[3] On these matters, as well as others in this section, I am indebted to discussion with Barbara Hall Partee and R. Bruce Freed, though I have not answered fully all the questions they have raised.

think, a very interesting semantic difference between nouns like 'reason' and 'justification' on the one hand, and, on the other, those like 'problem' and 'trouble'. In this respect, in so far as a comparison is available, nouns like 'argument' and 'excuse' go with 'reason' and are unlike 'problem'. What I have in mind here is the relation of simple sentences, where the possessive case is in force, to associated sentences with the verb 'to have', or 'has'. With 'has', we have these sentences to relate to those of our simple form. They concern a seller of sun-tan lotion who has closed his shop for the day:

> Ben has a reason, namely, that it was raining.
> Ben has a problem, namely, that it was raining.
> Ben has some justification, namely, that it was raining.
> Ben has some trouble, namely, that it was raining.

But, there is a big difference here. Especially if we tack on a uniqueness clause, e.g. 'and that is the only problem he has', the second and fourth sentences will entail, respectively:

> Ben's problem is that it was raining.
> Ben's trouble is that it was raining.

But the first and third sentences will *not* entail:

> Ben's reason is that it was raining.
> Ben's justification is that it was raining.

What's missing in the latter cases seems to be this: there are some features of each case which are such that, *if* Ben *were* aware of them, and if they were appropriately utilized, then his reason *would be* that p; but it is left open whether he is aware of them or not. Suppose that Ben has a reason (to close his shop), and the reason he has is that it was raining. Now, Ben's reason (for closing his shop) will be that it was raining only if (even given the uniqueness) he is aware of the fact that it was raining, that is, only if Ben *knows* that it was raining. With 'reason' and 'justification' we need the addition of relevant knowledge to get us from the 'has' sentences to the possessive sentences. With 'problem' and 'trouble' we need no addition. Perhaps this difference is connected with there being no sentence of the form *'Ben's problem *for* X-ing is that p.'[4]

---

[4] On these matters, I am indebted to Mark Glickson.

As I said, nouns like 'argument' and 'excuse' are here like 'reason', and not 'problem'. Even where we assume a reading of the simple possessive sentence where it is entailed that Ben has the relevant argument or excuse, we cannot logically infer such a sentence from the closest sentence with 'has'. That is, from:

Ben has an argument, namely, that it was raining.
Ben has an excuse, namely, that it was raining.

we cannot thus infer:

Ben's argument is that it was raining.
Ben's excuse is that it was raining.

The reason for this again involves the dominant work of the concept of knowledge: The sentences with 'has' do not entail that Ben even believes that it was raining, much less that he knows it. Thus, the greater syntactic closeness which the possessive allows may always be taken, I suggest, to indicate a greater closeness in reality which those sentences require for truth, but which are not required by the longer, more widely separating sentences with 'has'. When in Chapter IV, section 1, we remarked that the syntax and semantics of our language conspired to reflect the dominance of key concepts, this was the sort of phenomenon we could only hope to encounter.

To complete our linguistic parallel, we must examine our second hypothesis about nouns. The closest we can come to violating this hypothesis is with such nouns as 'error' and 'mistake' whose meaning seems made for the job. But, while 'Ben's error is *in thinking* (*that*) it was raining' and 'Ben's mistake was *to suppose* (*that*) it was raining' do indeed entail the negation, each is of a manifestly longer form and does not allow for shortening. If we try to shorten, to get sentences of our simple form, all we obtain are the deviant strings, *'Ben's error is that it was raining' and *'Ben's mistake was that it was raining.' While I'm not certain of it, I think the same happens with 'delusion', 'illusion', and other negative entailers.

Let's turn to nouns which don't need the extra words. Just as the verbal sentence 'John fancies that he is a prince' at least suggests that John is not a prince, so the nominal one 'John's fantasy is that he is a prince' at least suggests the same thing. But, just as the former does not clearly rule out John's being a prince—we can suppose that he has no idea of his prince-hood and firmly believes the opposite, so the latter does not clearly exclude it either. There are cases where fantasy is at one with reality. I suggest that in each case there is only a suggestion of falsehood. Why the suggestions work here needs to be understood, but, as remarked before, the same is true for suggestions generally. Though lacking this understanding, I suggest that no nouns clearly damage this second hypothesis.

At the same time, much as we had with verbs and adjectives, we do have nouns which entail ignorance, a very different thing to entail. We have 'hope', 'fear', and 'suspicion', which clearly go with associated verbs and, at the other extreme, 'hunch', which apparently has no relevant verb closely associated. And, they entail that their subject does not know *whether or not* the thing is so. Thus, in our simple sentences, nouns are like verbs and adjectives. They have a concern with knowledge and ignorance, and no great independent concern with truth and falsity. Among the nouns here concerned with knowledge are 'reason' and 'justification'. This completes the support for our Basis Argument. I should think it hard, at this point, for one who accepts our universal ignorance to suppose that he may yet be reasonable or justified in anything at all. A conservative sceptic about knowledge, however, may yet hold out such a hope. I turn to address him.

§7. *On the Connection between Partial Scepticisms of the two Types*

If our main points have so far been correct, we have shown that *universal* scepticism about knowledge entails *universal* scepticism about rationality. This in itself is, I think, quite an interesting result. But it is most interesting only if universal scepticism about knowledge is in fact correct. Now, we have argued at some length that our ignorance is indeed completely universal. But this universal position is so radical, and goes against so much epistemological teaching and training, that I despair that more than a very few will ever find it at all acceptable. If I have been moderately successful, however, then you might now well be at least a conservative sceptic about knowledge. You might, then, agree that you can know nothing of any external world, and also nothing of any other times. Yet you might persist in your belief that there are a few simple things which you do know: that you now exist; perhaps, that you are in pain; that one and one are two; and so on; but always along these meagre lines. Now, while I disagree with this conservative position, I have a certain respect for it. And, to further my sceptical philosophy, I should address those who, perhaps partly as a consequence of my arguments, are sceptical about knowledge but less than universal in that scepticism. Accordingly, I will now try to say what our Basis Argument suggests for our conservative sceptics about knowledge.

If a man even knows so little as only that he now exists, the argument so far given, you may think, leaves it very unclear how much philosophical interest our reflections will have. For so far as this Basis Argument is concerned, the man's reason for any number of very different things may in each case be that he now exists. Moreover, so far as our actual argument can tell us, that reason may in each case be enough for the man to be reasonable in the thing. The man may be reasonable in thinking it was raining and reasonable in running to the store, in each case his reason being that he now exists. This is of course most implausible, but our actual argument does not rule it out. I will now try to remedy this situation by looking into this implausibility.

While something's being known by someone is a requirement of something being that person's reason, or one of his reasons, it is quite clearly not the only requirement. There must be some relation of relevance between his reason—and so what he knows—and that for which it is his reason. This relation may depend on surrounding circumstances. But at least in almost any circumstances, comparatively few things will be related so that they might count as someone's reason. Even without having a defining criterion of this relation, we can still be pretty sure that in no circumstances of the actual life you have lived would your reason for running to a store be, say, that you existed at the time or, say, that one and one are two. In these actual situations, at least, that one and one are two is *no reason for you* to run to a store. Hence, it could not there be *your reason* for doing that. Similarly, that you exist is not, in situations like these, any *reason for you* to believe, say, that there are many people living in a land called 'China'. And, hence, in such situations, it cannot be *your reason* to believe this thing. This discussion is not conclusive. But, our view does, I think, appear a good deal more plausible than its negation. The same points apply, of course, to what justification you might plausibly have in any actual situations.

How do these points tie up with the position of our conservative sceptic? If his scepticism about knowledge is correct, then what is there in which you might still be at all reasonable, or justified? Might you be reasonable in believing that China is more populous than India? What would your reason or reasons be? If I were asked about my reasons here, I would say that at least one of my reasons was that I had often heard China referred to as being the most populous country on earth. But do I *know* that I have heard this? Since I don't even know that I have a past, I don't know this particular past thing. Perhaps, then, my reason is that *I believe* that I heard China referred to in this way, or that *it seems to me now* that I have. But, while I cannot say *why* it is so, it seems quite clear that these things miss out on relevance. While *someone else's* believing, or saying, that he heard China referred to thus might be a reason for *you* to believe this thing, that *you* believe you heard it does not seem appropriate. In most circumstances of life, in point of fact, that a given person believes a certain thing is no reason for him to believe that thing, or to believe something quite distinct. For example, there being certain cigar ashes in the living room may well be a reason for you to believe that Uncle Fred has been visiting. But, if there are no ashes, but only grey confetti, that you believe there to be ashes is no reason for you to believe that Uncle Fred has been around. The same points apply to what seems to you to be so. So, even if you might know quite a lot about what you believe, and about what seems to you to be so, it appears that this knowledge will be no adequate basis from which many of your reasons may be derived. For example, it does not seem adequate for any reason you might have for believing China to be more populous than India. Rather, with just this sort of knowledge, it seems that you will have no reason for believing any such thing.[5]

The trouble for your reasons, however, hardly stops here. For it does not seem that, given our conservative scepticism, you will know more than a very little bit about what you

[5] On this point, I am indebted to discussion with John Taurek.

believe, or about what seems to you to be so. If my believing or something's seeming to me are treated as relatively simple aspects of my present consciousness, as occurrent mental phenomena, something like sensations, then at any particular time there are exceedingly few things, if any at all, which I believe or which seem to me to be so. And, of course it is under just this traditional treatment that there is plausibility in the idea that I will *know* that I now believe thus-and-such, or that so-and-so seems so to me. In this occurrent 'sense', in which knowledge is possible for the conservative sceptic, it *might* be that, at a particular time, I believe that I heard China referred to as the most populous country. But, if so, then, at any *such* time, it is most doubtful indeed that *another* thing which will seem to me to be so, or which I will believe, will be, say, that I heard Abraham Lincoln referred to as having been a President of the United States. Indeed, it is most doubtful that anything pertaining to Lincoln will then be present to my consciousness. There is no strict necessity in this, of course, but it does seem quite certainly *true*. So, a time that I might be reasonable in believing that China is more populous than India will, almost invariably, not be a time when I am reasonable in believing that Abraham Lincoln was a President of the United States. Accordingly, by the most eminently plausible generalization, there will be no time when I will be reasonable in believing much more than hardly anything. More generally, as I am hardly novel here, there will be no time at which anyone will be reasonable or justified in much more than hardly anything.

Now it may be replied that neither believing nor even seeming to you now involve such strict conceptions. Rather, you believe many things at any time, and at any time there are many things which seem to you to be so. This is because the ordinary senses of 'seems' and 'believes' do not require anything to be occurring to your present moment consciousness nor anything of the like. With no need of such things, they allow for you to believe something, or for something to seem to you to be so. If one appreciates what these terms mean, one will admit that they are 'dispositional' terms, or something of the like. One will admit, then, that all the time almost every person of experience believes ever so many things, including that he has heard China referred to as being the most populous country, and that he has heard Lincoln referred to as having been a President. One will admit that these things and ever so many more seem to one to be so, not just occasionally, but all the time.[6] This is quite a sensible line of reply. But, sensible or not, it will only alter the location of the sceptical problem; it won't remove it. If I interpret these things 'dispositionally', then I can't also hold that I *know* them to obtain. For, on this sensible interpretation, what I believe, or what really seems so to me, needs a basis in certain things I will do, that is, in certain con-current counter-factual situations. Thus, while I may *suppose* that my belief is that I heard China referred to as most populous, in response to experience of people seeming to complain about too much reference to China, should that experience now have occurred to me, then, so far as I *know*, I *might* have said that I have never heard it referred to in ways which would help us have a proper concern for China, e.g. as the country with the most people in it. And, the same goes with all sorts of other sit-uations which might have been involving me now though in fact they are not. Now, as I should not be absolutely *certain* that I would not react in these untoward ways, I should not be *certain* that I believe these things which I suppose I do, e.g. that I have heard China so referred to. Hence, I don't *know* that I be-lieve that I have heard Lincoln referred to as a President, and so on. In trying to have believing both ways, for the conservative sceptic, we have made a dilemma: If he takes believing and seeming occurrently, it won't even be *true*, let alone *known*, that many things now seem to you to be so, or that you now believe many things. If we opt for a more relaxed treatment of these things, while it might be true that this seems to you to be so, and that too, and so on, you won't *know* that they do anyway. Even with questions of relevance pushed to the rear, then, if a partial but strong form of scepticism about knowledge is correct, it will be a rare occasion indeed when you

---

[6] This seems to be the motivation for taking some such line towards reasonable believing as that adopted by Roderick M. Chisholm. In his *Theory of Knowledge* (Englewood Cliffs, N.J., 1966), he advocates such principles as this (on p. 50):

(E) If there is a certain sensible characteristic F, such that S believes he remem-bers having perceived something to be F, then the proposition that he does remember having perceived something to be F, as well as the proposition that he perceived something to be F and the proposition that something was F, is *reasonable* for S. (The italics are Chisholm's.)

are reasonable or justified in, e.g. believing that Lincoln was a President. For the conservative sceptic about knowledge, our Basis Argument strongly suggests a very strong form of scepticism about rationality.

§8. *The Principle of the Possibility of Identifying Knowledge*

In the sense required by logic, there are, I think, no important holes in our work so far. But there is an area of discussion which our remarks here must have brought to mind, and about which we have yet to say anything of explanatory value. This area concerns the appeal of classical arguments against reasonable believing, which we entered into in Chapter I, section 11. It is now my purpose to explain their appeal. For this purpose, I will introduce, and try to support, a further necessary, analytic proposition about reasons, and a cor elative one about justification. I call them, indifferently, the Principle of (the Possibility of) Identifying Knowledge. Before this introduction, it will be useful, I think, to rehearse the appeal of these classical arguments.

The first argument, it will be remembered, uses a classically derived conclusion about knowledge as a sub-conclusion. It then goes on to conclude, further, that, from there being no possibility for us to know anything external, we can't, really, be reasonable in believing anything about any external matter. We levelled a criticism concerning certain 'pragmatic' reasons against this argument. But even if that may mean a more complex argument is required, the intuitions behind the present one may help point in the right complex direction. I think that the intuitive ideas behind the present argument are these: As we *can't* ever *know* anything external, there *can't* be any *reason for us* to believe anything about any external world. Accordingly, we can't *have* any reason to believe any such thing, and, so, finally, we can't be reasonable in believing any. I suggest, that these ideas are essentially sound, and I will try to show that they are. If so, they will explain the appeal as wanted, and they may get us a sound, more complex argument for a strong sceptical conclusion.

A second line of reasoning was also discussed. This did not make use of the sceptical conclusion about external knowledge, classically derived. Instead, it mirrored the form of argument for that conclusion. Briefly, this mirroring argument went like this: *If* you are reasonable in believing that there are rocks, then you *can* be reasonable in believing that there is *no* evil scientist who, by means of electrodes, is deceiving you into *falsely* believing that there are rocks. But, you *can't* ever be reasonable in believing that there is no such scientist thus doing such a thing. Therefore, you aren't reasonable in believing that there are rocks. Again, pragmatic reasons made this argument look too quick. But, again also, the underlying ideas may be basically sound. I suggest that here they are these: Because you *can't* ever *know* anything about the relation of your experience to the presence or absence of such a scientist, and so on, there can't be any *reason for you* to believe there to be no scientist. Hence, you can't have any reason for believing there to be none, and you can't be reasonable in believing that.

To account for these intuitions, and to vindicate them, I introduce my Principle of Identifying Knowledge. Concerning reasons, this principle runs like this: If there is something *r* which is a reason for someone S to X, then it must be *possible for* S to *know that r is a reason for him, S, to X.*[7] (Similarly, if there is something *j* which is a justification for someone S to X, then it must be possible for S to know that *j* is a justification for him to X.) This principle entails, I suggest, that it must be possible for S to know that *r* (or, that *j*). This last condition is nothing new for us, as our Basis Argument requires S actually to know that *r* and, so, *a fortiori*, that it be possible for S to do so. In any case, we may write our principle with this familiar entailment made explicit: If there is something *r* which is a reason for someone S to X, then it must be possible for S to know, not only that *r*, but that *r* is a reason for him to X. Whether or not a person must actually know what his reasons are even when something is *his* reason for X-ing, which is a much stronger idea, it must be *possible for* him to know of any candidate that it is a reason for him to X. Otherwise, the candidate won't, really, even *be* any *reason for* him to X, the weakest idea.

---

[7] We must always interpret this principle so that it does *not* imply that in the required possibility of knowing that r is a reason for him to X, it is required that S there knows that he is S, or that he is a he, and not a she, and so on. Most people would, I think, take the principle on this reading even without this cautionary note; but here it is anyway, for good measure. The same applies, of course, to the other ambiguous principles and premises of our essay, going clear back to our classical arguments.

There is nothing special about the words 'possible for' as this principle employs them. They have the same, ordinary sense they have in, say, 'It was possible for him to wash the car; he just didn't bother to do it.' Accordingly, there is nothing about the meaning of these words which prevents something from being possible for someone at one time but not at another. What prevents the consequent of this principle from ever holding, however, is that it is for reasons of logic, or analytic reasons, that it is not possible for people, at one time or another, to know that anything is so, in particular, that anything is a reason for them. As long as these points are held in mind, we may understand what this principle says, and also that it may explain our classical appeal due to those mentioned reasons of logic. While I realize that to put forward this principle is quite a bold action, even with these cautionary reminders, I will try to confirm it by means of a couple of examples. Then I will try to employ it in explaining the appeal of our classical arguments against reasonable believing. In so doing, I think, I will be confirming the principle in another way.

We often think that someone believes something without reason but that there is a reason for him to believe it. Thus, Ben may believe without reason that his ink-well was made in the sixteenth century even though there might be a reason for him to believe it was. The reason might be this: that a certain pattern used only in that century is on the base. If Ben couldn't know anything about such patterns, perhaps because of gross stupidity, then we would think something else: while the pattern's being there is a reason to believe that dating, it is not any reason *for Ben* to believe it. If, however, Ben does know something about such things, and he can find out a lot more, we do allow that there is a reason for Ben to believe here, even if none for far stupider people. Supposing this, we may further suppose that Ben hasn't in fact bothered to find out these other things about patterns, which he can find out, and, so, that he is not yet able to use his powers of observation to much avail here. Now, especially if he has not yet looked at the base, we would think that, while there may be a reason for Ben to believe the thing, Ben *doesn't* (yet) *have* any reason to believe that the ink-well dates from that time. If Ben does acquire this general knowledge, then we may well allow, I think, that Ben *has* a reason here, though, presumably, he is not aware that he does. This seems especially apt if the only trouble is that Ben hasn't done some small particular thing, like turning over the well, easy enough for him to do if he bothers. If he would only turn the well over to look at the base, and thus see that it has that pattern, then, should he believe that dating on this basis, we would allow that *his reason for* believing it is that the pattern is there. If the reason is a very strong one in this regard, and especially if Ben realizes that it outweighs anything else which bears on his present situation, then, finally, we may allow that Ben is *reasonable in* believing that his ink-well dates from the sixteenth century. It at least appears, and I suggest that there is, a logical ordering of conditions here, which we have just moved through from weakest to strongest.

At the beginning of this ordering, there are two points for our attention. First, if Ben is unable to discern the pattern on the base, perhaps because of a lack of '*gestalt* closure', and he can't know it's there by any more indirect means, then its having that pattern can't be any reason for Ben. And, second, if he can discern that it has that pattern but, perhaps due to extreme stupidity, he can't know that the well's having it is a reason for him to think that the well dates from that time, then its having the pattern can't be any reason for Ben to think that it does. If, nevertheless, the pattern's being there is a reason to believe this, that is because there are, or at least there could be, some other people who, perhaps through less stupidity, could know that this pattern is a reason (for them) to believe the dating. Of course, these people would at least have *gestalt* closure, or whatever else it took for them to know the pattern to be there. Now, if, through special surgery, our most lacking Ben acquired such closure, and became much less stupid, so that it became possible for him to know, not only that the base had that pattern, but that that was a reason for him to believe the dating, then, I suggest, we would say this: Now, for the first time, the well's having that pattern is a reason *for Ben* to believe that it comes from the sixteenth century. If, on the other hand, reasons of logic mean that no such knowledge is ever possible for Ben, and perhaps for no one else either, then there never is any reason for Ben to believe that his ink-well dates from that time.

In a grander vein, we may suppose that some scientists have

a certain theory about the distribution of matter in the universe. We may suppose that the fact that a certain planet rotates in a certain way is a reason to believe that this theory is correct. We may suppose also, however, that the scientists, who do believe the theory, *can't know* whether the planet rotates this way or not. They believe the planet does because they see certain patterns on their photographic Q-plates. While these patterns are usually associated with such rotation, they aren't always. Given these circumstances, I do not think our idea is that a reason *for these scientists* to believe this theory is *that the planet rotates in the favourable way*. For any who can know about the rotation, that may well be a reason here, but not for our isolated scientists. We may ask, next, whether they can *know* whether their Q-plates have those patterns on them. If they can know it, then we may think this: those plates having those patterns *might be* a reason for the scientists to believe that the planet rotates in that way, and it *also might be* a reason for them to believe the theory to be correct.

Let's suppose, further, that the scientists can associate such photographic patterns *sometimes* but not often, with the rotations of various other planets, whose rotations they can quite clearly discern. But, they can't get the patterns to correlate with observed rotations any better than that. For this reason, and others in the context, the scientists *can't know* that these patterns' being on the plate in this case *is a reason for them* to believe that the key planet rotates in the wanted way. I think that in such a case we would say what our principle dictates: that these patterns' being on their Q-plates is *not* a reason for them to believe in this planet's rotation, much less is it a reason for them to accept the theory.

If the scientists invent the spectroscope then they might be able to correlate well with the wanted rotation the *joint* factor of a planet's producing that pattern on the Q-plates and its also giving a spectroscopic reading of k. One might suppose, and we shall, that now the scientists can know this uniform correlation. As our principle would encourage, this would lead us to say this: Now, for the first time, there is a reason for the scientists to believe the planet to rotate in that way, and also a reason for them to accept the theory about matter's distribution. That reason, the same for both, would here be this: that the planet produced such-and-such a photographic pattern on the Q-plates *and* gave a spectroscope reading of *k*. We would say this, I suggest, because we think that now, for the first time, there is something such that the scientists *can know* that it *is a reason for them* to believe or to accept.

Our principle pushes us back, and back. It doesn't let us stop until we can find things a man *knows* and, then also, which he *can know* to be reasons for him. As we have already implied, this does *not* mean that reasons to believe things, or to do things, are based on other reasons. Nor does it mean that knowledge is based on reasons. On the contrary, we must dispense with these wrong ideas to get at the point of our principle. Rather, it is from among the things that we *know*, know with absolute *certainty*, that our reasons must come. They must come from things that are perfectly clear and obvious to us. And, of these things, it is only those which we can *know* to be reasons which might ever *be* reasons for us. If *r* is a reason for Ben to think that *p*, about his ink-well, then it must be possible for Ben to *know*, with absolute *certainty*, that *r* is a reason for him to think that *p*. In terms of our analytic condition, it must be possible for it to be perfectly clear and absolutely obvious to Ben that *r* is a reason for him to think that *p*. Otherwise, it can't be a reason for him to think that.

Our examples, and any others, I suggest, bear this out. We have just been at pains to treat some examples leniently, that is to allow that quite a bit of knowledge is instanced in them, at least once our later suppositions were made. Our intuitions about reasons followed suit, as our principle dictated. Sceptical arguments, in contrast, seek to make us treat *all* examples negatively, first, as concerns knowledge, next, as concerns reasons. In terms of this (correct) approach, our principle can, I suggest, give us just what we want to make this sceptical move. Before employing it to this potent effect, however, I should like to use the principle to help explain the appeal of two related near misses, our two classical-style arguments against reasonable believing. For that will help us in two ways. First, it will get us further support for our principle. And, second, it will give us an idea of what more must be done to get sound arguments to replace these appealing, instructive failures.

Here is how this principle explains our first sort of classical argument. We have already, we suppose, classically reached the conclusion that, e.g. no one can ever know anything about any external matter. Is there, then, any reason for you to believe anything concerning such matters? What might one such reason be? Perhaps that it now appears to you that there is a triangular object some distance before you. The following thoughts, repeated from Chapter I, section 11, may now run through your head: I know that things appear this way. And, I may *take* this to be a reason (for me) to think that there is such an object there. But my experiencing the appearance may be due only to a scientist's electrode operations. While all my experience makes it *seem* that there is an external world, it may have no effective relation to this world I believe in. If I can't know the general character of the source of my experiences, neither they, nor anything else, it seems, can furnish me with any reason for believing one way or another in any external matter. Even if a certain appearance or experience seems to be a reason for a certain belief, unless I can know it comes from some appropriate source, I can't *have any assurance* that my having it is a reason for believing here. And, if I can't have any assurance to this effect, then, it seems, there really *isn't* any reason for me to believe the thing.

What explains these thoughts? It is assumed that if you can't know the general character of your experiences' sources, you can't have any reason deriving from your experience. What makes this question seem important in the first place is your accepting the idea that you can and do *know* the character of your experiences themselves, which supposed knowledge your classical argument about knowledge has left alone and intact. On our principle, your experiences may, then, so far at least, furnish you with reasons. So far things look good; for example, you may know that r, where the value of 'r' is that there now appears to be a triangular object before you. But can you know that this appearance or experience, is a reason for you to believe there to be such an object there? The thought occurs that you can know this only if you can know something significant about the source of the appearance or experience. Whether or not this thought is correct, it does occur. But, by our already accepted conclusion, you cannot know anything about any appropriate, material source. Hence, this experience is *not* a reason for you to believe there to be a triangular object before you.

A similar explanation applies to the idea about not being *able to have any assurance* that a certain thing really is a reason for you; there is now only greater complexity. Taking the matter most liberally, you want a reason, r', to think that something else, an 'apparent reason', r, really is a reason for you to believe something external, say, that p. But, to satisfy this want, by our principle, it must be possible for you to *know* that this r' is a reason for you to think that the apparent reason r is a reason for you to believe that p, say, that a triangle is out there. As it is natural to suppose that r, if a reason here at all, must be an evidential reason, it is natural to suppose also that r' must be. But, then, presumably, r' will be that you experience a certain appearance; otherwise it would seem to be irrelevant. This being so, r' is in no better position than r was, in our explanation before, concerning its possible sources. Hence, you *can't know* that r' is a reason for you to think that r is a reason for you to think that p. Accordingly, you conclude, by our principle, that r' can't be a reason to think that r is a reason for you to think that p. But, if you can't even have any reason to think r a reason to think that p, you surely can't *know* that r is a reason for you to think it. Finally, you conclude, again by our principle, r isn't really any reason for you to think that a triangular object is out there. And, as these things have been chosen arbitrarily, you conclude that there is no reason at all for you to believe that a triangle is before you.

We turn to explain our second classical argument against reasonable believing, with premises parallel to arguments against knowledge. Negatively put, the first idea here is that, if you can't have any reason for believing there is *no* scientist deceiving you into *falsely* believing there to be a triangle before you, you can't be reasonable in believing that such an object is out there. If evidential reasons were the only ones, this thought would, I think, be all right. But, as I said before, I believe this thought to be incorrect. The other thought, of course, is that you can't ever have any reason to believe this negative thing. This thought, I believe, is correct. What lies behind this second thought, is, I suggest, your thinking like this: As you can't *know* of anything, r, that it is a reason for you to think that no such operations are going on, there never even is any reason for you to believe any such thing. This is just an application of our principle, with the lack of knowledge vividly clear. The second premiss thus accepted, it is conjoined with the first to deduce the sceptical conclusion against reasonable believing in external matters.

In its ability to explain these two related sorts of argument, I suggest that our principle receives added support. However, to be most satisfied that genuine progress has been made, we should like to employ this valid principle in constructing a sound form of argument. We should like one such argument to have the conclusion that no one is ever reasonable in believing anything about any external world. And, finally, we should like some of the motivation behind the classical type arguments just discussed to help advance the new form. To this joint end, I now turn.[8]

§9. *A Form of Sceptical Argument Employing this Principle*

With our Principle of the Possibility Identifying Knowledge, we can construct sound arguments which exhibit more directly those ideas which underlie our classical arguments against reasonable believing. But, more than this, we can employ the principle soundly to deduce, in the realm of reasons and reasonableness, a more strongly sceptical conclusion than any we have drawn from our Basis Argument. Along both of these lines, we will have some news even for our more conservative sceptics about knowledge. And, in examining these arguments, we will see how our principle helps defeat the challenge of 'pragmatic' reasons, an effective challenge to our classical arguments concerning reasonable believing.

The challenge of pragmatic reasons was also introduced, along with the arguments challenged, in Chapter I, section 11. This challenge must be ineffective against the arguments we are now to construct. As we may recall, those (alleged) reasons worked like this: Even if you know nothing which can give you any evidence, or any 'evidential' reasons, for believing, say, that there are rocks, you might know certain things, say, things about yourself, which *can* give you *another sort* of reason to believe there to be rocks. For example, without knowing about

---

[8] As regards the section just completed, I have been helped by discussion with Robert Hambourger, and also with Michael Slote.

an external world, you might know that if you (now) believe there are rocks you will (now) be happier than if you do not. And, this last, it seems, might be a reason for you to believe that there are rocks; it might even be quite a powerful reason. Accordingly, without having any evidential reason for the belief, you might still be reasonable in believing something about an external matter. But, while the (alleged) existence of such pragmatic reasons demands some thought, we intuitively feel, I suggest, that their challenge is at best temporary. Rather than letting the issue rest, we are inclined to keep thinking that the classical arguments against reasonable believing are on the right track. What we want is something to counter this pragmatic suggestion to the contrary. Our Principle of the Possibility of Identifying Knowledge is, I suggest, the very thing for us to do this with.

Employing this principle, we may construct the following Argument from the Principle of the Possibility of Identifying Knowledge. In this present case the Argument concerns beliefs regarding an external world. The first premiss is our principle itself, here, for convenience, confined to the topic of believing. Thus confined, the principle concerns, not only belief in matters regarding an external world, but in any matters at all:

(1) For any propositional value of '*p*', if there is a reason *r* for someone S to believe that *p*, then it is possible for S to *know* that *r* and, moreover, to *know* that *r* is a reason for S (for him or her) to believe that *p*.

The second, and the only remaining premiss, is this:

(2) For any propositional value of '*p*' which concerns any external world there may be, it is never the case that it is possible for S to *know* that *r* and, moreover, to *know* that *r* is a reason for S (for him or her) to believe that *p*.

Our conclusion will follow validly straight away. But, before letting ourselves draw it, we should provide some discussion on behalf of this premiss. For, given our principle, it is on this premiss which the argument turns.

Concerning reasons to believe, the normal case is of course the evidential one. For this case we may just repeat thoughts we explained in the previous section; their only lack was in their not concerning the case of pragmatic reasons. In short, even a conservative sceptic who thinks he can *know* his own experiences (ostensible memories, and so on) will have to admit that we cannot *know of* any such plausible candidates *that it is a reason* for him to believe anything external (anything about other times, and so on). There remains to consider the case of pragmatic reasons. We consider our typical example. We suppose that a certain man *knows* that his believing there to be rocks is more conducive to his (present) happiness than his not so believing. This is our value of '*r*'. But, can he *know* that this is a reason for him to believe there to be rocks? It seems clear that, so far as he can *know*, his believing such a thing might also be more conducive to the much greater misery of many others. If this is so, it *might* mean only that the conduciveness to his own happiness is a poor, bad, or weak reason for him to believe the thing. But, perhaps also, the misery to others is so overwhelming that it means that its effect on his own happiness is no reason at all here for him to believe that there are rocks. There is, I think, at least a moderate amount of plausibility in this latter alternative. And, suppose our voice (from Chapter 3, sections 7, 8, and, especially, 9), after impressively establishing its credentials, assures him that in the present case his happiness means no reason for him at all. How can he *know* that it is a reason; how can it be *obvious* to him that it is, so that he may be justifiedly *certain*, absolutely *certain*? No way, I submit. As he can't possibly *know* that it is, this pragmatic thing can't be a reason for our conservative to believe that there are rocks, and so for any other alleged pragmatic reason. The same idea which motivated, and explained, our over-quick classical arguments against reasonable believing, the Principle of Identifying Knowledge, now vindicates our feeling that those arguments were on the right track. It not only figures as our first premiss in our new, sound, argument; it helps show why the second premiss is correct.

From our two premisses, we may validly deduce:

(3) For any propositional value of '*p*' which concerns any external world there may be, there is never any reason *r* for anyone S to believe that *p*.

And, from this stronger sceptical statement, our weaker conclusion about reasonable believing follows straight away:

(4) For any propositional value of 'p' which concerns any
external world there may be, no one ever is (at all) reasonable
in believing that p.

Parallel arguments can, of course, equally establish conclusions
in other domains, e.g. concerning other times. And, the same
can be said for being justified. Accordingly this new form of
argument closely ties our present chapter to our first one. Also,
it means a good deal of scepticism about rationality for even
quite a conservative sceptic about knowledge, more than we
could imply in section 7 of the present chapter. Beyond this,
we may notice that the full form of our Principle of Identifying
Knowledge may be coupled to our thesis of universal ignorance.
These two jointly entail that there never is any reason for
anyone, to do anything, to believe anything, to want anything,
and so on. They establish this as a necessary truth, of course, as
both of them are necessary propositions. And, as we have
remarked, the idea of there being a reason for someone appears
to be the weakest one in the whole area of personal reasons
and reasonableness. Hence, it appears that in this entire philosophic domain, our universal ignorance means that the strongest
sceptical conclusion holds with strict necessity. The same, of
course, applies to our thought about justification.

§10. *Irrationality*

By our Basis Argument, as well as by our Argument from the
Principle of the Possibility of Identifying Knowledge, we have
derived some very severe and sweeping sceptical conclusions.
At the very least, we have concluded that no one can ever be
reasonable in anything, not even in the least degree, and that
no one can ever be justified either. In our terms, we have
established the thesis of scepticism about rationality.

The notions of being reasonable and of being justified are not,
I suggest, isolated ones. While I cannot prove the point, the
following conditional seems correct to me: If no one can ever
be reasonable or justified in anything, then nobody can ever
be rational, or sensible, or wise, or intelligent, or prudent, etc.,

in anything.[9] Now each of the predicates for these properties has the appearance of a relative adjective, as does 'reasonable' itself. Someone may be wiser in saving his money than in wasting his time, just as he may be more reasonable in the first than in the second. And this doesn't look to mean that he will be closer to being wise in the one than in the other, or that he will be closer to being (?) absolutely reasonable in saving than in wasting. Like 'reasonable', however, 'wise' and its companions may well prove on examination to be defined absolutes. If so, their connection with a basic absolute will be even less direct than that of such words as 'happy' and 'sad'. If someone is happy that p, it follows that he knows that p; the absolute term 'knows' comes in pretty directly here, and, therefore so does the basic term 'clear'. He cannot, however, be *reasonable that p, or *wise that p. Slightly further removed, he can be reasonable or wise *in believing*, or *in saying*, that p. From this, however, it will not follow that p, or that he is certain that p, much less that he knows that p, or that it is *clear* to him. Indeed, no basic absolute seems so directly to follow. But as with 'reasonable', with 'wise' also, I suggest, it will follow that there is at least some q such that he knows that q. His saying it, or his believing that p, 'on the basis of this knowledge, of this clarity' is what is to make him reasonable, or wise, in saying it or in believing it. It is in this more indirect way, I suggest, that 'wise', 'intelligent', etc., like 'reasonable', are defined absolutes after all. If this is right, then it will not be surprising if no one can ever be wise *simpliciter*, or intelligent *simpliciter*, and so on. For how can anyone ever be wise or intelligent at all, if no one can ever be wise or intelligent in anything? Our ignorance, then, seems to

---

[9] I have some inclination to think that if there is never any reason for anyone to do anything, nothing is ever the *right* thing for anyone to do. And, if there is never any reason for anyone *not* to do anything, nothing is ever the *wrong*, or a wrong, thing for anyone to do. On these same conditions, I think, in the relevant sense, it is never the case that anyone *ought* to do anything, or that anyone *ougt not* to do anything. This is getting pretty close to the position of our normative nihilist, introduced in Chapter III, section 12. Such a result would completely undermine ethics and morals, or at least almost completely undermine them. In such a case, however, the more important points in ethical thinking could, I suggest, be recaptured in certain relative terms, perhaps something like 'good' and 'bad', which future philosophers may construct for the purpose. All of these ideas are so sweeping, of course, and I am so unconfident of them, that I confine them to this footnote. An argument for them, or one against them, might form the basis of an entire book, even a large one.

mean that a very strong and comprehensive thesis will fall under our rubric 'scepticism about rationality'.

But things do not stop here. For, in the realm of believing at least, it appears that we may conclude that there is *irrationality* on the part of every person. If a person *believes* something, then, at least on the assumption that he *doesn't know* the thing to be so, there had better be a reason, or reasons, for him to believe it. Otherwise, it seems clear, he will be *unreasonable* and, thus, *irrational* in believing the thing. We take an ordinary sort of case: Ben believes that silver sunglasses will be the big thing this summer in beachwear. As is ordinary, we assume that he does not *know* this. And, for our example, we assume that there is no reason whatsoever for Ben to believe this about silver sunglasses. It is quite plain, I submit, that Ben is unreasonable, and irrational, in believing silver sunglasses will be big this summer. Now, we take an ordinary case, but made it extra-ordinary by importing what we have already established: scepticism about knowledge. We return to the case of our friend, Norman Malcolm, and his looking at his familiar ink-bottle. His perceptual view of things is clear; the bottle may even be in his right hand; it is a bottle with which he has had much experience. We would ordinarily *say* that he knows there is an ink-bottle here in his hand, before him. But, having imported our scepticism about knowledge, we now deny that this is in fact true; on the contrary, Norman *does not know* that there is an ink-bottle before him. We now suppose, further, that there is *no reason at all* for Norman to believe that there is an ink-bottle there; not that there so clearly seems to be one; not that he has had extensive experience of the relevant desk furnishings; nothing. If with *no reason* for him to do so, Norman *still believes* that there is an ink-bottle before him, then, I think it plain, he is unreasonable and irrational in believing that simple thing.[10]

This ready slide into irrationality, it seems clear to me,

[10] This situation seems to be more relaxed with, say, animals, that is, those which are not persons. Supposing that animals believe things, and that they often or sometimes do so without there being any reason for them to believe the things, it still does not *seem* to follow that they are unreasonable or irrational in believing these things. While we may well be animals, we are not, perhaps unfortunately in these regards, among those which are not people or persons. On this, as on other points in this section, I am again indebted to Michael Slote.

attends not only believing, but also like states or aspects of persons: states or aspects most directly concerned with truth and falsity. Thus, the same severity of alternatives applies to being confident that p, thinking that p, and so on. In many cases, however, it does not apply to actions, or to states or aspects like desires. Thus, a man may stroll along the boardwalk and, even if there is no reason for him to do it, it does not follow that he is unreasonable or irrational in strolling along. And, a man may desire to swim without there being any reason for him to desire this, but it does not follow from this that he is unreasonable in desiring to swim. Whatever the explanation, believing seems quite different from these things as regards people's being unreasonable and irrational. I should think that any theory of these matters will have to yield an argument which explains the difference; it is far less likely, I suggest, that such a theory can afford to deny a difference here.

While irrationality in our actions does not follow so directly from the lack of reasons for us, in a less direct way, we are saddled with this result as well. The result may not apply to actions of ours which are reflexive, or 'totally unthinking'. But regarding any action which is based on beliefs, a man must be unreasonable and irrational in doing the thing, I suggest, if the beliefs on which he acts are themselves things such that in the believing, he is unreasonable and irrational. This last consequent condition, we have quite directly found upon us. Accordingly, as regards any actions but the most brute and unthinking, in a slightly less direct way, we conclude that people are always irrational in doing what they do.

Along the line of these conclusions, finally, I suggest, we may validly draw the inference that all people are irrational *simpliciter*. For we have already agreed that of necessity, every person is irrational in anything he may believe, and, except for the most unthinking actions, in anything he may do. Now, it seems to me that if a person is such that, for whatever reason, he is irrational in anything he may believe, and in any of his possible 'thinking' actions, then that person is irrational. Even if the reasons which explain his plight are logical or analytic, and even if his condition is logically necessary and, so, no fault of his, this conditional appears quite true. Hence, there is nothing but to conclude that of necessity, any person there may be is irrational. Accepting our ignorance, our language requires that we then accept our universal irrationality.

§11. *A Second Problem of what to Say and Think*

According to our sceptical view, no one can ever be reasonable in anything. Consequently, if someone believes this view itself, then he will not be reasonable in believing it. And, indeed, from what we have more recently said, the view implies that he will be unreasonable in believing the view. Doesn't this mean an overwhelming paradox? Doesn't it mean that this much scepticism must thus be self-defeating, and, so, that it need not be taken seriously after all? Indeed, in terms of these arguments, even a rather conservative sceptic about knowledge will have these difficulties. What are we to say to this charge?

These thoughts were, of course, anticipated rather near the outset of our present chapter. But an early and easy realization of them does only a little to disarm. In fact, I do find these thoughts quite disconcerting. But, while I do it with some hesitation, the force of all our arguments inclines me to treat these ideas in a way in which they are not regarded as decisive against scepticism.

In general terms, what I shall say is this: As remarked repeatedly, our language embodies a theory which makes much depend on an impossibly demanding concept of knowledge. Having thought for so long in this language, and having no other comparable means available, anything which looks radically to undermine the theory and, so, our language, looks to be crazy, and also threatening to logic itself. But, I would believe that the look of craziness, and the appearance of a total threat to logic, owes more to our tremendous involvement with our language than to any real craziness, or any genuine threat to or defiance of logic. The thing for us to do, I suggest, is to break out of this involvement.

A bit more particularly, I will speak a bit more boldly: to think that these charges of paradox devastate scepticism is to miss the point of both scepticism and paradox. The sceptic proposes that serious inquiry into the idea of knowing will end in the result of at least a partial but strong scepticism about knowledge. And, he proposes that such an inquiry pursued also into the ideas of being reasonable and being justified, will end in the result of at least a partial but strong scepticism about rationality. If this should prove the result of these inquiries—and who can be certain that it won't—then this will be the situation: Due to the nature of our ideas of *knowing*, of being *reasonable*, and of being *justified*, nobody can ever *know*, or be *reasonable* or *justified* in believing much more than hardly anything, including this very thing. But this will only be because the concepts prove so demanding that people can, at most, hardly ever satisfy them. The sceptic isn't the culprit, nor the position he advocates. It is the concepts themselves that mean the trouble. If anyone is to be blamed, likely it will be the originators of such seemingly lenient but actually demanding conceptions. The same thing goes for our concepts of being unreasonable, irrational, and unjustified, only their demands are less direct.

Instead of despairing in the face of these results, instead of feeling bad when thinking ourselves irrational, the thing for us to do, I suggest, is to devise alternative locutions to do the jobs of appraisal which, willy nilly, it appears that we in fact use our impossibly troublesome locutions to do. For even if we do not speak the truth in so doing, we may well make an important discrimination, in fact, at such times as when we say, e.g. one is more reasonable in accepting the astronomers' predictions of eclipses than the astrologers' prescriptions of what we should do for greater personal success. As I have argued, the man who accepts the former is not at all reasonable in that and, so, not more reasonable than the client who accepts the latter. But even so, I am eager to allow there may well be a difference between the two. We may in fact point to this difference in saying the false comparative thing about these people, however oblique the falsity will make the pointing. What we want to do is to mark that difference, perhaps even to describe it adequately, without saying anything false. What, then, are we to say and think here?

Our problem here is quite similar to the one encountered in Chapter IV, section 12, where we saw the need for new locutions for describing many of our emotional and other mental states and relations. Some philosophers will feel the present problem to be more acute, however, because some philosophers have denied the possibility of fruitfully making the comparative appraisals we want. While I allow that they may be right, despite my radical scepticism, I am not one who denies this possibility. On the contrary, I am eager to allow that it may not only be possible, but actually quite important to make these discriminations fruitfully, and while saying nothing false.

As in the previous chapter, I have no important statements to make along positive lines. But the following thoughts, which highlight our problem, may prove suggestive. While we might just as well think of continuously operating electrodes, these thoughts will concern a man who arrives in the world *à la* Russell, in the manner familiar to us from Chapter I, section 12. Let us suppose, first, that this man is an exact qualitative duplicate of yourself. Accordingly, we may further suppose, he mirrors, not only your every molecular constituent, but the qualitative character of all your beliefs, your attitudes, and so on. Unlike you, of course, the man will believe many false things about himself. He will think that he has turned knobs and then seen pictures on nearby connected screens. This of course is false, as he has had no experience whatever. Partially 'based' on this first false belief, he will believe correctly we suppose, that he can now see pictures on such screens if he turns such a knob. In other words, as supposed, he has qualitatively the same belief as you. We have, I suggest, a strong inclination to think that this man must be *just as reasonable* in this belief of his as you are in believing that you can see pictures if you turn such knobs. We are inclined to think that the two of you are identical as regards reasonableness, and so, identically very different from many other people. We would distinguish you two thus, for example, from a denizen of an underdeveloped land who, having unfortunate experience of Westerners, unreasonably believes that if he turns the knob his soul will be saved.[11]

When thinking about traditional sceptical problems, however, our inclinations run differently. At these times, I suggest, your thinking tends to run like this: For all you know, *you* may be such a man, arrived *à la* Russell, whether a duplicate of anyone else or not. If your 'basis' beliefs are incorrect, because having arrived you lack all experience, you can't really be

---

[11] Saul Kripke has long said to me that these two qualitatively identical men are reasonable, and thus equally reasonable. As a sceptic, while I think him wrong, I will shortly try to make what I take to be the valuable point behind this judgement of his.

reasonable in believing very much at all. You can't, for example, be any more reasonable in believing that such a knob on such a box is a way of bringing pictures to a screen than, say, that the knob only will involve the saving of your soul. There is of course a certain inconsistency in these two sorts of inclination.

If our Basis Argument is on the mark, the latter inclination is a truer guide to what most fundamentally goes on with our concept of being reasonable: the requirement of some appropriate *knowledge*.[12] The former inclination comes from focusing on the relative dimension(s) of the concept, unfortunately, to the point of overlooking the necessary condition of knowledge. Once this is realized, we need not overlook any longer. And, we may learn some good lessons from this first inclination. For example, if we elect to replace 'reasonable' with a new word 'queasonable', the inclination directs us like this: A man who arrives *à la* Russell, or who is made in a laboratory, and who is the exact qualitative duplicate of an existing man, is just as queasonable a person as the first. And, more particularly, he is just as queasonable in believing each of the things he believes, no more and no less, as is the man he duplicates. The import is quite clear. What matters for our wanted discriminations are certain qualitative features of the person himself. One thing of importance might thus well be the relations among certain present beliefs of his; another might be the relations among these and certain current *attitudes* of his, like an interest in getting closer to the truth, a willingness to think hard about opposing claims, and so on. The important points do *not* concern, in any case, the relation of the person to things at other times or, by any easy parity of reasoning, to things outside his mind, that is, to things in the external world. In this respect, the important best parts of our ideas of being reasonable, being justified, wise, etc., are all subjective. I suspect, however, that these subjective features require a description of beliefs and attitudes which is very complex and subtle, if the important features are to be adequately described. And, I suspect, further, that in that complex description there will be crucial reference to a certain attitude the subject has towards his own beliefs, an attitude which will prompt us to say, 'He is an objective sort of person.'

12 I am indebted here to discussion with Dennis Stampe.

VI

Where Ignorance Enjoins Silence

IT is common to feel that there is something wrong where a sceptic about knowledge states his own sceptical view. I want to explain the frequency of this feeling in a way which vindicates the feeling as sound, and which does justice to the circumstances which arouse the feeling. At the same time, of course, my explanation is not to reflect badly on scepticism about knowledge. Rather, I suggest, the culprits will be revealed to be our notion of stating itself, and our like notions of asserting and declaring. The problems with these 'illocutionary acts' will suggest some extremely sweeping problems with our accepted ways of expressing our thoughts. The upshot of the problems is that our ignorance enjoins us, rather than give expression to our thoughts in any familiar way, to be silent. An alternative, of course, is to find new ways to express our ideas.

§1. *Some Feelings we have towards the Statements of Sceptics*

I have just mentioned the common feeling that there is something wrong with a sceptic about knowledge who states his own sceptical thesis, who states, that is, that nobody ever knows anything to be so. Even right near the beginning of introductory courses in the subject, both teachers and many bright students of philosophy often have some feeling to this effect. Moreover, it is felt that the sceptic shouldn't state *anything*. Sometimes, though less frequently, the feeling is this: In that he thinks there is no knowledge, this sceptic shouldn't even so much as suggest that something is so. Given the truth of his view, it is felt, in so far as his speech or writing involves putting forward anything as even possibly true or correct, he had better be silent.

Here is an example of the sort of thing I mean. A teacher may say that the following assertions are quite consistent, and for that reason, they provide consistent possibilities for the sceptic about knowledge. First, he may assert his view. And, second, he may assert, *not* that he *knows* that it is sunny outside, but just that it *is* sunny. But the students and often even the teacher, I suggest, feel that there are problems here. First, there seems to be some sort of inconsistency involved in *asserting* that nobody knows anything to be so. And, second, it also seems to be inconsistent with this proposition to *assert* that it is sunny outside, even if *what is asserted* is not thus inconsistent. Whatever this sceptic should do, it is felt, it should be 'less' than this. Accordingly, in more open-minded moods, the teacher may go on to correct himself. In retreat, he may say that the opportune assertions for our sceptic are these: First, that he *believes* that nobody knows anything to be so, and, second, that he *believes* that it is sunny outside. The idea here is, of course, supposed to be this: The sceptic thinks only that things can't be known, not that things can't be believed. But even though this idea is correct, it is out of place here. As many feel, there is no real advance in these alleged opportunities. Given that our sceptic's view is that we don't know *anything* to be so, then one thing which he doesn't know is what, if anything at all, he believes in a particular matter. On his view, he does not know that he believes that nobody knows anything. And, further, he does not know that he believes that it is sunny outside. Accordingly, he should refrain from asserting that he believes either of these things, much less both. While the locus of our problem has been shifted, the problem itself remains.

As I think these feelings are on the mark, I want to explain their soundness as well as their frequent and early occurrence. The conclusions we reached in section 10 of the preceding chapter present one sort of explanation. But I do not think it will account well for the frequency or the early occurrence of these feelings we experience. That overpresumptuous explanation would run like this: From scepticism about knowledge, it follows that there is no reason for a sceptic about knowledge to believe anything. Thus, he is irrational in anything which he may believe. But asserting and stating are, in some sense, 'thinking actions'; they are in some sense based on beliefs of the subject, even when they are not done intentionally. In that our sceptic is irrational in these beliefs, he is irrational also in asserting or stating anything. In particular, he is irrational in stating his sceptical view, and also in asserting that it is sunny outside. Accordingly, he should not do these things. While this is, I think, a good argument, it offers little in the way of our wanted explanation.

In the first place, thinking that this argument may lie behind their feeling asks too much of most of our bright students. As we have been supposing, and as so often does take place, the feeling against our sceptic occurs before the topic of scepticism about rationality is even introduced. Without this introduction, I doubt that many students would quickly think far, if at all, along the lines of our offered explanation. And, to get someone to the point of feeling a prohibition against asserting, that explanation requires him to think rather far along these lines. He must get beyond the absence of reasonable believing, to the unreasonableness in believing and, then, all the way to the irrationality of 'thinking' action, here, the assertion of something. I do not think that this goes on nearly often enough to explain the frequency or the early occurrence of feelings against our sceptic about knowledge. In the second place, our students feel that the sceptic does *better* by being silent, that he does better to *refrain* from asserting anything. This feeling is, I submit, most common in these cases. But, refraining is a 'thinking' act. And, as the students normally envisage the case, the sceptic is supposed to refrain intentionally. But according to the explanatory argument deriving from our preceding chapter, the sceptic about knowledge will, on his own view, eventually be irrational in (intentionally) refraining. For any belief on which this refraining is based will be one in which the sceptic is irrational. This gives us too much. For, I submit, those who would think through the offered explanatory argument would, in most cases, think this much further as well. Thus, they would *not* feel that the sceptic does *better* to refrain. On the contrary, they would feel that he is completely irrational *in either case*. The feeling we want to explain is of course more selective than this. Accordingly, the material we developed in our preceding chapter is too powerful for our present purpose.

§2. *An Hypothesis concerning Asserting and Like Acts*

One of the most common things we do with our language is to assert that something is so. Another is to state that something is. While declaring something to be so may not be so common, even here we may be expected to have some pretty good intuitions. I mean to put forward an hypothesis about these things which will uncover an important element they have in common, whatever the further features that may distinguish them. The hypothesis is this. If someone asserts, states, or declares that something is so, then it follows that he represents himself as *knowing* that it is so.[1] Schematically, if S asserts, states, or declares that *p*, then S represents it as being the case that he *knows* that *p*. It seems plain enough to me that this hypothesis entails the weaker condition that in asserting that *p*, S represents it as being the case that *p*. In any case, we may give a fuller statement to what we hypothesize: If S asserts, states, or declares that *p*, then he not only represents it as being the case that *p*, but he represents it as being the case that he *knows* that *p*. I think that a wide variety of sentences and examples serve to confirm this hypothesis. Among these are the 'negative' examples of our classroom situations, where feelings are aroused against the sceptic about knowledge. I begin to test the hypothesis by seeing how well it explains these philosophically familiar feelings.

On this hypothesis, when our sceptic asserts that nobody knows anything, he represents himself as knowing that nobody knows anything. Accordingly, he represents as actually being the case something which is inconsistent. He thus *represents* an inconsistency even if he does not actually assert anything inconsistent. This serves to explain the direct negative feeling towards him, or towards what he is doing. Moreover, as he represents himself to know what can't possibly be known, as a matter of necessity, he *falsely represents* himself, at least in this one respect. As we all have a general feeling against false representation, and, just a bit more particularly, against a person falsely representing himself, it is not surprising that we feel something to be wrong with this sceptic here.

There is no obvious necessity of false representation in someone's asserting that it is sunny outside. But, given the truth of scepticism about knowledge, and given our hypothesis, it

---

[1] In response to some rather confused remarks I made on these topics, Donald Davidson suggested such a condition with the single difference that he had believing where I have knowing. While I take this difference to be important, my debt to Davidson here is obviously very large indeed.

follows that one who asserts even this must falsely represent himself. For in asserting it, he represents himself as knowing that it is sunny; if nobody knows anything, then it is false that he knows that. Similar remarks explain the feelings against the sceptic when he would state what he believes. Whether he states that he believes his sceptical thesis, or whether only that he believes it to be sunny, the sceptic, like anyone else who would make such a statement, represents himself as knowing what he believes. On his own position, he cannot know even this. And so, rightly I think, we feel that there is something wrong with even such a statement on his part. This explanation requires no very radical or advanced sceptical thinking, nothing, that is, like the thinking done in coming to be a sceptic about rationality. In short, I suggest, it is just the right sort of explanation for what has been going on in our classroom.

Our hypothesis receives some support from explaining these negative examples. This is hardly a surprise, as the hypothesis was advanced for just this purpose. What would be more impressive is any support it might get from examples and sentences which have much less to do with the issues of scepticism. To pave the way for our considering these other phenomena, I shall make a few remarks.

A man may often assert that p, while fully believing that he does *not* know that p, perhaps, even, that it is false that p. Furthermore, the man's intended audience may fully believe as well that the man does not know that p. The man may in turn fully believe this to hold of his audience, and so on. None of this is denied by our hypothesis. For an example, we may consider a man who sells widgets for an eccentric millionaire, the latter wanting his salesmen to give widgets the 'hard sell'. He wants this, and will pay for it, even though he is as aware as the next man that his salesmen and the public think widgets to be no good; his salesmen are apprised of this, and so on. In a typical circumstance, one of his salesmen may say, 'These widgets are the greatest gadgets in the world. Try one for thirty days with no obligation on your part.' I think that, typically, a salesmen would have asserted that the widgets are the greatest gadgets, even with the complex network of beliefs (or, if you like, knowledge) to the contrary. I also think, however, that he would have *represented* himself as *knowing* the widgets to be the greatest gadgets. So far, so good, for our hypothesis.

Assertion is often unintentional, and we even mean to assert nothing. Thus, a patriotic fan of debating may resolve to listen quietly to a debate about the economic merits of his country's system as compared with a radically different one. Upon hearing something grossly false, he may loose control and say 'That's not true, *their* growth rate was only 2 per cent last year and *ours* was 12 per cent; you've got it backwards.' Without intending to, indeed while intending to do no such thing, this man may have thus asserted that this country's growth rate last year was 12 per cent. But, then, while intending to do no such thing, he represented himself as knowing that it grew that much.

At least in our fuller formulation of it, our hypothesis says this: If someone asserts, or states, that *p*, then he represents it as being the case that *p*. We ask: Does anyone ever assert that anything is so without, at the same time, representing that thing as being so? If someone asserts that it was raining and then goes on to say that he didn't *mean* to represent it as being the case that it was, what are we to ask of what he says? To make any sense of it, we must suppose that he means to take back what he first represented as being the case, or we must suppose something very similar. Suppose, now, that someone asserts that it was raining and then goes on to assert that he *isn't* representing it as being the case that it was. This time it doesn't look so much like the speaker is taking back what he said at first; rather, it looks as though he just contradicts it. All of this strongly suggests that when one asserts that something is so, one must always be representing that thing as being so.

We may help make the point clearer by way of contrast. Now, philosophers have pointed out to the point of boredom that we can do things in and with language that do not involve asserting that anything is so. What is a bit less boring, perhaps, is that we can do such things in the way of 'putting forward a proposition' while still not actually asserting anything to be so. For example, without actually asserting that it was, one might *suggest that* it was raining.[2] In this case, one would not be so

---

[2] I owe the idea of contrasting assertion with (the appropriate form of) suggestion, and of making the contrast along the lines that follow, to Dennis Stampe.

likely to use the unqualified words 'It was raining,' though if the context were right, perhaps one might: 'Can you suggest a possible explanation for their having caught a cold? Anything which may have happened; any suggestion will do.' In most contexts, however, we use words like these to suggest: 'Let me suggest that it was raining,' 'It might have been raining,' 'Perhaps it was raining; I don't know.' Now, if someone suggested that it was raining, he needn't have represented it as being the case that it was; after all, he just suggested it. There is all the difference in the world between saying, on the one hand, 'It was raining, but I'm not representing it as being the case that it was' and, on the other, *'Perhaps* it was raining, but I'm not representing it as being the case that it was.'

Even if someone only suggests that *p*, it may follow that there is *something* that he represents as being the case, though it will (at least generally) not be the same thing as that which he suggests. I suggest that what might thus always be represented is this: that it might be the case that *p*; that it is possible that *p*. Perhaps that is why it sounds inconsistent to say 'I suggest that it was raining, but I'm not saying that it was possible.' In any event, there is a clear enough contrast between actually asserting something and just suggesting it. The contrast is clear enough, I think, to make the point that, of the two, only the former requires that one represent that very thing as being the case.

§3. *Support from Problem Sentences*

We want to argue that asserting that something is so entails not just representing the thing as being so, but representing oneself as *knowing* that it is. In addition to our explanation of feelings against the sceptic, I will try to support our strong condition along two main lines. The first of these involves the proper treatment of some otherwise puzzling sentences.

There is a famous phenomenon which occurs with certain sentences and which often passes under the name of 'Moore's Paradox'. The sentences express consistent states of affairs, but they sound as though they say something inconsistent. A typical example is the sentence 'It's raining, but I don't believe it.' What the sentence standardly expresses is indeed consistent, that is, one who standardly utters it expresses a consistent proposition or state of affairs: it may be raining even while the utterer does not believe that it is. But, nevertheless, the sentence does sound inconsistent. The problem is to account for the inconsistent sound.

The first step of an account seems to be this: Upon seeing or hearing the sentence, we think of it, however implicitly, as being used by someone to assert, or state, or declare that it's raining but he (or she) doesn't believe it. More particularly, one may think of it as being used by oneself to assert that it's raining but one doesn't believe it. We think of the sentence in these ways, I suggest, even when we are quite well aware that it is in fact being used in some quite different way, e.g. as an example for philosophical discussion, where rain is hardly the issue. It is no accident, I suggest, that the standard grammatical name for such sentences is 'declarative', that philosophers standardly think of them as expressing 'statements', and as our means for doing so with 'assertive' or 'assertoric' force. This thought of asserting, stating, or declaring is the first step of our account. But where do we go from here?

In line with our hypothesis, I suggest that when one asserts that it's raining, one represents oneself as *at least* believing that it is. This allows that one may say the thing without actually representing oneself as believing it, say, perhaps, if one represents oneself as knowing the thing. In case knowing precludes believing, which I cannot determine, one will still represent oneself as at least believing the thing, though not as believing it. In line with this suggestion, the following sentences do *not* sound inconsistent: 'It's raining, but I don't believe it; I know it is' and 'It's raining, but I don't just believe it; I know it.' It may be that in hearing the first of these, we interpolate a 'just' and in that way hear it as equivalent to the second. In that case, we may even allow that knowing entails believing. But, of course, this interpretation has not been argued to be necessary. Indeed, in contrast, it may be that when we hear the original sentence, 'It's raining, but I don't believe it,' we interpolate an 'even' so as to hear it as 'It's raining, but I don't even believe it.' It may be that only this last sentence fully gets us the paradoxical phenomenon. In that case, we may even allow that knowing precludes believing, as I suggested (but certainly did not assert) before. So, while we are not sure we want to accept this suggested condition *without* the 'at least', *with* these words we may continue our explanation: If one says that *p*, one represents oneself as *at least* believing that *p*.

Our explanation is now quite straightforward: We first think of an utterer as asserting that it's raining and, so, as representing himself as at least believing that it is. We then think of this utterer as going on to assert that he doesn't even believe that it is and, so, as going on to represent himself as not even believing the thing. We thus think of the utterer as representing all of the following as being the case: that he at least believes that it's raining and he doesn't even believe that it is. But, then, as this last is quite clearly inconsistent, we think of the utterer as *representing something inconsistent* as being the case. This is why Moore's sentence sounds inconsistent even though nothing inconsistent is ever said to be the case.

An ability to explain Moore's Paradox gives us support for a proposition about asserting: If one asserts that *p*, one represents oneself as *at least* believing that *p*. The question now is this: can we similarly gain evidence for our stronger proposition: If one asserts that *p*, one represents oneself as *knowing* that *p*? Sentences involving 'believe' cannot help us much here. We must now look to other sentences for our support.

For some reason or other, it is not nearly so often noticed that an apparently inconsistent sentence also results from by following a simple indicative clause by a denial of things much stronger than mere belief in the proposition.[3] For example, it seems inconsistent to say, 'It's raining, but I'm not absolutely sure it is' though what one standardly says with these words is perfectly consistent: It may be raining even while the utterer is not absolutely sure that it is. It seems inconsistent also to say, 'It's raining, but I don't know for certain that it is,' or to say, 'It's raining, but I don't know that it is.' Like Moore's sentences with 'believe', there is a problem here, or by far the greatest problem, only where the first person and present tense are employed: it's quite all right to say and hear 'It was raining, but I didn't know it' or 'It's raining, but she isn't certain of it.' So, these less noticed sentences present phenomena quite on a par with those of Moore's Paradox. We may solve the problem

---

[3] A notable exception in the literature is Jaakko Hintikka's *Knowledge and Belief* (Ithaca, N.Y., 1962), pp. 78ff.

of explaining the apparent inconsistency in this yet more puzzling case by appealing to our desired condition.

We may begin by explaining the oddness of 'It's raining, but I don't know it is.' First, of course, we think of someone's asserting that it is raining but he doesn't know it is. Our hypothesized condition now tells us that, in asserting the first part, the speaker represents himself as knowing that it is raining. When he goes on to assert the second part, by our weaker condition, he represents himself as *not* knowing that it's raining. Thus, he represents himself as both knowing and not knowing this simple thing. If we are implicitly accepting our condition all along, this pattern of thought may well be in our heads. And, if we all accept this condition, that is probably because it is analytically correct.

We may explain the peculiarity of 'It's raining, but I don't know for certain that it is' by identifying knowing and knowing for certain. There are other ways, to be sure. But their appeal is small when we realize that we must account in any case for the apparent inconsistency of both 'He *knows* it's raining, but he doesn't *know for certain* that it is' and 'He *knows for certain* that it's raining, but he doesn't *know* that it is.' Having to suppose that knowing and knowing for certain entail each other, and that it takes no great faculty to sense this, we may allow that there is but one knowing here. Thus, we may allow that the following is just a restatement of our desired condition, and that it is accepted by us all as such: If one asserts that p, one represents oneself as knowing for certain that p. The explanation for our newer problem sentence then follows as did the first.

We may explain the apparent inconsistency of 'It's raining, but I'm not absolutely sure it is' by making an assumption about knowing and being absolutely sure. We need only suppose that one's knowing something to be so entails one's being absolutely sure of it. It is to be expected that this is so, and that we accept it as such, since we accept the idea that knowing is the same as knowing for certain. It seems that this condition must be accepted anyway. For, as we noted in Chapter II, section 9, we must explain the inconsistency of 'He *knows* it's raining, but he's *not* absolutely *sure* of it,' 'She *knew* it was raining, but she *wasn't* completely *certain* of it,' and so on. On the basis of accepting this entailment, I suggest, we accept the condition: If one asserts that p, one represents one-self as being absolutely sure that p. And, once again, the ex-planation of the puzzling sentence follows as before. Of course, we may explain the sentence in similar ways which do not re-quire this last condition of assertion. We may think, for example, that the person just represented himself as knowing that p, and not as being absolutely certain of it. Understanding this representation, we in turn quickly realize that what he rep-resented entails that he is absolutely certain that p, which he then goes on to deny. This is another way in which we may get the idea that our speaker had put forward an inconsistency. But I see no reason for not taking the stronger, simplifying line that in asserting that p, he did represent himself as being abso-lutely certain of it. And, so, I shall continue to write my ex-planations in a way which is friendly to such assumptions, while mindful, of course, that alternatives are open to us. No further discussion should be needed to figure out, for example, some explanations for the inconsistent sound of 'It was raining, but it's not completely clear to me that it was,' nor should any be needed to assess which is the simplest of them. Accordingly, I submit, the consideration of a variety of difficult sentences lends support to our idea that if one asserts that something is so, one represents oneself as *knowing* the thing. Thus encouraged, we look to support our strong condition in other ways.

§4. *Support from Conversational Situations*

If the evidence from problem sentences is striking, it may also be called, in a certain sense at least, trifling. It would be good to have evidence which, in some sense, is of a more serious sort. We get just such more serious support when we consider our reactions and thoughts in ordinary conversational situations.

Suppose that someone did not just suggest but actually as-serted to you that you will get a substantial rise in salary for the coming year. If this was said during normal, serious conversing on things, how would you think of this person if he did not *know* the thing to be so? And, if the speaker was very *confident* that the thing was so, but also suspected that he did *not know* the thing, how would you think of and treat this individual? If this man were only very *confident* of this thing, your thought is, I take it, that he shouldn't have asserted it. If he is to say something on the matter, he should assert some weaker thing, something of which he is *sure*. Depending on the situation, he might assert that it is *almost* certain that you will get the rise, or that he is quite confident that you will, or, perhaps, that you will get one if anyone will. But, if he *doesn't know* that you will, he shouldn't assert, state, declare, swear, or claim that you will get the rise.

It is not simply whether the thing he says is true which is at issue. Nor is his being justified in thinking it true enough to get him off the hook. Suppose that the man who said you'll get a rise did so on the basis of a talk with his superior, the president. The president himself did not know whether you'll get a rise and admitted as much. Accordingly, the man who spoke to you could not have known. What the president said was that it was extremely likely that you will, that you will barring only the most incredible turns of events. This is all your 'informer' could know. Now, your informer is justified, if one ever is, in thinking and even being quite confident that you'll get a rise. But, then, he should just say something to that effect; at any rate, he shouldn't assert that you'll get it. Even if it turns out that you do get the rise, that makes little difference here. As the man didn't know it at the time, he shouldn't have asserted it. Assuming that he was rather aware of what he was doing, he was, I think, even open to some blame for having done it. The reaction to what this man has done is not that he has just made a mistake, misused language, or broken any particular rule or convention. He may also have done those things. But our reaction is that, in a more fundamental way, he has acted wrongly. What he did, in so far as it was intentional, was of a piece with lying, though perhaps it was not quite so badly wrong as that. How might we best account for our thinking this about this man?

On our condition for asserting, this man represented himself as knowing something which he did not in fact know. In so far as he realized that he did not know it and realized that he was so representing himself, he represented himself in this way quite consciously. This is something which is dishonest. We may quite clearly bring this out by noticing that in stating this thing without knowing it to be so, the man falsely represented things and, in particular, quite consciously *he falsely represented himself* as knowing the thing. It is our thinking this last thing, I suggest, which lies behind our reaction to the man of this example, and to real people who assert things without knowing them to be so. If these speakers *think* they know, or are otherwise innocent about the facts, the worst we think of them is that they are unduly incautious: they do not mean to represent themselves falsely; they should then take the proper precautions not to do so. But, if they are as well into the relevant matters as we think anyone could be, and act on the idea that they do not know the thing, then in asserting, they misrepresent themselves on purpose or do something to the same bad effect. This false representation is, I suggest, what is dishonest, and worse than making a mistake or breaking a convention. I can think of no other explanation of our reactions which quite compares with this one. If this is no defect of mine, our reactions here are support for our strong claim about asserting.

We just considered an example of someone's bad behaviour which concerned one's own future. But the important features do not concern any particular time or person. For example, one might think of a colleague asserting that *his* manuscript *had* just been accepted by a certain publisher or periodical. Now, suppose that though the colleague believes this, and justifiably so, and though it is true that his work has been thus accepted, he doesn't really *know* that it has. He can't rightly be *sure* of it. For example, his secretary might have told him that he has an envelope from the publisher which looks to be of the sort in which they send their acceptances—but she can't be absolutely sure, she says. Or, perhaps, he has a letter before him which says that if he makes some small changes in his work, which the editors think he can make, then it is almost certain they will publish it. It may be that from this publisher, strangely enough, these words constitute an acceptance. But assuming that our colleague *doesn't know* that, he *shouldn't assert* that his work has been accepted. In asserting it, he falsely represents himself. And we are bound to think the worse of him for it.

Finally, think of someone who just says something about the world, e.g. that Bob Hope is richer than Nelson Rockefeller. Now, I believe that I have read things from which this can be easily deduced, but I am not certain that I have. In any case, you may take it that I do *not know* that I have read them and, so, I do not *know* for certain which man is the wealthier. In such a case, if I *asserted that* Hope is the richer, you would think poorly of me—even if I reasonably believed the thing and even if it was in fact true. What I *should* assert is that I *believe* that Hope has more money; or I might assert some still further thing. But, if I simply asserted that thing, which I only believe, I would falsely represent myself. This is because when one asserts that something is so, one represents oneself as knowing the thing, and in the present case I do not really know. Now, I suppose that this all may come as something of a surprise to many philosophers. For many seem to think that, overriding considerations aside, whatever is enough to make it all right for someone to believe something is also enough to allow him properly to assert it. But, putting aside for the moment our extreme difficulties with reasonable believing, this thought, it seems, must go by the board.

Perhaps the most striking evidence for our condition comes from its ability to explain otherwise puzzling facts about the way we allow our conversations to proceed.[4] It is exceedingly common, of course, for someone to say something in conversation in way of asserting or stating the thing. So far, there is nothing very puzzling. A puzzle, however, is that faced with such an assertion or statement, even if it is impolite or boorish, so far as the logic of the discourse goes it is appropriate to respond by asking whether the asserter is *absolutely sure* of what he said, or by asking whether he *knows* the thing *for certain*. Thus, if someone says 'I had eggs for breakfast on Monday' so as to assert that he did, appropriate challenges may be standardly made by asking, 'How do you *know* you had eggs?', 'Are you perfectly *certain* you did?', 'Do you know that for certain?', and so on. Though the original asserter *said nothing about knowing*, or even about being certain of anything, these questions are felt by all to be a challenge to his assertion and, so, to him for making it. The puzzle, then, is to account for how the questioning of such strong, demanding conditions can be a challenge to making an assertion whose content is quite undemanding. Why can't the asserter get off the hook by saying

---

[4] The importance of these otherwise puzzling facts was urged on me by Michael Slote.

'I never said I knew it?' Our epistemic condition resolves the puzzle: Though he never *said* he knew, in asserting what he did, the speaker represented himself as knowing that he had eggs then. In asking the question, we question what he represented in asserting what he did. It is for this reason, I suggest, that we manage to challenge his assertion even when the content of what he asserted is quite weak and undemanding.

If after having his assertion challenged in this way a speaker can make a good case for the thought that he really does know the thing, his assertion will be allowed to stand. If he feels he can't make such a case, however, he can withdraw his assertion and stop asserting things for the time being. But a more usual response here is for him to replace his first assertion by another. What he asserts instead is usually, I think, that he at least thinks or believes that the thing is so e.g. that he had eggs for breakfast then. This assertion is generally not challenged. Why is that? Our explanation is this: Now, the asserter represents himself as knowing that he at least believes the thing to be so. And this is something which, generally, it is allowed that he does know. Without this explanation, the appropriateness of this assertive retreat is almost as puzzling as the original challenge. A further, more particular point now calls for our attention. Why do we think of a man's later saying what he believes as being a *retreat* from his assertion that he ate eggs? Why are the two placed in the *same scale*, with the former weaker than the latter? For they seem to be about entirely unrelated topics: one about what the person *ate*, the other about what he *believes*. Our condition explains these feelings also. While the person first only asserted eating on his part, he represented himself as knowing and, thus, as being certain. Later he asserts and represents himself as just believing the same thing. The latter is weaker than what he first represented, and very much in the same topic area. In explaining these puzzles, our condition gains at once a triple strand of evidence. Indeed, it seems that, whether the matters involved are trifling or serious, the evidence from sentences and conversations alike fairly conspires to support our epistemic condition of assertion. And this means that the evidence from classroom situations, where it is granted that scepticism is in force, joins neatly with that from the more ordinary situations of our lives.

Before drawing this section to a close, I should like to explain some remarks I made quite early in this essay, in fact, in section 8 of the first chapter. Discussing a Moorean who would try to reverse the classical argument against knowing about an external world, I suggested that he would seem wrongly dogmatic in *asserting*, even to himself, not necessarily that he *knew* there to be no evil scientists deceiving him, or that he was *certain* there was none, but even in asserting *that there is no evil scientist who is deceiving him into false belief.* The experience as of having electrodes removed from his head, and as of having such a scientist explain some of the deceptions to him would, I submitted, rather forcefully make this Moorean consider the over-positive and dogmatic nature of his asserting ways. It would do this for this simple asserting just as much, or very nearly as much, as for the dogmatism inherent in his thinking himself to know. We may now explain our intuition to this effect by means of our condition of asserting. When the Moorean asserts there to be no evil scientist, he represents himself as *knowing* that there is none deceiving him. Imagined experiences to suggest the possibility of the scientist run counter, then, to what this philosopher represents himself as *knowing*.

It hardly matters whether or not this last represents a new strand of support, or whether it falls under the category of conversational situation. With it, and with our other cases, we have, I suggest, supported our hypothesis to the point where we had best accept it. If someone asserts, declares, or states that something is so, it follows that he represents himself as *knowing* that it is so. From this, in conjunction with our thesis of universal ignorance, it follows in turn that whenever anyone asserts, states, or declares anything to be so, whether he has any idea of it or not, of necessity he falsely represents himself in so doing. And, even if only a more conservative scepticism about knowledge may be maintained, it will follow that at least in virtually every circumstance of assertion or statement, the speaker will represent himself falsely.

§5. *More Representational Difficulties*

It is no business of mine here to try to place any metaphysical limits on language or our uses of it. But our accepted ways of using our language do, I believe, let our ignorance mean for

us a sweeping problem of false representation. We have seen
such a problem to occur with such 'strong' sorts of accepted
linguistic act as asserting, stating, and declaring. I now want to
suggest that, in a somewhat less direct way, the same happens
with all of a crucial set of (kinds of) linguistic act. Not only
is my idea of these acts rather vague but my suggestions
concerning them are intended largely to be programmatic.
Accordingly, I will not argue for these suggestions at length,
though I will take the liberty of drawing some quite sweeping
conclusions from them. My hope is that they are at least plausible, and that they may spur some positive research in certain
parts of the philosophy of language.

The sort of acts I have in mind coincide, at least roughly,
with J. L. Austin's 'illocutionary acts'.[5] His idea, while itself
somewhat vague, was roughly this: When a person produces an
utterance, in speaking, writing, or whatever, we are given to
understand the utterance, and what the person meant by it,
in terms of a certain sort of act, or acts, he performed *in* uttering the thing. These acts are somehow above the level of the
merely grammatical; they go beyond the adherence to rules of
the language, though they at least generally presuppose some
such adherence. These acts are not causal consequences of
the utterance or its production, nor of the adherence to rules.
Knowing that his utterance is to be taken as a piece of English,
even as the sentence, say, 'You will get off the steps,' we want
further to know if it is to be taken as a (predictive) statement,
as an order, as a request, or whatever. These last are each
necessary products of certain linguistic acts the person may have
performed in uttering what he did. These illocutionary acts are
stating (to you) (that you will get off the steps), ordering (you
to get off the steps), requesting (you to get off the steps), and
so on. When you understand him to be doing one or more of
these things, in uttering what he does, then you may first understand him, in some full sense, as speaking (to you) (in English),
communicating (to you) (in English), and so on.

[5] The basic work here is Austin's *How to Do Things with Words* (Oxford, 1962).
More recent work on these acts includes P. F. Strawson's 'Intention and Convention in Speech Acts', *Philosophical Review*, lxxiii (1964); John R. Searle's
Speech Acts (Cambridge, 1970), Stephen R. Schiffer's *Meaning* Oxford, 1972),
especially Chapter IV, and Zeno Vendler's *Res Cogitans* (Ithaca, N.Y., 1972),
especially Chapters II and III.

In addition to asserting and company, we may start to list the sorts of acts we mean here in terms of verbs we have for 'naming' them. With a few omissions, here is a list I borrow from another writer on the subject: 'advise', 'affirm', 'answer', 'apologize', 'ask', 'assure', 'command', 'correct', 'deny', 'describe', 'entreat', 'interrogate', 'object', 'order', 'predict', 'prescribe', 'promise', 'question', 'report', 'reply', 'request', 'suggest', 'tell', 'thank', and so on.[6] More specific classification can be achieved by embedding certain of these verbs in larger contexts, and then taking different acts to be indicated by the different resulting expressions as follows. His telling *me to leave* is different from his telling *her that I would leave*. I think that saying that *p*, and also saying for someone to X, are also illocutionary acts, though perhaps, in some appropriate sense, very general ones. And, of course, in no sense is our list meant to be exhaustive.

My first programmatic suggestion for such acts as these is this: In the performance of any of these acts, a subject must represent, not only that something is the case, but that he knows that something is the case. In asserting, stating, and declaring, of course, we have the clearest and most direct sort of case: something represented as known is indeed the very same thing (or logically parallel to it) as the thing asserted, stated, or declared. In asserting that *p* our S must represent himself as knowing that *p*. In *suggesting* that *p*, however, say, that there is no danger, our S need not represent himself as knowing *that there is no danger*. And, importantly, I think, nor need he do so in *saying that p*.[7] But, then, I suggest, he must represent himself as knowing some other thing, or things. Hazarding to be more specific, I think that one thing he must represent himself to

---

[6] This list is borrowed from Schiffer, *Meaning*, p. 99.

[7] But for discussion with Gilbert Harman, I would have thought *saying that* to have the same strong condition as asserting and the like. But saying that *p* does not seem to require representing oneself as knowing that *p*. One of Harman's examples against such a condition is this: People may bet on various outcomes of an event, as in a pool. One person, invited to express to the nearest minute the length of a certain train ride, may say 'An hour and 38 minutes,' or he may say 'I say it will take an hour and 38 minutes'. Another may then say, 'And I say it will take an hour and 42 minutes'. It seems that the second man said that the ride would take an hour and 42 minutes, but did not assert, or represent himself as knowing that it would. In having said this, though, the man represented himself as knowing that it was at least possible that the ride would last that long. (Harman thinks even this to be too strong.)

know is that it is at least possible that there is no danger. In more personal terms, I think he thus must represent himself as knowing that he does *not know* that there is at least some danger. This will account for the inconsistent sound of 'Look, I suggest that there is (or may be) no danger, but there is danger,' or 'Perhaps there is no danger, but perhaps I know that there is.' (With the second sentence, being charitable, we may understand the utterer as taking back in the second part what he put forward in the first.) Being for a moment a bit more conservative than our whole programmatic suggestion, I suggest that such an epistemic condition holds at least for all those illocutionary acts which provide ways, however, strong or weak, of 'putting something forward' as true, or even as possibly true. If even this much is right, then there is no appropriately accepted way for a sceptic about knowledge to express his view without falsely representing himself in the process.

In *ordering* someone to do something, or in *saying for* him to do it, a subject must, I think, represent himself as knowing that it is possible (for his audience) to do the thing. This accounts for the apparent inconsistency of 'Get off the stairs, though, of course, it may be impossible (for you) to do so.' For most naturally, we take the first part as expressing an order, or something relevantly like, and the second as a suggestion to the effect that, for all the speaker knows, the hearer can't do the thing ordered. In *questioning*, I think, a subject represents himself as knowing that he wants an answer: to know it, to be told it, or whatever. This can be overridden by surrounding context, so that a resolution takes place. But an inconsistency is first felt to obtain anyway. Thus there is an inconsistency in 'Where are the stairs? Though maybe I don't want an answer; maybe I just think I do.' To be charitable, we may allow that in the second part of what he says our subject is taking back something which he represented in saying the first part. To get the point, we need only compare our offered discourse with another, always consistent: 'I think I'd like to know, or to be told, where the stairs are; though maybe I don't want this; maybe I just think I do.' While I can't canvass all our illocutionary acts, I think you will feel a certain plausibility by now in this programmatic suggestion of mine. If it is right, then, for our ignorance, we must falsely represent ourselves, not only in accepted ways for advancing things as true, or as possibly true, but in all the illocutionary acts we have available to perform. In a very general way, then, our ignorance enjoins our silence.

While it leads to this hard conclusion, our programmatic suggestion helps me think of a stronger one which may prove promising for positive research. In each (kind of) illocutionary act, the subject must represent himself to know a different thing, or different set of things; what is represented as known in each case is characteristic of that act and, thus, in some sense, serves to define the act. Now, it seems clear to me that, as in ordering, also in *requesting* someone to do something, the subject must represent himself as knowing that it is possible for the thing to be done. As ordering and requesting are patently different, this hypothesis predicts that either in ordering one represents oneself to know something else as well, or in requesting one does, or in both. This clearly seems so. For example, in ordering, one represents oneself as knowing something like this: that one has some sort of right (perhaps relative to certain institutions, conventions, etc.) to expect his audience to do the thing. In requesting nothing so strong as this is represented as known, whatever else may or may not be. Is ordering different also from commanding? As I believe, but am not very sure, that it is, I believe, but only believe, that there is a difference in what each requires the subject to represent as known. Our strong programmatic hypothesis of course predicts a difference in case they are distinct kinds of act. But I will not now try to uncover such a difference. For that would be to proceed some of the way with the programme of this hypothesis, and I just want to suggest such a programme for those interested in working programmatically in this area of language study.

In addition to there being requirements on our illocutionary acts, I think there are informal rules, or 'nests of expectations', which regularly are in force when we try to communicate, speak our language, and so on. An adherence to these rules, I think, also requires us to represent ourselves as knowing something. Thus, for our universal ignorance, it requires us falsely to represent ourselves.

Here is one such rule. I express it in two steps or parts, the latter, stronger part entailing the former. In uttering an expression 'M', first, the subject must *know*, and not just believe, that 'M' is indeed meaningful (in the relevant sense); and, second, the subject must *know* what 'M' means, and not just believe that, say 'M' means thus and so. Thus, I break this shared rule if I say 'Stop squiggling; but maybe, while I believe it does, "squiggling" really doesn't mean anything'. Of course, here I have broken the first, or minimal, part of the rule. If I remember a sentence of French, but am not sure of its meaning, I may say, '*Enlevez-vous de l'escaliers* (= Get off the stairs). I *think* that means "Get off the stairs," but I really don't *know*.' Now, I have broken the second part of the rule, though not necessarily the first part. To make sense of such an act, we do something like this. We suppose the first part of the discourse, '*Enlevez-vous de l'escalier*,' to be directed at one audience, say, some Frenchman whom we may suppose to be monolingual. And, we suppose the rest to be directed at another: our companion or ourselves. This bespeaks our acceptance of this suggested rule, or so we may most simply explain matters.

I shall not look into further examples here. For I do not want to make a great deal of my suggestion of such a rule. Indeed, while it seems much less plausible to me, perhaps this requirement of representing meaning to be known is built right into *all* of our illocutionary acts. Perhaps, then, there really is no additional rule. But on the more likely event that this requirement is not built into all these acts, such a rule will explain a feeling which, while not so common as the one we encountered at the beginning of our chapter, wants some account from us in any case. This feeling is that there is something wrong where a sceptic about knowledge, not just states or asserts something, or where he tries to put something forward as true or possibly true; but even wherever he might try to speak or write meaningfully in any way at all. The existence of such a rule as this, with no detriment to scepticism, does justice to this feeling.

Now, if the suggestions of this section prove correct, then, for our universal ignorance, philosophers of language have some quite general work cut out for them. For we do not want to falsely represent ourselves. And, thus, we want to have available illocutionary acts to perform, and perhaps informal rules to follow, which need not involve us in any activity on the perimeter of fraud. We want linguistic institutions and practices where our ignorance will not enjoin silence.

Of course, holding all of this, however tentatively, a sceptic who would communicate is in an unfortunate situation. Again, we are skirting paradox, whether or not we are actually confronting any. But I shall not pause again, as I did in section 11 of the preceding chapter, to defend my scepticism explicitly against any such charge. For my final chapter will contain the most straightforwardly paradoxical results imaginable, and, along with that, my most radical critique of our language and our thought. I beg, then, to proceed at once to the most sweeping, thoroughgoing problems which we are, finally, to encounter.

VII

The Impossibility of Truth

ACCORDING to our account of it, knowing about something is a very special state or position, so special, indeed, as to be impossible. Now, it is a commonplace to allow that this knowing, in so far as it may obtain, is never a state 'internal' to the subject, in the sense in which at least some believing may be. In knowing, there is some relation between the subject, on the one part, and on the other, the thing which is known by that person or being. This known thing is supposed to be 'external' to the subject, at least in the great majority of cases. Unlike believing, then, the state or position of knowing is, in quite a strong sense or way, a relational one.

Though we have said a few words on the matter, we have not yet inquired seriously into the question of the nature of those things which are supposed to be known, known, that is, when someone is supposed to know something about something. In that this knowing is such a special, impossible relational state or position, we might suspect at the outset that its putative objects, the things supposedly known, are also thus special and impossible. I shall argue, on independent grounds, that this is indeed so. This will give us an independent, confirming argument for our universal scepticism about knowledge, and thus also, for the many consequences of this thesis exhibited in the three chapters just preceding this present one.

I shall argue that in each case, when someone knows about something, or knows something to be so, what he knows is either the whole truth about the world or, if less than that, something which is part of that first thing. The former is of course the far more exotic case, occurring only where there is true omniscience. The latter is supposed to occur in our daily lives. My contention will be the rather obvious one that there really is no thing which is the whole truth about the world. For this reason, there can be nothing either which is any part of the whole truth about the world. Accordingly, nothing can ever be known to be so, for the non-existence of these things is hardly a contingent matter.

I think that this non-existent object, by way of its parts, is the central entity in a metaphysics of knowledge and truth which is embodied in our language. Not only, according to this embodied theory, is this entity to provide the objects for knowing, it is at the same time to provide the standard of truth for what may be asserted or believed, for statements, propositions, and the like. In terms of this guiding idea, I shall offer an account of truth: truth is, at least roughly, the property of being in agreement with (or in accordance with) the whole truth about the world. As this latter does not exist, there is nothing which is in agreement with any such thing. Accordingly there is no truth and, in the relevant sense of the term, there is nothing whatsoever which is true. Along the same lines, I shall argue that no one ever believes or thinks that anything is so, or asserts or says that anything is so. Finally, I will develop straightforward paradoxes and contradictions. I take these disconcerting results to be no criticism of my sceptical position, though they *may* be that, but rather to show that our language is in need of radical change. This leads me to make some suggestions about what philosophers may best do to help contribute to our thought about things. With these admittedly vague suggestions, my essay draws to its close.

§1. *The Whole Truth about the World*

At various points in this essay, I have mentioned, hinted at, or implied a certain conception of our language and thought. According to this conception, the common words of our language group into connected systems. With an eye towards both syntax and semantics, certain structures may be seen as providing frames for words to exhibit their analytic connections, and thus their entailing powers. Taking things further, these systems serve to embody a theory or view of the world. Sentences which exhibit these important analytic connections, and which are thus themselves analytic, give principles or theorems of this theory. One such theorem is this: If someone is happy that something is so, then he knows that it is so. Another, more central theorem is this one: If someone knows that something is so, then he knows something which is part of the whole truth about the world, namely, that that thing is so. As vague as it may be, this is my conception of our language and thought.

I often continue to conceive of these things along the following bold, shall we say, anthropological lines. This embodied theory, with its rigid theorems, was the developed view of certain persons who were instrumental in creating an important ancestor, or ancestors, of our language, of English. I place no strict limit on how far back these thinkers go, but I should be surprised if they did not operate, and complete (at least most of) their contribution, a very long time before the Greek thinkers who are commonly taken to represent 'ancient' philosophy. In trying to make sense of things, and in trying at the same time to satisfy certain other deep needs or drives, they developed a theory which in certain respects badly failed in various places, of necessity, to fit the world. While new meanings have sometimes been added, the central meaning of our common words does not differ from theirs, however much pronunciation may differ. While syntax has shifted, deep syntactic relations have been preserved. Accordingly, even if it is without our realizing the fact, their incorrect theory is always on the tips of our tongues. When we make statements we often give expression to it. And, more important, what we state, through analytic connection with the theorems of this theory, always will have entailments which are not true and which fail 'to fit the world'. Thus, what we state is never true and fails 'to fit the world'.

At the heart of the theory, or of much of it, we may find the aforementioned metaphysics of knowledge and truth. It is my aim now to display this embodied metaphysics. In doing this, I will begin by focusing on the word 'truth', in what I take to be the central meaning of and context for this key word. Later on, I will look to find the most important connections of this word with 'know', and with other importantly related words. In the process, I will look to support my contention that our chosen sense of 'truth' is indeed the central one. With this sense of 'truth' in mind, I look now to exhibit the central entity of this metaphysics: the whole truth about the world.

In the central sense of 'truth', we may speak of the *whole* truth about something as well as of various things each of which is *part* of the whole truth about the thing. This is entirely smooth and colloquial. Though it may not be so colloquial, we may, if only for expository convenience, speak of each of the latter things as *a part* of the former and, so, speak of them as *parts* of it. It is easy to translate back to get the facts of colloquial speech which I will use this convenience to record.

In the central sense of 'truth', we may speak of the truth about one thing as well as the truth about another. Generally, this will be the same as the whole truth about the first, and then, again, about the second. The only possible exception here, apart from elliptical usage, occurs where the thing in question is a 'yes–no matter', or something to be specified, when we can specify it at all, by an expression of the form 'the matter of whether or not *p*' or, more shortly, of the form 'whether *p*'. (The letter '*p*' is, as is standard, to be replaced by a propositional clause, in the standard sense of the expression.) Thus, the truth about China is, really, the whole truth about China, and the truth about China's size, the whole truth about China's size. Perhaps, the truth about *whether China is larger than India* is *not* the *whole* truth about that; perhaps *nothing* is such a thing. This goes with the apparent fact that there is nothing which is part of the truth about whether China is larger than India. This last thing, which has no parts, at least none which are each the truth about something, itself is simply either of two things: In case China is larger, it is that China is larger; in case it is not, it is that it is not. There being no suitable parts, there at least *seems* to be nothing which is the *whole* truth about whether *p*, just the truth about it.

In contrast, the truth about whether China is larger than India *is* part of the truth about China's size. And, *each* of these two things is part of the truth about China. What is this last part of? The truth about China is, amongst other things, part of the truth about the world, even in the grand, as against the planetary, sense of this last word. That is, it is part of the truth about the universe, or about everything. Thus, each of these things is the *whole* truth about something, and, except for the last, each is *part* of the whole truth about something else. Finally, in every case, when 'truth' is used in its central sense, it is used to talk about the whole truth about the world or else about something which is part of that.

The whole truth about the world is itself but part of the (whole) world, just as is a book about the whole world, or a toad, or a toothpick. And, further, we should also note that *the whole truth about* the whole truth about the world is itself but *part* of the whole truth about the world. As such, it too is, then, but part of the world. And so, too, for anything of the form: the whole truth about . . . the whole truth about . . . the whole truth about the world, and for any of the infinite number of things that are each part of any such thing.

The whole truth about the world is different from the whole truth about any entity in it. This may be shown even in the face of the following: It may well be that in order to *know* the whole truth about, say, me, you must know also the whole truth about the whole world. But even if for one to be known the other must also be, and vice versa, the two things known will be different things. For, we have as a sentence descriptive of the truth about the world:

Part of the whole truth about the world is the truth about whether China is larger than India.

But we do not have any such descriptive sentence about the truth *about me*, not one that makes any sense, anyway:

Part of the whole truth about me is the truth about whether China is larger than India.

There is something, then, which is part of the one but not of the other. And, so, the two are not the same. What we do have as a perfectly sensible sentence which *is* descriptive of the whole truth about *me* is this:

Part of the whole truth about me is that I exist in a world (or as part of a world) in which there is also something which is the truth about whether China is larger than India.

And, while we don't have as any sentence which makes sense:

Part of the whole truth about me is that China is larger than India,

we do have this sentence to talk some sense with:

Part of the whole truth about me is that I exist in (or as part of) a world in which (the truth about whether China is larger than India is that) China is larger than India.

Indeed, it is this last sort of sentence which brings to our attention the idea that *so much* must be known in order for anyone to know the whole truth about me. But, then, it leaves intact our distinction between the whole truth about the world, on the one hand, and the whole truth about me, which is but part of that first thing.[1]

All of this presents a metaphysical theory. At the same time it records, or manifests, many quite obviously related facts about perfectly grammatical and even rather natural discourse in our language. Thus, we may be encouraged to surmise that this theory is embodied in our language. Of course, this suggestion needs much more evidence if we are to be much more serious about it. Indeed, such an attempt to be so literal in our interpretations faces obvious problems. I turn now to present and treat the most important of these.

We often say things which look to cause trouble for the idea that our ordinary speech makes references to (things which are) parts of the truth, and that these are to be taken as genuine entities, with intelligible 'conditions of identity', just as people and rocks are supposed to be. For example, we may say that in telling Mary that he quit school, Ben may be telling her the truth. And, in telling her that he likes macaroni, Ben may also be telling Mary the truth. If we take this talk of the truth quite literally, then the most direct inference is that Ben may be telling her the very same thing each time. But, of course, this is absurd: that Ben quit school is one thing, that he likes macaroni another. How are we to interpret these remarks so that we may, less directly, understand them as making quite literal references to the whole truth or parts of it?

In the first case, what Ben is really doing is telling Mary the truth *about whether he quit school*. In the second case, he is telling her the truth *about whether he likes macaroni*. These are two different things: the first is that he quit school, and the second is that he likes macaroni. So our typical use of 'the truth' here is elliptical. For example, in the first sentence, the phrase 'the truth' is elliptical for the longer phrase 'the truth about whether he quit school'.

Other sentences require but a bit more ingenuity to provide

[1] On these points I have been helped by discussion with William Barrett, and also with Michael Slote.

the completion for the ellipsis. In telling Mary each of these things, Ben was also telling her *the truth about himself*. But, again, he is not telling her the same thing each time. The point is, though, that in neither case does Ben tell Mary the *whole* truth about himself. That would involve his telling her the truth about whether he is tall, about whether he likes ravioli, and infinitely or indefinitely much more. So, the first time Ben tells her *part* of the (whole) truth about himself, *namely*, that he quit school. And, the second time, Ben also tells her *part* of the (whole) truth about himself, but *this* time, it is that he likes macaroni. He tells her, in each case and context, the relevant or key part of the whole truth about himself.

It often happens, of course, that in telling someone that something is so, one does not tell them the truth at all. That is, one does not then tell them the truth about *anything*. Thus, one will not then tell them part of the truth (about anything either. In such cases, the propositional clauses which express what was told do not purport to refer to part of the truth. Their function is quite different. But, when we say *the truth was told*, we may always provide the completions to understand things quite literally: *These* propositional clauses *do* purport to refer to part of the whole truth about everything.

§2. *Parts of the Truth, Facts, and some things which are True*

When we dig down into the parts of the truth, we come upon parts which have no other such parts. These may be denoted by expressions of the form 'the truth about whether (or not) p'. They may *also* be denoted by an appropriate propositional clause, or that-clause. Indeed, it is only in this latter way that such 'ultimate' parts of the truth may be most explicitly specified by us. We have already noted as much in the case of China and India: if China is larger than India, then the truth about whether China is larger than India is that China is larger than India. Otherwise, it is that China is not larger than India.

Unlike some other propositional clauses, the ones just employed do *not* mean to denote anything which is true (or false). If we take a relevant sentence which *does* have such a that-clause:

That China is larger than India is true.

and try to connect it with one of our sentences:

> The truth about whether China is larger than India is that China is larger than India,

the result is deviant:

> ?The truth about whether China is larger than India is true.

This is no mere redundancy, as the acceptability of such redundant tautologies as the following helps make clear:

> The true statement that China is larger than India is true.

For, even on its relevant interpretation, this last sentence only seems an unusual one to offer.

We may get further evidence to the effect that our key that-clause indicates nothing which is true by looking at sentences with the verb 'believe'. This verb's that-clauses always seem to purport to denote the appropriate *sort* of thing for being true, but never any part of the truth. For example, in this simple sentence:

> He believes that China is larger than India.

the that-clause means to denote something true, as the following connecting sentences serve to make plain:

> In believing that China is larger than India, what he believes is that China is larger than India.

> In believing that China is larger than India, what he believes is true.

We may expect, then, that what someone believes, while it may be denoted by a that-clause, is never the same thing as any which is part of the truth. Accordingly, if we should try to say of someone that he believes something which is part of the truth, deviance should result. To see this result, we compare:

> ?Ben believes the truth about whether China is larger than India, namely, that China is larger than India.

> Ben remembers the truth about whether China is larger than India, namely, that China is larger than India.

It appears, then, that while what is believed is at least often true, anything which is part of the truth never is.

Now, facts also are things which seem never to be true (or false). Especially for facts of the sort purportedly denoted by that-clauses, we may notice the following deviance:

?The fact that China is larger than India is true.

Much as noted before, with our sentence which has 'true statement' where this string has 'fact', this deviance is not the same as any mere redundancy.

The fact that relevant facts are also never relevantly true raises the idea that when that-clauses denote parts of the truth, it is a fact which, in each case, is being denoted. Accordingly, we have the idea that certain parts of the truth might just be certain facts. If this idea is right we would have some unity, and a large thrust towards the philosophically familiar. But, unfortunately, when we try to say of a promising part of the truth that it *is* an equally promising fact, only marked deviance is the result:

??The truth about whether China is larger than India is the fact that China is larger than India.

Relevant connecting sentences only serve to confirm:

Part of the truth about China is the truth about whether China is larger than India.

??Part of the truth about China is the fact that China is larger than India.

It appears, then, that parts of the truth are no more facts than things true or false. Rather, they appear to be some third sort of thing, which despite their neglect by philosophers, may well be the most deserving of our most careful attention.

§3. *The Objects of Knowing*

We are to inquire into what are the things which are known if anyone should know anything about anything, or, what I take to be the same, should know that anything is so. What are the objects of such alleged knowing? Many philosophers have said that these objects are facts, which we have just seen to be different from our parts of the truth.

Now, it may be that sometimes, or even always, when someone knows that something is so, he knows a particular fact, namely, the fact that the thing is so. Various locutions incline me to think that this is indeed always the case. At the same time, the attempt to construct the most direct form of sentence to this effect inclines me against thinking facts ever to be proper objects of this knowing:

Ben knows that China is larger than India.

*Ben knows the fact that China is larger than India.

In contrast, it is always in order to say directly that a person knows the relevant part of the truth:

Ben knows the truth about whether China is larger than India, namely, that China is larger than India.

In trying to analyse knowing something about something, I think that parts of the truth are the objects that we want. To begin the analysis, we say that someone S knows that p if, and only if, S knows the truth about whether p, namely, that p.

When in Chapter III, section 10, we introduced our analysis of knowing, we noticed the difficulty in treating the that-clause as purporting to refer to a particular fact. At the same time, we left it quite unclear what role that clause might have. We may now clarify its role: it purports to denote an 'ultimate' part of the truth. In giving that analysis, we said that when S knows that p, that means that it is (absolutely) clear to S that p. Accordingly, we may now spell things out further: What is here (absolutely) clear to S is the truth about whether (or not) p, namely, that p. Someone's knowing something to be so, then, is just the relevant part of the truth's being absolutely clear to him.

When analysing sentences of the form 'S knows that p', we gave parallel analyses for related sentences with 'know'. I think that these sentences also expressed states of affairs where someone knew something *about* something: sentences of the forms 'S knows how many X's there are', 'S knows where Y is', and even 'S knows how to X', 'S knows where to Y', and so on. Thus, for example, for S to *know* how to X is just for it to be (absolutely) *clear* to S how to X. We may now spell out these conditions in a parallel way for their objects: what is clear to

S here is the (whole) truth about how to X. This gets us to look at strings like:

He knew the truth about how to ride a bicycle,

which, while pompous and unusual, are, I suggest, grammatically quite sound.

Now, before, in arguing for scepticism about these cases of knowing something about something, we didn't need to worry about whether they could be treated as special cases of knowing something to be so. But, now we have a stake in doing just this, for our purposes have begun to encompass the metaphysical. In terms of our metaphysics, we want to treat all cases of knowing something about something as knowing *some part of the truth*. But, then, the object must be constituted of ultimate parts or else itself must be an ultimate part of the truth. We have already said, however, that the only ultimate parts are ones of the form 'the truth about whether (or not) *p*', or in more specific terms, of the form, 'that *p*'. Accordingly, we must now understand knowing the truth about how to X, about where to Y, and so on, as knowing something, or some things, of this simple ultimate form. In cruder terms, we must now, for the simplicity of our embodied metaphysics, treat knowing-how, and so on, in terms of knowing-that.

I think that, in the only way relevant, we may understand such a treatment to be in order. Zeno Vendler, who takes this position, puts the point rather well, and I agree with him in all the essentials:

It will be objected here that in some cases of knowing how it is impossible to tell, in words, what one knows. . . . I grant this, but but point out that this situation is possible with nearly all the *knowing wh* forms. I know . . . what the color magenta looks like, where it itches on my back, . . . I could not tell you in words alone. I must have, however, some other means to supplement the words: pointing, offering a sketch, a sample, a demonstration. . . . By these means I can tell you, or show you what I know: I know that magenta looks like this (offering a sample), that it itches here (pointing), that. . . . The need for non-linguistic media affects knowing how, and *knowing wh* in general, exactly because it affects the corresponding knowing that.[2]

<hr>

[2] Vendler, *Res Cogitans*, pp. 104–5. Along with linguists, Vendler classifies 'how' as a *wh* word, even though it does not begin with the two letters 'wh'.

In essence, at least, we faced the same sort of point when we defended the second premiss of our Basis (in Knowledge) Argument (for Scepticism About Rationality), in Chapter V, section 3. We said there that if something is Ralph's reason, then it is something 'propositionally specific', even if we don't have the words to express the matter adequately. John's reason, or his belief, may be no better indicatable than by saying it is that things are *that* way. And if John knows how to wiggle his ears, he may just know that the way to do it is *that* way, with *that* sort of effect, or whatever. Once we do not wrongly expect too much in way of descriptions our available words can give, the truth about how to wiggle one's ears need be, for our metaphysics, no more difficult than the truth about China. The knowing of each, in so far as it obtains, may be understood equally, in terms of the knowledge of our ultimate parts of the truth.

While I have implied my doubts regarding the idea that in knowing that *p*, someone knows a fact, I am prepared to allow that this may always go on. Perhaps the deviance of the form *'S knows the fact that *p*' should be discounted as an anomalous deviance. But even if the fact that *p* must be known by S, whenever S knows that *p*, the new doubts we are building towards won't be much affected. For, as we have already agreed, whenever S knows that *p*, he will *also* have to know the relevant part of the truth about the whole world. And, as we have also agreed, this latter is nothing so solidly familiar as any fact. If *any* relevant knowing is to transpire, there had better be these parts of the truth around; otherwise nothing will be known to be so, and no fact will be known either.[3]

If facts are allowable objects of our knowing, it is a bit bad, I admit, to speak of our parts of the truth as *the* objects of knowing; they are some and facts are others. But, as these parts look to be the objects which most clearly will cause problems, and as these problems are my main concern, I hope that I may then be allowed such a false reference for convenience. If necessary, the change to a more accurate description may always be made rather easily.

[3] On these points, I am indebted to discussion with Gilbert Harman.

§4. *The Truth and Truth*

The whole truth about the world has a dual role in our embodied metaphysics. On the one hand, it provides the objects for knowing about things. On the other, it provides the main standard for such things as believing and asserting; it provides the standard of truth for them. I mean to give an account of truth with this idea as the guiding theme. On this account, the truth of such believed things as are relevantly true consists in, indeed, just is, their being in a certain relation to the whole truth about the world. This relation is that of their being in agreement with the whole truth or, for short, their relevant relation of agreement. Truth, then, is the property of being in agreement with the whole truth about the world. Let me begin to motivate this accounting by trying to elicit certain intuitions which, I believe, are based in our tacit acceptance of the metaphysics it is my purpose to articulate.

When a man believes something which is *true*, then what he believes is *in agreement with* what might be known in the matter, in so far as anything might be known there. Putting the point more abstractly, and perhaps a bit more vaguely, the things which might be *objects of knowing* will, at the same time, be or constitute or serve as the *standard of truth* for things which might be believed, for what might be asserted, and so on. In particularly tricky or difficult cases, perhaps nothing may ever be known in a matter. Still, if there is a genuine question or matter, the relevant object or thing may be there even if nobody can ever know it. In a universe with no beings at all, the truth about whether there are any beings would be that there are no beings. And this would be part of the whole truth about the world. Now, of course, nobody would ever actually know this thing; that is now the simplest matter of logic. But we might acknowledge that the statement that there are no beings would nevertheless be true. And this will be to acknowledge that the statement will be in agreement with what is there, appropriate for knowing, even though, in the nature of the case, nobody is there to know it. Its truth will consist, then, in its being in agreement with the whole truth about the world. Our account of truth thus motivated, we look to the relevant linguistic data, so that we may more fully articulate the account, and may, perhaps, even give it some exclusive support.

At the outset, one thing seems pretty clear: Whatever else may be said about truth, truth is bound to be the purported referent of our own word 'truth' in at least one important sense of this quite common common noun. On my reckoning, as with other great, grand things, like knowledge, freedom, or goodness, the evidence for testing any account of truth is likely to be largely linguistic. More specifically, it will concern facts about our own language, English, in which this purportedly referring word occurs. It should also be pretty clear that the word to look at first and last, indeed, most closely, is the word 'truth'. Facts about this word are the ones we most want to explain. For a variety of more or less obscure reasons, which I will try neither to discern nor to excuse, this word has been avoided by contemporary philosophers of truth, even when they have an eye towards our own actual language. This has hardly been an unconscious omission, as the following quote from Austin illustrates:

'What is truth?' said jesting Pilate, and would not stay for an answer. Pilate was in advance of his time. For 'truth' itself is an abstract noun, a camel, that is, of local construction, which cannot get past the eye of even a grammarian. We approach it cap and categories in hand: we ask ourselves whether Truth is a substance (the Truth, the Body of Knowledge), or a quality (something like the colour red, inhering in truths), or a relation ('correspondence').[1] [There is here a footnote which reads: [1] It is sufficiently obvious that 'truth' is a substantive, 'true' and adjective and 'of' in 'true of' a preposition.] But philosophers should take something more nearly their own size to strain at. What needs discussing, rather is the use, or certain uses, of the word 'true'. *In vino*, possibly, *veritas*, but in a sober symposium *verum*.[4]

My own belief, on the contrary, is that many contemporary philosophers have missed out on a correct account of truth largely because, like Austin, they have neglected to look carefully at 'truth'. If we look first at 'truth', we might hope later to give a better account of the relevant meaning or use of the

---

[4] This is the first paragraph of J. L. Austin's 'Truth', originally published in the *Proceedings of the Aristotelian Society*, Supplementary Volume xxiv (1950). In fairness, I should also refer to his 'Unfair to Facts' in his *Philosophical Papers*, ed. J. O. Urmson and G. J. Warnock (Oxford, 1961).

adjective 'true'. We might also hope to explain what distinguishes a relevant use of 'true', as in 'Her statement to him was true,' from uses less directly relevant to the topic of truth, as in 'Her love for him was true.' We proceed, then, to look at 'truth'.

There are, I think, exactly, three main uses or, better, *senses* of the word 'truth'. Each of them connects rather directly with the philosophical topic of truth. They are manifest in the following three sentences:

1. The first thing he uttered was a truth, but the truth was not as informative as the lies he later produced.

2. The truth of what he said cannot be denied, and truth should always be valued.

3. At first, I didn't think he was telling me the truth, but then I remembered the truth about it all and realized that he was.

In the first sentence, 'truth' is, in both occurrences, a sortal or count noun. A necessary condition for a thing to be a truth is that it be true, in the relevant sense of 'true'. To dispense with talk of 'the relevant sense', we may say that a thing is a truth *only if* we may speak of the *truth* of it. It seems to me that not all things which are thus true are truths: the sentence 'Though what he said was *not* true, there is something true *in* what he said' will not mean ?'Though what he said was *not* true, there is a truth *in* what he said' (especially, perhaps, if what he said is, simply, that all men are created equal). But, whatever further refinements are needed to get a definition for 'truth' in this first sense, I will try to show that one will understand the first sense of 'truth' in terms of the second.

In the second sentence, 'truth' is, in both occurrences, used to talk about, or to try to denote, a certain *property*, namely, the property of truth. This is a property which all truths have (whether or not only those things have it.) In the first occurrence, we talk of a property *of something*, namely, of what he said. In the second occurrence, we talk of the same property but more abstractly, detached, so to speak, from any things which might have it. There is of course nothing at all unusual in this, nor anything peculiar to talking of truth. Talk of properties manifests this distinction quite generally: 'The innocence of the peasants was charming, but, then, innocence can be a curse.' In any case, this is evidently the sense of 'truth' which most directly relates to the philosophical topic of truth; indeed, we just now used the word in that way to mention our topic. If we can define 'truth' in this sense, we will have provided, at least in the main, a definition of truth itself. (We will then need only 'to cast things in the material mode'.)

Now, for reasons already surveyed, facts are not the only relevant objects of knowing; indeed, they *may* not be proper at all here. Wanting to have objects of knowing for defining truth, we are happy to have parts of the truth at hand. For the evident linguistic closeness of 'truth' to 'the truth about . . .', and the evident disparity with 'the fact that . . .', makes a definition of truth in terms of facts look comparatively forced. This brings us to our third sentence.

In this third sentence, we find, in both occurrences, what I take to be the key or central sense of the word. This sense is given in part by the sorts of facts we displayed in our previous sections. The function of the word in this sense, determined by the sense, is to denote the whole truth about the world, and also such other entities as are part of that thing. It is important to note, I think, that this sense gives us a way, both simple and quite natural, of defining the other two main senses. For, if what someone said was true, so that one might refer to the truth of it, then it was in (complete) agreement with the truth. Thus, truth may be defined as agreement with the truth, or as the property of being in agreement with the truth. And, then, this is the relevant property which all truths share, in virtue of which they are each called a truth. No other way of starting, or proceeding, allows for so simple or so natural a way of relating the main senses of 'truth'. This alone is some pretty strong support for the idea that this third sense is the central, indeed, the primitive one. It is also some evidence for our account of truth which is, in short, that truth is agreement with the truth, that is, with the whole truth about the world. But, then, what is that? We have already said rather a bit about our key entity, the whole truth about the world. So let's now try to say something about our key relation, that of something's being *in agreement with* something else. And, let us see how well this relation may account for our intuitions about the nature of truth.

§5. *Agreement and Truth*

The relation of agreement is much stronger than the philosophically more familiar one of consistency. If one thing is in agreement with another, then it follows that the first is (at least) consistent with the second. But something can be consistent with something else even while failing actually to be in agreement with it.

If we all jump up and down, and our policy does not prohibit this, says nothing about such an action, then what we do is perfectly consistent with our policy. But it is not in agreement with it. If our policy is that we should jump up and down a lot, then what we do is, not only consistent with our policy, it is actually in agreement with it (or in accordance with it). When one thing *is* in agreement with another, then it is always in perfect, absolute, and complete agreement with that other. In this way, agreement is an absolute relation, just like the weaker relation of consistency. If what I say is not in *complete* agreement with what you say, at least *some* of what I say will not be in agreement with what you say. And, so, what I say will not be in agreement with what you say. Also, of course, if what I say is not *completely* consistent with what you say, then at least *some* of what I say will not be consistent with what you say. And, so, what I say will not be consistent with what you say.

If what I say is that China is larger than India, and what you say is that India is larger than Denmark, then what I say is completely consistent with what you say but it is not in agreement with it. If I say that China is larger than India, and you say that China is at least as large as India, then, while what you say is also completely consistent with what I say, I don't think that it is so much as in *agreement* with what I say. So, the relation of agreement is indeed a very strong relation. That is why it can play such a major role in an adequate account of truth.

The standard theory of truth, still maintaining its popularity, is the *correspondence* theory of truth. In its standard formulation, this theory has it that truth is correspondence with the facts, or, perhaps, that the truth of a particular statement is, or consists

in, that statement's correspondence with the appropriate particular fact. Now, facts, we have agreed, are already to be
placed outside of an account of truth. But, then, this correspondence formula may be altered only slightly to give the pre-
ferred place to our new candidates: truth is correspondence
with the truth, or the truth of a particular statement is the
statement's correspondence with the appropriate 'ultimate'
part of the truth. Our account would further change the
formula by replacing correspondence with agreement, leaving
little indeed of the original correspondence theory. But, even if
agreement is as strong a relation as we have indicated, what
motivates this further change?

First, I think that 'agreement' better captures the *positive
character* we intuitively feel truth to have. The term 'correspondence' is too neutral and colourless to do this feeling justice.
When a statement is true, then the way it has things *is the same*
way as the truth does (or as the facts do). In other words, as
our account has it, the true statement is *in agreement with* the
truth (or with the facts). In short, 'correspondence' is a technical term any ordinary meaning of which has little to do with
truth; in contrast 'agreement' gives us a natural way of expressing our embodied metaphysics.

Our recent reference to the correspondence theory raises an
important point, which retains its importance even after we
have settled on the preferability of agreement over correspondence. For everything we have said so far may appear to
speak as much for the following theory of truth as it does for
the account I offer: Truth is agreement with the *appropriate,
or corresponding, thing which is part* of the whole truth about everything. In the case of the statement that China is larger than
India, its *truth* is its agreement with the truth about whether
China is larger than India, for in *this* case *that* is the appropriate thing which is part of the whole truth about the world.
On this perhaps more modest alternative, when two things are
both true, the property which they share is, not (being in)
agreement with the same thing, but (being in) agreement with
something which corresponds with *the thing in question*.[5] Except
for the obvious metaphysical statements, anything which is

---

[5] This alternative theory, as well as the fact that I should consider it, was
suggested to me by Rogers Albritton.

true on our account will be true on this one, and anything which is not, not. On our account the truth of something *is* its agreement with *the whole truth about everything*, and it has that property just in case it is, and, even, by its being, in agreement with the relevant part of the truth. On the alternative its truth *is* that latter. But, then, we can think of the former; what of *it*? Does agreement with the whole truth about everything have no name, no simple expression to mention it?

While still other alternatives suggest themselves, perhaps as compromises between or mixtures of these two, the dichotomy presented now allows us to ask the key questions which our account should be especially well designed and suited to answer. The first key question is this: Which account allows for the simplest and most natural sounding statement of what truth is, or definition of truth? Of the promising contenders, ours is the clear and obvious winner. But, then, why is that important? Well, first, one wants a simple account of something anyway; that's good methodology. But, in the present case, that's hardly the *main* point. For, we are not after a theory of galactic formation or insect behaviour. We are after a theory of *one of our own common concepts*, and of *the meaning of one of our own common words*. Thus, we do well to ask, 'When constructing a theory of things, and a language to express it, what would men do? Would they place in so apparently a central part of their thought and language a concept, and a term, whose definition we, and so presumably they, could easily, simply, and naturally formulate? Or, would they put in such a place a term and concept whose definition would require a rather complex, awkward, and difficult formulation?' I think that the former course is by far the more likely one. Especially given my general conception of our language's development, but really, in any case, this speaks rather heavily, I think, in favour of our simply expressed account of truth.

There is another large factor to favour our account, though it is closely related to the first. Especially when we look at 'truth' in relatively splendid isolation, and not confine our attention to 'the truth of this' or 'the truth of that', our own account gives a much better paraphrase than any more atomistic contender. When we say things like, 'One must always seek truth,' or 'Truth is often not easily attained,' our sentences have a meaning which gives them a certain inspirational, indeed, awesome flavour. Our own account provides paraphrases which capture this flavour rather well, 'One must always seek agreement with the whole truth about everything' and 'Agreement with the whole truth about everything is often not easily attained.' More atomistic accounts do us no justice here. But then, they, unlike an adequate account of truth, were never really designed to do any such thing in the first place.

I will close this section by examining how a relational term like 'agreement', when brought to the forefront, may solve what might otherwise seem an insuperable problem, and may do so in a way that even gains further support for our account of truth. When someone says something which we take to be true, we are wont to say:

What he said is the truth.

But, on our account, if what he said is true, then it is in agreement with the truth. Must we conclude, then, that the truth is in agreement with the truth, or is *in agreement with itself*? That is a puzzling, and an unwanted conclusion. We must conclude, since what he said is true, and is also the truth, that the truth is true? That would also be puzzling, and unwanted on any account. Are we to conclude that for something to be true *is just* for it to *be* the truth? Unless we are prepared to say that being the truth may be the same thing as being in agreement with the truth, which seems absurd, this conclusion contradicts our account of truth. How, then, are we to explain such a sentence? I take that sentence to mean:

What he said is *in agreement with* the truth.

This will solve our problem, as the short sentence will now present no problems for our account. But is this move perhaps only an *ad hoc* manoeuvre? I think not. Indeed, we can show that we need some such paraphrase in any case. We can show that taking the short sentence to be literal and complete leads to nonsense.

If what he said is anything, it is surely something which he *said*. If there is anything to say about this thing, then one such thing is this: He *said it*. In other words, we have:

He said what he said.

Now, if we take our short starting sentence so seriously as to think we have problems, we must also think that we must conclude:

*He said the truth.

But, this last is nonsense. So, our starting sentence must be treated delicately, rather than swallowed. Our paraphrase provides just such a treatment. Along the lines of our paraphrase, we have these connecting sentences:

He said something which is true.

He said something which is in agreement with the truth.

What he said is something which is in agreement with the truth.

What he said is in agreement with the truth.

What he said is the truth.

It would be clear that something like this is indeed what is needed here.

The problem we encountered in section 1, with telling, has nothing to do with this problem with saying. For example, we get just as much of a problem with:

What he said is the truth about whether China is larger than India.
*He said the truth about whether China is larger than India.

The problem here, then, has nothing to do with relevant parts. More particular sentences just require more particular paraphrases.

What he said is *in agreement with* the truth about whether China is larger than India.

And connecting sentences will be similarly more particular. Perhaps this is enough:

He said something about whether China is larger than India which is in agreement with the truth about whether China is larger than India.

For we must realize that what he said is now said to be in (complete) *agreement* with that particular thing, and surely not just (completely) consistent with it. In any case, certain related sentences will demand a more ingenious treatment. We must consider, for example:

What he said was only part of the truth about that, even though everything he said was true.

But, this might be paraphrased as:

What he said was in agreement with the truth about that but, though everything he said was in agreement with the truth, it was only part of what might be both said and in agreement with the truth about that.

In any case, whatever the details for more detailed sentences, it appears that they may run smoothly along the lines of my account of truth.

This means more support for my account than one might first think. For we don't even have as data to be treated any such sentences as:

*What he said is the fact
*What he said are the facts,

and so on. And, a perfectly fine sentence like:

What he said is a fact (we shall now have to make apologies for its insulting character).

means only something like

It is a fact that he said what he said (we shall now have to make apologies for its insulting character).

Thus that fine sentence is obviously quite irrelevant to our topic. So our original sentence, 'What he said is the truth,' which began by looking to be a problem, proves to be an asset in disguise. The very fact that the words 'the truth' turn up in such a connection with 'what he said' indicates that it is our chosen entities that are to have the parts in an adequate account of truth.

§6. *The Predication of Truth and the Relevant Sense of 'True'*

Truth is a certain property. It is a property of precisely those things such that, in each case, there is *the truth of* that thing.

ICS—L

When we talk about a thing, e.g. a particular statement, and say that truth is a property of that thing, we may say that we are predicating truth of the thing. Parallel remarks can be made about any other property, for example, redness. Redness is a property of precisely those things such that, in each case, there is something which is *the redness of* that thing. When we talk about a thing and say that redness is a property of it, we may say that we are predicating redness of the thing.

By far our most common and important devices for predicating properties of things are adjectives. The standard form of sentence for predicating begins with a referring expression, goes on with a tensed copula, and ends with an adjective. Thus, 'That is true' and 'This is red' are standard sentences for predicating truth and redness of that and this. In particular, it is the adjective 'true' which, in relevant uses, is our most common device for predicating truth of things. We ought, therefore, to look at 'true'.

While it has not always been for such a good reason as this, philosophers of truth have concentrated enormously on this adjective. (Our quote from Austin gives an example.) They have not, however, tried to separate systematically the relevant uses of the word from the other uses which it has. That is, they have not tried to demarcate just those uses which pertain directly to the topic of truth, giving a rationale for this demarcation. Much less have they tried to define the word for those uses, to specify the meaning which it has in them and them alone. We will now try to support our account of truth by using it to remedy this situation.

The most natural extension of our account says this: Among those uses of 'true' which pertain directly to our topic, the most central is its use as a predicating adjective in standard sentences for that purpose, e.g. as in the sentence 'That is true.' Other relevant uses, as in 'It is true that that is red,' derive from this central one and are, accordingly, to be best understood as being so derivative.[6] The meaning of 'true' is the same for all relevant uses; it means, at least roughly, 'in agreement with the truth'.

[6] I suppose that this means that the prominent contemporary philosopher of truth from whom I differ the most is my former tutor, Peter F. Strawson, especially in his early paper 'Truth' in *Analysis*, vol. ix, No. 6 (1949). Of course, one should also see his later 'Truth' in the *Proceedings of the Aristotelian Society*, supp. vol. xxiv (1950), which is part of the famous symposium with Austin.

Accordingly, 'That is true' means 'That is in agreement with the truth' and, there being no qualification, we take what it expresses to be logically equivalent to what is expressed by 'That is in agreement with the whole truth about everything.' The sentence 'What you said was true about him' then means the same as 'What you said was in agreement with the truth about him.' The meaning of 'What you said was true of him' cannot be expressed in a sentence obtained by direct substitution. But it can be understood in our terms; we only need say that it means (at least roughly) the same as the sentence with 'about'. For in these sentences, 'of' and 'about' mean (at least roughly) the same. Perhaps we may even say that 'true' means (just as roughly) this much: 'is in agreement with the *whole* truth *about everything*'. In that case, we would paraphrase 'What you said was true about him' in this way:

> What you said was, in so far as it was about him, in agreement with the whole truth about everything.

I will take this latter, bolder line on the relevant meaning of 'true'.

If anything, the sentence: 'It is true that that is red,' while philosophically familiar, presents even less of a problem. First, we may paraphrase it by the predicating sentence:

> That that is red is true (is in agreement with the whole truth about everything).

Additionally, we may also paraphrase by a direct substitution:

> It is in agreement with the whole truth about everything that that is red.

Now, *if* one always *demands* direct substitution, *of course* some problems occur with various relevant sentences:

> It is a true statement that that is red.
> *It is a in agreement with the truth statement that that is red.

But such a failure of substitution does not count against our definition. For this typically happens when a predicative adjective is moved to a pre-nominal position. A good definition of 'illegal' is 'against the law'. The sentence 'That was illegal in France last year' means, at least roughly, 'That was against the law in France last year.' But, however good this definition, we get no sentence at all by trying to substitute in:

That illegal act was worth doing.

We get only:

*That against the law act was worth doing.

So, if our definition of 'illegal' is a good one, all we should expect is this: First, we can directly substitute our defining expression in a set of central sentences with (virtually) no change in meaning, and secondly, we can understand other sentences where the word is used (and not just mentioned) in terms of their relations to the central ones.

With certain words, adhering to this criterion leaves many sentences unexplained. We might then expect either that our offered definition was not a good one or else that the word to be defined has more than one meaning, the offered definition then being, at best, good for only one of the meanings of the word. I think that the second alternative is what we find with the word 'true' and our offered definition of what it means. Now, if this is right, our definition, and so our account of truth, may be tested in yet another way: by how well it separates uses of 'true' which have much to do with truth from those which have much less (directly) to do with our topic. This is no empty claim. When we compare the two sentences:

Her statement to him was true

Her love for him was true,

we cannot help but feel that the first has much to do with truth, while the second has little to do with it. What explains this difference? Two routes join together. First, the first sentence can be paraphrased in terms of our offered definition, but not the second:

Her statement to him was in agreement with the truth.

??Her love for him was in agreement with the truth.

And, taking now the second route, we may say that only in the first of these sentences is 'true' being used to predicate truth. In that sentence, what we are bringing to the fore, and may go on to talk about is *the truth of* her statement to him. But, in the second sentence, we are predicating no such thing; it is badly substandard at best to try to talk of ??*the truth of* her love for him. What we *may* speak of here, and perhaps *are* predicating, is faithfulness, or even *trueness*. Thus, we may speak of *the trueness of* her love for him. But of course this is a different matter; *our* topic is *truth*. Accordingly, our definition of 'true', along with our account of truth, lets syntax and semantics join in explaining the division between relevant uses of 'true' and those which do not belong to our topic.

§7. *The Modification of 'True'*

One cannot over-emphasize, I think, our intuitive idea that truth is some sort of *absolute* and, so, that matters of truth are not really matters of degree. Matters of truth may be closely *associated* with certain matters of degree, for example, with matters of accuracy. But, then, we can be intuitively quite sure, for this reason alone, that truth and accuracy are different.

In classes in philosophy, elementary as well as advanced, students are often criticized for bad grammar when uttering a sentence like:

What Mary said is truer than what Ben said,

where a modification of 'true' makes matters look relative. But, the students' sentence is perfectly grammatical and even may make good sense. The way to explain and preserve our intuition that truth is an absolute is not to bar that sentence, but to understand it properly. We do have the three forms with 'true' even in relevant uses, just as in ones far from our topic: 'true', 'truer', 'truest'. That is data which must be handled, never denied. The students' sentence being proper, we must give an intuitively accurate account of its meaning.

Looking at that sentence, the first thing to notice is that it is clearly entailed that what Ben said, at least, is *not* true. The next thing to notice is that it is *at least suggested* that what Mary said is not true. If we suppose that it is even *entailed* that what Mary said is not true, we may paraphrase our sentence in this way:

What Mary said is closer to being true than what Ben said.

If we suppose, on the other hand, that it is *only suggested* that what Mary said is not true, we may paraphrase by beginning with the quite unproblematic disjunct:

What Mary said is true and what Ben said is not (true).

We then get:

Either what Mary said is true and what Ben said is not or what Mary said is closer to being true than what Ben said.

This paraphrase also suggests, though not quite so forcefully, that what Mary said is not true, but it entails only that what Ben said is not true. I am inclined to think that this is all that is entailed. Accordingly, I am inclined to go along with such a longer, disjunctive form of paraphrase.

Where intuitively relative properties are compared nothing like this does any justice. If we take, for example, the similar looking sentence:

What Mary said is wiser than what Ben said.

it is *not* entailed, or even suggested, that what Ben said is *not* wise; it might have been wise also, just *not as* wise as what Mary said. Indeed, it is suggested that this is the case, that Ben said something wise. At the same time, no parallel to our vital disjunct even begins to do any justice to our sentence with 'wise':

What Mary said is closer to being wise than what Ben said.

For this last does entail that what Ben said is not wise, and even that what Mary said is not wise. Accordingly, our form of paraphrase at once lets in modifications of 'true' and also preserves our intuition that truth, unlike wisdom and the like, is always an absolute. But, then, how are we to explicate our sentence with 'truer' still further; how are we to bring it explicitly into agreement with our account of truth?

As the first disjunct is easy to handle, everything depends on our doing more with the second disjunct. Now, according to our account, the only *way in which* what is said might be closer to being true is *by* its being closer to being in agreement with the truth. Accordingly, we paraphrase our second disjunct as:

What Mary said is closer to being in agreement with the truth than what Ben said, and, so, our way of paraphrasing our original sentence becomes the long but faithful:

Either what Mary said is in agreement with the truth and what Ben said is not or what Mary said is closer to being in agreement with the truth than what Ben said.

Thus, what *are* matters of degree here are matters of *how close to* the truth things are, that is, really, of *how close to being in agreement with* the truth.

We may close this section with a few brief remarks about adverbial modification of 'true'. We do say things like: 'What he said was very true.' So, there are *some* adverbs of degree, like 'very', which grammatically modify 'true' even in relevant uses. But what are we to make of their function here? Concerning *truth*, no *logical* modifications are produced. When something which is said is very true, so far as truth goes, it is just plain true: it is also absolutely, perfectly, and completely true. There are no other possible things to be said which, while true, are *any less true* than it. So, when adverbs and adjectives are properly understood, there are no degrees of truth.

Because it works with comparative forms to look like a relative term, but not with adverbial modification, the behaviour of 'true', in its relevant sense, is similar to such an absolute limit term as 'perfect'. Still, it is a basic absolute term, and gives us further reason for saying, as we did in Chapter II, section 2, that these forms give us a more sensitive test than adverbs do. Now, when we think of 'true', we almost automatically think of its opposite, 'false'. The adjective 'false' is not an absolute limit term, and so in our restricted sense, it is not an absolute term at all. It is not a basic absolute term, because it never gives the appearance of a relative: *'What you said is falser (more false) than what he said.' And, I can't see that it is a defined absolute, for which basic absolute would serve to define it? I will talk more about 'false' quite shortly, when we talk about the relation between truth and falsity. But, first, I want to discuss some puzzling locutions involving 'truth' for which no counter-parts exist on the side of falsity.

§8. *The Appearance of Amounts of Truth*

I now come to the most perplexing locutions involving 'truth'. An example is given by:

There is a lot of truth in what you said.

Here, it looks like we talk of amounts of truth, much as though truth were some sort of stuff. I will offer a perhaps over-bold account of these locutions. This account will bring in my beliefs on the way we may instructively view our language to have been developed, and what theories and functions it was thus made to serve.

Now, the very first thing to notice about our sample sentence is this: It *at least suggests* that what you said is *not* true; that there is *nothing* which is the truth *of* what you said; that you have here said *nothing* which is in *agreement* with *the truth*. Now, I am inclined to think that our sample sentence only suggests this, that it does *not* actually entail it. For the following seems, while a bit unusual, consistent:

> What you said is true; there is, indeed, a lot of truth in what you said.

Still, even if our original sentence does not have the harsh entailment, its suggestion in that direction is extremely important. It must be attended to in further thought about the sentence.

Another thing to notice is that parallel remarks can be made right down the line for paraphrases of our sample sentence. We also have such talk of amounts with agreement, even if the sentences for that would not so commonly occur:

> There is a lot of agreement with the truth in what you said.

This too suggests that what you said is not true, but it doesn't seem to entail that either:

> What you said is true and, indeed, there is a lot of agreement with the truth in what you said.

But, while this all gives support to our account, it barely scratches the surface in understanding the function of such sentences.

Now, perhaps the most important thing to notice about these sentences is that they provide nice, encouraging, praising ways of describing what someone said *in terms of truth* even when what he said is *not* true:

There is a lot of (a fair amount of) truth in what you said, even if what you said isn't (completely) true.

In fact, these sentences seem our best common device for doing this. Compare the former with:

What you said is very close to (fairly close to) the truth, even if what you said isn't (completely) true.

That first is more the sort of thing one *wants* to hear. And, the same difference emerges with:

There is a lot of (a fair amount of) agreement with the truth in what you said, even if it isn't (completely) true.

What you said is very close to (fairly close to) being in agreement with the truth, even if it isn't (completely) true.

So, our account captures the power of amount talk in praising what is said, and so the sayer, in terms of truth. But, how does it do this; what is going on here?

Talk of amounts of agreement can be just as puzzling as talk of amounts of truth. For, as we have noted in section 5, we feel that just as truth is an absolute, so is agreement an absolute thing. Indeed, this has motivated our account all along. If, as we say, you and I agree about something, but *not completely*, and, so, only in part, then we *don't* really agree about that thing. If your report and mine are, *in the main*, in agreement about that affair, then the two reports are *not* really in agreement about the event. So, what can be going on with all this praising talk of amounts, which seems so puzzling in the case of these absolutes?

I think that the fundamental idea is very simple. If your report and mine are, in the main, in agreement about the affair, then there are *things in* my report which actually are in agreement with *things in* your report, and, so far as these reports go, *these* things are the *main* things about the affair. Now, the things I'm talking about are exceedingly elusive. The reports may not be in agreement in so far as the content of their respective sentences is concerned. The things, which agree, go deeper than what is said by any particular sentence. The sentences are just means by which we can say certain things. The sentences are important because there can be other things, vital third parties, *in* the things *we* manage to *say*. Certain of these third things, according to our language, really do agree. And, so, it is that they allow, as we say, the two reports to 'agree in the main'.

While we like our reports to agree with each other, at least in the main, it is our concern for truth which is the point. We turn, then, from agreement between reports to agreement of something with the truth. We have already noted our lengthening paraphrase for: 'There is a lot of truth in what you said', namely,

There is a lot of agreement with the truth in what you said.

But, a shortening paraphrase is also worth noting:

There is a lot in what you said.

Now, if we are to take things seriously, we must ask what the words 'a lot' may mean to refer to here? In other words, a lot of what?

I think that these words are used here to refer to a lot of importance or value. But, it is not just importance in the abstract. It is the importance or value *of something* which *is in* what you said, or *of some things* which *are in* what you said. So, *the amount of truth in what you said* may be best understood by some such paraphrase as this: The amount of importance of *whatever is true in* what you said. This is born out, I think, by the *inconsistency* of such sentences as these:

There is a lot of truth in what you said, but there is very little that is true in it.

There is some truth in what you said, but there is nothing true in it.

There is a lot of truth in what you said, but there is very little importance in what you said,

There is not much truth in what you said, but there are many important things in it which are true.

So, we treat 'amounts of truth', or 'amounts of agreement with the truth', as ways of talking about the amounts of importance of certain things which are true, that is, which are in agreement with the truth.

It is something of a mystery to me how these true things might be *in* what someone said, or believed, or in anything of the like. Indeed, it is a mystery as to what exactly these true things might be. These things do *not* look to be statements, or propositions, or even truths:

?What you said isn't true, but there are many truths (?true statements, ?true propositions) *in* what you said.

A solution to this mystery would, for me at least, consist in a further elaboration of the metaphysics embodied in our language. But, whatever the details of the solution, I think that what has already been brought to light may be seen to serve an important purpose. That purpose is the successful resolution of the following deep human conflict.

It often happens that a man says something which is not true, and what he says is of such a nature that nothing can be formally deduced from it which is both true and important. I take it that this is generally what happens when someone says something bold, fresh, new, and general, says the sort of thing which 'contributes to our understanding in an original way'. I take it that this occurs with what Newton said about the world, or with the most important, interesting, general things he said about it. I take it that the same is true of Einstein, of Marx, and of Freud.

I think that there is in each of us a powerful motivating force which our language has put like this: First, we want to know as much as possible. But, if we can't know various things, we would like to believe, with reason, as much as we can which is true. We would like to believe what is in complete agreement with what is there to be known. The truly creative thinker is driven by this force. He boldly strives to know as much of the truth as he can, at least to say and believe as much as he can which is in complete agreement with the truth. But, the bolder and the more creative his thinking and theorizing, the slimmer the chance that what he actually says and believes *will* be true. The truth, or at least truth, was his goal. Must his creativity almost certainly frustrate him in these terms? Do we have no place in our thought of these things to help resolve this conflict?

I think we may do well to view things this way: The ancient developers of our language were, intuitively, sensitive psychologists. They felt this motivating force very strongly. They also appreciated that their limited minds, together with a relatively impoverished language, provided them with a conflict, encouraged frustration, and would lead to an inhibiting fear of that impending frustration. This fear could inhibit creative thinking. At the same time, they provided a relatively satisfying way of dealing with this problem, a relatively effective way of freeing future creative thinkers from this fear of frustration: the idea of there being a lot of truth *in* what a man says or believes. This is the idea that *in* what these men say or believe are many things, specifiable or not, which *are* in complete agreement with the whole truth about everything. In this way, the ancients let us express this powerful motivation. And at the same time, they pressured us to talk about the creative thinker coming out *well ahead* of the cautious bore *even as judged in these powerful terms*. Granted, they may have employed a certain amount of obscurity to accomplish this task. But, even so, their expression of this fundamental motivation, and their resolution of its conflict with creative thinking, must still remain a considerable achievement.

§9. *Falsity and Truth*

Many properties have opposites. Goodness has badness; truth has falsity. Just as badness is not the mere absence of goodness, but actually is the opposite, so falsity is not the mere absence of truth. This is patent in the case of, say, a stone, which is neither true nor false. While truth is absent, that does not mean that the property of falsity is instanced in the case of the stone. The same holds, I suggest, for more suitable objects, for example, statements. According to many philosophers, when a statement lacks truth, it follows that it has the property of falsity. But even if this be so, the statement's falsity is not just its lack of truth. This intuition, I think, must be admitted by anyone fair to his own ordinary thinking.

A second intuition about falsity is this. Just like truth, falsity is a relational property. A statement which is false has its distinctive property in virtue of its bearing a certain relation to something, or some things, other than itself. I suggest that the statement's falsity just is its bearing the relevant relation to this external entity, or group of entities.

Thirdly, falsity is not just felt to be the opposite of truth but, of the two, it is deemed clearly the negative, and the inferior, property. This is not just a matter of associations, as may be the case with, say, openness and closedness, or wetness and dryness. Here, as with goodness and badness, there is a definite ranking implicit in the properties themselves.

As with other opposite properties, no single entity can, at any given time, possess both at once. If a statement is true, then it is not false; if false, it cannot then be true as well. But, at the same time, we should not suppose, as many philosophers do, that, from their logic alone, one or else the other of these two properties must apply to every object 'of the sort to which they properly pertain', for example, to every statement, or proposition. Perhaps for some external reason, however deep, this dichotomy will in fact apply to every statement after all. But this universal application should not owe its explanation just to an adequate account of truth and falsity. I want now to account for all of these intuitive facts by giving an account of falsity, indeed, one which is a most natural extension of our account of truth.

Truth, as we have said, is agreement with the truth. I propose to define falsity as the opposite relation to the same object. Right away, we may notice that, on the side of falsity, there is no expression to match the whole truth about the world. Only in its third and central sense does 'truth' have no opposite word that shares a root with 'false'. There are falsehoods, matching the referents of the word in its first sense, and, then, there is the falsity of those things, matching the referent in the second sense. But falsehoods are not in agreement with the *falseth, or with anything of the like. Indeed, this asymmetry in the case of the third sense alone is further reason, I suggest, for thinking that sense central.[7] In any case, this linguistic

---

[7] Not myself speaking German, but according to the account I have received of him, Frege speaks of the True, which all true propositions are supposed to denote, and also of the False, which is supposedly denoted by all false propositions. Neither of these seems implied by ordinary English or thus contained in its embodied theory. On the side of Frege's True, however, English does have the truth, the whole truth about the world. On the side of the False, I submit, English has nothing at all. Unlike Frege's theory, then, English is relevantly asymmetric. I suspect German of being like English here, and unlike this distinguished German speaker. See Gottlob Frege, 'On Sense and Nominatum', in *Readings in Philosophical Analysis*, ed. H. Feigl and W. Sellars (New York, 1949).

asymmetry indicates that in our embodied metaphysics, there is no object opposite to the truth about the world. The oppositeness of falsity, then, comes from the oppositeness of its relation. What relation, we ask, is relevantly opposite to that of agreement? I suggest that it is the relation of conflict or, more familiar to philosophers, and here amounting to the same thing, the relation of inconsistency. If a statement is, then, false in the relevant sense, that statement is in conflict with, or inconsistent with, the whole truth about the world. And, its falsity just is its (being in) conflict with, or its being inconsistent with, the truth.

Intuitively, the whole truth about the world is, if not positive, at least not a negative object. The positive character of truth, then, may be explained in terms of that of the relation of agreement. For that is a positive relation, we intuitively feel. By the same token, the negativity of falsity is explained by that of conflict, or that of inconsistency. For these or this are, intuitively, negative relations. Unless it is a negative thing with which something agrees, agreement (or accordance) with a thing is something positive, superior to conflict, or inconsistency with it. And, just as agreement is superior to conflict and inconsistency, so truth is superior to falsity.

At the very same time, nothing can be both (completely) in agreement with the truth and also inconsistent with it. Accordingly, I submit, nothing can be relevantly true and, at the same time, thus false. But why can't something, even a statement or proposition, not to mention a stone or fish, be neither in agreement with the truth nor yet so much as actually inconsistent with it? I see no reason in the nature of these relations to rule this out. Indeed, I believe them to allow for a third status, even for statements or propositions. While examples concerning the past may not be as clarifying as one would like, an example concerning the future may make our thought here clear enough.

If the whole history of the world is already laid down, as it were, is already completely determined, then, perhaps, every statement must be in agreement with the truth or, if not that, then inconsistent with the truth. Perhaps in such a case, but then only in such a case, every statement or proposition must be true or, if not that, then false. But, if the future is genuinely open and not determined, or if at least certain parts or aspects of it are, then it seems there may be statements with neither of these two properties. For example, let us suppose that it is not yet determined whether or not I will jump up and down in the next hour. If this be the case, then the statement that I will, along with the statement that I will not, is not (yet) true nor (yet) false either. Neither the one statement nor its negation is in agreement with, nor inconsistent with, the truth. I should say that, in this case, *each* of these statements is *consistent* with the truth, but, again, neither is so much as in agreement with it.

On our account, a statement is in agreement with the truth only when it is in agreement with the appropriate 'ultimate' part. It is inconsistent with the truth, we may now add, when it is inconsistent with such an appropriate part or, what amounts to the same, with *any* ultimate part of the truth. Lastly, we may say that it is consistent with the truth when it is not inconsistent with the truth, and so, not inconsistent with any ultimate part of that great entity. In the present case, there is as yet nothing at all which is the truth about whether I will jump in the given interval of time. Accordingly, the statement that I will cannot possibly be in agreement with such a thing; it thus cannot be true. For this statement to be inconsistent with the truth it must be inconsistent with that ultimate part, which, again, as yet doesn't even exist. Thus, it cannot be relevantly inconsistent, nor relevantly false. With respect to all of the ultimate parts which as yet do exist or obtain, that statement, along with its negation, is perfectly consistent. But, perhaps to repeat ourselves, when a statement is consistent with every 'ultimate' part of the truth, that is, with every one which actually does exist or obtain, then that statement is consistent with the whole truth itself. Thus, this statement, that I will jump in the next hour, is consistent with the whole truth about the world, as also is its negation. If this account of three relations may be accepted, then we have explained our idea that from the logic of our properties alone, we cannot deduce that every statement must be true or, if not that, false. In the case of statements involving 'vague predicates', not necessarily about the future, I think that our account also does a good job in explaining our intuition that neither truth nor falsity apply. But perhaps this is not so clear as our result with future contingencies.

I trust that we now have a rather good account of falsity. Before finishing the topic, I should like to give our account a last bit of confirmation by examining the way we modify 'false', in the relevant meaning of that predicating adjective. As with 'true', adverbial modification is, when apt at all, never indicative even of the appearance of any degrees. Unlike with 'true', in the meaning relevant to our topic, there are no comparative forms for 'false': *'What he said was falser (more false) than what you said.' On our account, this is quite all right, for we do not have either: *'What he said is more inconsistent with the truth than what you said.' Nor do we have with 'false', though we do with 'true', relevant locutions for indicating some appropriate nearness or closeness: ??'What he said is more nearly false (??closer to being false) than what you said.' Our account predicts this as well: ??'What he said is more nearly (??closer to being) inconsistent with the truth than what you said.' What we do have with 'false', and most directly relevant to our topic, is this: 'What he said is more badly false than what you said.' And this agrees perfectly with what our account produces: 'What he said is more badly inconsistent with the truth than what you said.' Of course, this sentence with 'false' wants further analysis for us to achieve any understanding of it worth the name. But, our account, at least, provides a first step in the right direction, and it is thus further confirmed.

§10. *Some Paradoxical Consequences of this Account*

The central entity in our account of truth is the whole truth about the world. It plays its part, as we have seen, by way of things which are each part of it, eventually, by way of its ultimate parts. These last are things which must be known if anyone is ever to know anything about anything. Now, I must confess that, metaphysically, I am quite nominalistically inclined. I am quite doubtful that there are facts or states of affairs, or propositions or statements. I even have some reservation towards thinking that there are actually any sentences, as opposed to patterned inscriptions and streams of sound. But, in the present context, these must be adjudged very mild doubts on my part. For I find it almost incredible that there should actually exist or obtain what must be a much greater abstract thing, our central entity, the whole truth about the world. Indeed, I am quite as confident that there really is no such thing, nothing such at all. And it follows from this, of which I am thus confident, that there really isn't anything either which is any part of that first, that is, there really is nothing which is any part of the truth. The consequences for us of this rather simple and uncontroversial idea now look to be remarkable. As this non-existence is, I suppose, strictly necessary, these remarkable consequences will also hold of the strictest necessity.[8]

In the first place, we must now conclude that for the relevant knowing, these needed objects are not there to be known. It follows straight away, then, that no one ever knows anything about anything, for that is the knowing we have just called relevant. By denying the possibility of needed objects for knowing, we have again derived, in another way now, our thesis of universal ignorance. Accordingly, the parts of our essay are mutually supporting. On our conception of our language and thought, this should come as no surprise. For if we may find the relational state of knowing to be incredible and impossible, we might expect objects to which this state is supposed most directly to relate us also to be quite incredible and impossible.

In that our account of these objects leads to scepticism about knowledge, any consequences of the sceptical view will of course also follow from our account. One such consequence is this: If someone regrets that he did a certain thing, then he knows that he did it. Now, even if the objects of regret are different sorts of things from our most dubious objects of knowing, as facts are different from parts of the truth, a suitable *parallel* may hold between the objects, so that the conditional here will hold. (This reminds us of the second premiss of our Basis Argument, discussed in Chapter V, section 3.) Thus, as nobody ever knows he did anything, nobody will ever regret his having done anything either. Likewise, nobody will ever be happy or

---

[8] I provide no argument for thinking that there is no such entity as the whole truth about the world, that no such thing really exists or obtains. But, I trust that none is needed. If you think that there really is such a thing, then you may consider the previous sections to exhibit a series of genuine metaphysical disclosures and, no doubt, you will not be much impressed by what is to come next in this present one.

sad, upset or elated that anything was, is, or will be so. And many similar consequences will also follow in like manner. What were, in Chapter IV, given as consequences or wages of our first three chapters equally follow from this present one.

It further follows, from our account of truth and of falsity, that nothing can ever have either of these properties and, so, in the relevant sense of each term, that nothing can ever be true or ever false. The reason that these properties are impossible should be quite plain. As there is nothing which is the whole truth about the world, there is nothing relevant for something to be in agreement with, nor to be inconsistent with. Just put the other way around, nothing can be in agreement with the truth about the world, nor inconsistent with any such thing. That is, in the relevant sense of each term, nothing can be true and nothing false. This applies as much to the offerings of the present essay as it does to anything else. But even if what I have placed before us is not true, it may well be worth your while to focus on it, to be influenced by it, and even to be guided by it in the construction of some new, better intellectual approach to the world. This new approach, of course, will have no involvement with these impossible properties.

The impossibility of truth, and of falsity, is not our only notable new conclusion. In Chapter V, we argued that no one could ever be reasonable or justified in believing anything to be so. Now we may argue for a far more radical conclusion: no one can ever think or believe anything to be so at all. We have agreed that what may be believed to be so need not be true or else false, so this conclusion will not follow from the one we have just previously reached. But in terms of our account, what does constrain these alleged things is this more liberal condition: what is believed to be so must be either consistent with the truth or else inconsistent with the whole truth about the world. As there is nothing which is the whole truth about the world, nothing can satisfy either of these alternatives. And, so, there really is nothing which is thought or believed to be so, nor can there ever be. Finally, from this, it follows straight away that no one ever can think anything to be so, nor ever believe any such thing at all.

This sort of argument is not confined to 'mental states' such as believing. It applies equally to such 'illocutionary acts' as asserting, and even saying something to be so. In Chapter V, we argued that these acts, along with all 'thinking acts', were never reasonable for us. We even argued, as we articulated at the start of Chapter VI, that they meant unreasonableness and irrationality on our part. Later on in Chapter VI, we argued that asserting, and even such saying, must always involve us in false representation. Now we argue, more radically, that such acts as these are actually impossible. As with what is believed, what is asserted or said to be so must be consistent with the whole truth about the world or else inconsistent with it. As before, nothing can be either of these, for the needed entity cannot possibly exist. Nothing, then, can be asserted or even said to be so; no one can assert or even say that anything is so or not. Of course, though no one can say that there are rocks, this is not to deny that someone might say (the words), 'There are rocks.'

Though the many foregoing consequences of our account are puzzling, to say the least, we have not yet come to the most perplexing and, indeed, to the utterly paradoxical consequences of our account of truth. These consequences begin to present themselves when we begin to consider grammatically sound versions of strings made famous by Alfred Tarski. Accordingly, we begin to consider the Tarski-inspired equivalence:

What is expressed by the sentence 'Snow is white' is true if and only if snow is white.[9]

Much as Tarski would have it, this equivalence looks quite pristine. It looks, at least, relatively unmetaphysical, possibly quite unproblematic. But, our own account of truth brings forth a rather longer equivalence with the same left-hand side:

---

[9] I have in mind Tarski's paper 'The Semantic Conception of Truth', originally published in *Philosophy and Phenomenological Research*, vol. iv (1944). There Tarski has such at least mildly deviant strings as:

?The sentence 'snow is white' is true if, and only if, snow is white.

Our slight change converts such Tarskian strings, I think, into perfectly non-deviant sentences. But, of course, that is a very small move. Of more importance perhaps is the apparently dire consequence of our account for theories of meaning, etc. which would put truth at or near their centre. I have in mind, of course, such Tarski-inspired attempts as those for Donald Davidson in such papers as his 'Truth and Meaning', *Synthèse*, vol. xvii, No. 3 (1967).

What is expressed by the sentence 'Snow is white' is true if and only if what is expressed by the sentence 'Snow is white' is in agreement with the whole truth about the world.

Now, I cannot see that any speaker and user of our language, English, can at this point fail to accept *either* of these equivalences, unless of course he refuses to accept what his language has to offer. If he is to accept its sanctioned implications, he cannot reject either of these equivalences. But the two together entail a third, which, while it looks innocuous from one end:

What is expressed by the sentence 'Snow is white' is in agreement with the whole truth about the world if and only if snow is white,

shows itself for what it is when the short side is put first:

Snow is white if and only if what is expressed by the sentence 'Snow is white' is in agreement with the whole truth about the world.

Now, as there is no such thing for what that sentence expresses to be in agreement with, we must conclude that snow is *not* white. For *this* case does not allow a third status.

That we should be able, indeed required, to reach such a substantive extra-linguistic conclusion from what may *appear* to be *mere* considerations of language seems shocking; the fact that we would generally consider it a *false* substantive statement makes matters look even worse. But, of course, we could take a parallel course starting from equivalences concerning the sentence 'Snow is not white.' And, we would thus be led equally to the conclusion that snow *is* white. Putting two and two together, we must conclude, finally, that snow *is* white *and* snow is *not* white. Any case not involving future contingencies, or the borders of vague predicates, will get us a contradiction.

Encountering such blatant paradox must force us to think hard. But, then, so must our previous result that, in the relevant sense of the term, nothing can ever be true. Criticism of our sceptical philosophy is now quite easy to come by, whether or not that criticism will be genuinely deep and devastating. No one, I think, is more painfully conscious of our present situation than myself. Indeed, anticipating as much, this is why I said less than might be wanted about the lesser troubles we encountered in earlier chapters. I wish that I could now satisfy all such wants quite fully, especially those concerning our present situation. Instead, I will close my essay with but a few programmatic remarks. My hope is that these may help others towards some empirical research, some imaginative construction, and, in short, perhaps, to a more open and fruitful approach towards the work of philosophy.

§11. *An Approach to Philosophy*

We have encountered great difficulties. But it has been the aim of our essay to bring us to the point where we might face these difficulties openly. For I believe that the problems are not of my own making, however disturbing the contradictions I have just exhibited. Rather, as I said in my Introduction, I believe the problems to originate from quite another source. Having now exhibited a great many difficulties which I could there do little more than hint at, I will try to bring my essay to a more pointed close while always maintaining the spirit with which I began it.

Going against beliefs or assertions of 'common sense', even scepticism about knowledge may be considered a 'crazy conclusion', and probably will be by most professional philosophers even at this point. The same goes, only more so, for later conclusions we have reached, especially, perhaps, for the paradoxical contradictions just recently displayed. But, if inferences to crazy conclusions may be made to look natural and compelling, and in a variety of connected ways, this may be due more to the language in which premises receive substance than to any tendencies on the part of one who might arrange them for our consideration. At the same time, our language is a useful social instrument of thought, expression, and communication, with a long history of effective service. How, then, might so much bad thought be embodied in it; how might this ever have come to pass? In order that our scepticism gain acceptance, and for more than a brief moment, some plausible account of this must be suggested. Thinking better than to use the terms, but having no better ones available, the account must, sooner or later, be supported, evidenced, or confirmed. Of those I can think of, I will now suggest the account which seems to me most plausible. This is essentially the account outlined in my

Introduction. While the account is quite vague, it is not so vague, I think, that we can have no idea as to what sort of experience might help pressure us towards it, and what sort might pressure us to deem it less acceptable. As in so many other cases, perhaps an actual search for pertinent evidence will be our best stimulus towards giving the account a more definite shape, towards lessening its vagueness.

At various points in this chapter, I have mentioned as useful a certain conception of our language and our thought in the language. Excepting my Introduction, up till now, this conception has been offered mainly as a helpful viewpoint for spurring certain analyses of our locutions, analyses which are systematically congenial to our scepticism. At this point, however, I shall begin to offer the conception in a much more substantial vein. Accordingly, I now hypothesize that our present language embodies a badly wrong theory of things, however good in other respects it may be, and that this theory is inherited by us from an ancestor language, or languages, which embodied it in the first place. For this hypothesis to be taken seriously, it needs rather a fair amount of support. A small beginning towards this amount is given, I think, in our present essay. For our essay appears to bring out a great many of our linguistic intuitions, or our deeper linguistic tendencies. And, it serves to relate these systematically, while making whole systems of analytic propositions seem to appear in the process. The systematization of these feelings also pressures us to accept certain existence statements, like 'There is something which is the whole truth about the world.' Fortunately, in relevant respects, we can think beyond these pressures, and so deny these existence propositions. A good explanation of these forces, I suggest, is that involvement in the language means pressure to accept a theory embodied in it, a theory of which these analytic propositions are theorems, as are (certain of) our necessary existence statements. Pressure to accept the existence propositions is pressure to think that this theory actually applies to things, even quite regularly so. But, even if the systematic collection of our linguistic feelings may thus give us some support, a great deal more is needed.

To get more, I suggest that we actually look into the historical roots of our contemporary language. My hunch is that as we go further and further back, the sorts of analytic connections for which I have had to dig so hard will be more apparent, closer to the surface, so to speak, and similarly with the relevant necessary existence statements. While I have been at great pains to make an embodied theory appear for us, I of course realize that present-day English has no obvious look of containing any such theory, much less an entire metaphysics of knowledge and truth. Indeed, with hardly any exception, those who speak our language, and who think in its terms, have had no conscious thought of any theory here. Indeed, for such reasons as this, I am not all that confident that many of my offered propositions are true, let alone that they are so for an analytic reason of meaning. Quine notwithstanding, then, we may observe that the ease or the rationality with which one will give up belief of what is expressed by a certain sentence, for example, 'If she is happy there are rocks, she knows there are,' this does not even correlate well with how plausible it is to think that the sentence is analytic; much less should it ever be thought any defining criterion.[10] If we look far enough back in

___

[10] In his famous paper 'Two Dogmas of Empiricism', *From A Logical Point of View* (Cambridge, Mass., 1961), W. V. Quine denies that there are any analytic sentences. As far as I can tell his reasons are two: first, we have no satisfactory account of what it is for a sentence to be analytic and, second, any sentence, or belief in what it expresses, may be given up, or best or rationally given up, under appropriate conditions of experience, especially if one has appropriate other beliefs. The first of these I pass over quickly: 'sentence *S* is analytic' will go over *roughly* into 'sentence *S* is true in virtue of its meaning alone.' Apart from smaller difficulties, the problem here is that we have no good theory of a sentence's meaning, of what sentences mean, or anything of the like. Any good beginning at defining 'analytic' awaits the fulfilment of this more fundamental need. As for the second reason, which looks to me more like an argument, it seems to miss its mark. What Quine does seem to challenge successfully is a certain idea of the *a priori*; a reverse *a priori*, if you will. This *a priori* has to do with the conditions for giving up beliefs; the more usual notion, just as bad I think, has to do with the conditions for coming to have beliefs or knowledge. In any case, an idea of the *a priori* is an epistemological one, that of the analytic, a semantic notion. Quine's argument, it seems to me, trades on mistakenly conflating the two.

In one of the most interesting studies to follow in Quine's wake, Hilary Putnam seems to make the same bad conflation, though perhaps to a lesser extent. Putnam draws the interesting conclusion that there are analytic sentences (or statements) but they form a philosophically unimportant class. I have argued to the contrary throughout; that class is quite important. If Putnam looked at verbs like 'regret', and adjectives like 'clear' and 'happy', he might have been more friendly to the possible importance of this semantic class of sentences. See Putnam's 'The Analytic and the Synthetic', *Minnesota Studies in the Philosophy of Science*, vol. iii, ed. H. Feigl and G. Maxwell (Minneapolis, 1966).

time, however, I think we will find a period where such propositions would not be easily abandoned at all, though of course that is only a clue to whether they were and are analytic.

In those earlier times, I continue to hypothesize, people spoke a tongue or tongues whose simple, explicit structure and semantics made fairly explicit their embodied theory of the world. As most simply and best translated, their analytic sentences, I predict, would be those analytic sentences I have claimed to express theorems embodied now in English.

Now, vague as they are, these hypotheses are still quite bold, I realize, and hardly what one would expect from a contemporary American philosopher. Of course, the hypotheses are not absolutely necessary to our sceptical critique, for other sceptical explanations for defective thought may be offered. But I think that hypotheses at least a lot like these will offer our best bet for a scepticism which may be widely accepted and long maintained. Accordingly, it is of importance to me that the sort of empirical research here indicated be undertaken with some vigour and with a friendly seriousness of purpose. But my research inclinations are too typical of one with my training and social associations. Accordingly, with a hope which may well be vain, I leave that work to philosophically inclined anthropologists, linguists, and others, and perhaps to sceptically inclined philosophers with a penchant towards mastering the methods and materials of such more directly empirical areas of inquiry.

If my contentions prove by and large correct, what work is left for those like me, for philosophical analysts only on the margin of most empirical inquiry? Two areas of endeavour suggest themselves. The first is to undertake new sceptical essays in other philosophical topic areas. Again, one will favour the 'crazy conclusion', for example, perhaps, that no one ever does anything of his own free will. One will look first for classical arguments for the conclusion. Then he will seek to explain the feelings aroused in terms of demanding meanings of key terms in the arguments. The rest of the strategy will also follow the present lines, if not in detail, in general direction. And, then, further hypotheses will be suggested for researching anthropologists, linguists, and others.

A second area of inquiry is perhaps the most creative; and

the most trying. The need for it will depend on whether there is available to us a natural language, present or past, which, while rather rich in the ways we should want, avoids the difficulties we encountered without, of course, having others which are at least rather nearly as bad. If there is at least one such language, and we can find it and show it to be so good, then there is no very creative task left in connection with our present problems. But I suppose it more likely that no rich natural language is all that much better than English in the relevant respects. Accordingly, to solve our problems, either a new language should be developed and made available or at least an existing language should be radically changed in creative ways. This is the second area of inquiry to which I referred.

It should be pretty plain that this constructive task will really not be any simple or easy one. As I took pains to make clear, in Chapter IV, section 12, in Chapter V, section 11, and elsewhere, much more must be done than to eliminate, or even to replace, 'truth', 'know', and a few close cognate expressions. There are important problems here which want a systematic and a sensitive answer. Now, neither my inclinations nor my aptitudes, I think, are strongest in this most constructive area. If my sceptical ideas prove correct, if empirical, historical research supports them, my grandest hope would be for my rather destructive efforts to stimulate such constructive action in others more well suited to the task.

I should think that these constructive thinkers must be dexterous logicians, but with a subtle appreciation of the function and workings of a natural language. As I have tried to point out, our own language contains locutions which may help to resolve certain difficult human conflicts, fostering better thinking, and perhaps even better action, in the process. The helpful features of these locutions had best be preserved in any new or altered language which, in other ways, may be much better than ours now is.

If this grand hope of mine is not in vain, then some day someone may write an essay like mine, one about knowledge, reasons, truth, and the rest, without any paradox or contradiction on his part. In a new language, or in a reconstruction of an existing one, he will write about things to which his crucial, working terms make no purported reference of any troubling sort. When, for example, he uses 'know' or 'knowledge', he will also have better terms to use more essentially. Indeed, he might do well to underline or italicize, but he need not emphasize, the topic terms, as I might do when writing about something the Greeks thought to exist or obtain, say, *episteme*. For me, of course, there is no opportunity of writing a sceptical essay so consistent and pristine. But, unless my sceptical approach is badly wrong, this lack of present opportunity is not something which we should feel defeats us. Nor should we let paradoxes or contradictions lead us into a continued embrace of our present comparatively provincial situation.

In my Introduction, I said that I wanted to confront and remedy two dissatisfactions of mine with philosophy, at least as now conducted. The first concerned the arguments for scepticism, which people encounter in their first weeks or months of involvement with philosophy. These never seem adequately rebutted by later, more 'sophisticated' developments which we encounter in the subject. At least, any appearance of adequate rebuttal rather quickly passes. Indeed, these later developments seem less deep than the original negative reasoning; compared with it, they often quickly look to be quite superficial. The second dissatisfaction was this. According to certain currently dominant trends, due to philosophy's rather recent enlightenment, there seems little left for the subject beyond the analysis of just so many words, beyond the understanding of their meaning or, more generally, of various features of their behaviour. For the most part, philosophy leaves, not only science, but the common sense beliefs on which it grows, quite unchanged and intact. While we first thought it might help towards bettering our comprehensive view of things, philosophy's rather recent developments make it look to be a quite insubstantial discipline.

Regarding the first dissatisfaction, I have tried to resolve it most simply. I have argued that in epistemology, the originally encountered arguments are essentially sound, and that their 'crazy conclusions' are actually to be accepted. Though it is for the simplest of reasons, that is why the rebuttals later encountered end by seeming so unsatisfyingly superficial. But, then, this means that philosophy helps show that many of our common sense beliefs are inadequate. While they may serve the growth of science, there might be other things to serve that goal at least equally well, which lack the problems encountered with our common sense beliefs. This resolves my second dissatisfaction. Philosophy need not leave our view of the world almost wholly unchanged. Rather, it may help in reshaping a goodly portion of our developing comprehensive view of things. While this last resolution of dissatisfaction need not be thought a strong reason for following the lead of any of my arguments, loving philosophy as I do, I derive some pleasure from this remedy which they suggest. For at the present time, with as much plausibility, I can think of no other way in which philosophy might prove so constructively substantial.

Index